DEVELOPING READERS AND WRITERS IN THE CONTENT AREAS: K-12

DEVELOPING READERS AND WRITERS IN THE CONTENT AREAS: K-12

DAVID W. MOORE
University of Northern Iowa

SHARON ARTHUR MOORE
University of Northern Iowa

PATRICIA M. CUNNINGHAM
Wake Forest University

JAMES W. CUNNINGHAM
University of North Carolina, Chapel Hill

Longman
New York & London

Executive Editor: Raymond T. O'Connell
Developmental Editor: Naomi Silverman
Production Editor: Pamela Nelson
Text Design: Laura Ierardi
Cover Design: Steven August Krastin
Photos: John Wedman
Production Supervisor: Judith Stern
Compositor: Pine Tree Composition, Inc.
Printer and Binder: The Alpine Press, Inc.

Developing Readers and Writers in the Content Areas K–12

Copyright © 1986 by Longman Inc.

Longman Inc.
95 Church Street
White Plains, N.Y. 10601

Associated companies:
Longman Group Ltd., London
Longman Cheshire Pty., Melbourne
Longman Paul Pty., Auckland
Copp Clark Pitman, Toronto
Pitman Publishing Inc., Boston

Library of Congress Cataloging-in-Publication Data
Main entry under title:

Developing readers and writers in the content areas.

  Includes bibliographies and index.
  1. Language arts—Correlation with content subjects.
2. Content area reading.   I. Moore, David W.
LB1576.D455   1986   428.4'0712   85-19739
ISBN 0-582-28518-6

86 87 88 89 9 8 7 6 5 4 3 2 1

Contents

PART II
. . . IN THE CONTENT AREAS: K-12   183

Preface

Developing Readers and Writers in the Content Areas: K–12 is an introduction to a fascinating aspect of education—students' reading and writing during the study of school subjects. Of the many responsibilities that teachers assume, teaching students how to read and write effectively certainly ranks near the top. Our introduction to this aspect of education contains several noteworthy features. First, our audience for this text consists of teachers who work with primary- through secondary-grade students. Although students certainly change as they move through the grades, they remain the same in fundamental ways. This text emphasizes the similarities of students across the grades.

Another feature of this text is that both reading and writing are emphasized. Written language deserves to be treated in an integrated fashion. Even though separate chapters are devoted to comprehension and composition, you will find that reading and writing are combined within each chapter. Third, individual chapters are devoted to literature, student researchers, and classroom complexities. These chapters help distinguish this text from others in the field. A fourth feature is that methods of instruction are thoroughly explained. We assumed that our audience did not already know what we were presenting, so we sought to develop our topics clearly and completely. Finally, basic learning processes are stressed. Chapter 1 describes nine thinking processes that contribute to learning. The remaining chapters then demonstrate how those processes underlie the learning strategies and teaching methods that are presented.

This book consists of two parts. Part I includes seven chapters written in expository form. That is, the information is explained in a straightforward, objective fashion. The closing comments in Chapters 2 through 6 address concerns frequently expressed about the information contained in the chapters. The title of each comment begins with the phrase *What about;* we have noticed that teachers and students usually introduce their concerns with this phrase. The final four chapters, which make up Part II, follow a nontraditional form for textbooks; they are written in narrative style. Each of these chapters is a fictional account of how one teacher spends a school year developing readers and writers in the content areas. These narrative accounts are meant to show how the principles and strategies of instruction presented in Part I operate in the classroom.

Several learning aids are included. We inserted boxed activities throughout Part I to help you understand and retain the information presented. These activities are labeled with at least one of the essential thinking processes described in Chapter 1. We encourage you to participate in these boxed activities to become actively involved with the contents of the text. In addition, each chapter in Part I ends with a list of suggested readings. The books and articles listed are meant to amplify the material presented in the chapter. An aid we included in Part II is locators. Locators are meant to specify the relationship between Parts I and II. The locators that are listed in the index will help you find where a particular topic from Part II is explained in Part I.

We thank the teachers and students at Malcolm Price Laboratory School, Cedar Falls, Iowa, who allowed us to take the photographs in this book. Joan Duea, Joyce Hornby, Cheryl Lubinski, Steve Rose, and Betty Strub willingly allowed us to photograph what teachers and students do in order to develop reading and writing proficiencies. John Wedman provided timely, expert advice on placing photos in a textbook and took the pictures presented here.

David W. Moore
Sharon Arthur Moore
Patricia M. Cunningham
James W. Cunningham

DEVELOPING READERS AND WRITERS IN THE CONTENT AREAS: K-12

PART I

DEVELOPING READERS AND WRITERS . . .

C H A P T E R 1

Essentials of Content Area Reading and Writing

Students in elementary, middle, and high school learn an incredible amount of information. They learn that Confucius was a Chinese philosopher, that lizards are reptiles, that yeast causes dough to rise, that an isosceles triangle has two equal sides, and countless other facts. Such information comes from many sources. Personal experiences; pictures and movies; conversations and lectures; and books, magazines, and newspapers all provide information to students. In addition, students learn about the world by engaging in many activities: reading, writing, listening, speaking, viewing, touching, smelling, and tasting. This textbook addresses learning through one source, written language as it is processed through reading and writing.

Classroom teachers can use typical school-related content areas to help students learn about the world through reading and writing. Content areas are bodies of knowledge that present information about the world in a systematic fashion. Some content areas are science, mathematics, and fine arts. It is important to remember that content areas consist of language and that language involves writing and reading. Teachers and students who study school subjects actually are studying language. Postman (1979) presented the case this way:

> Biology is not plants and animals. It is language about plants and animals. History is not events. It is language describing and interpreting events. Astronomy is not planets and stars. It is a way of talking about planets and stars. (p. 165)

This chapter presents some basic facts about what is needed to develop readers and writers as they learn content area information. The remaining chapters address specific topics in detail.

THE CHALLENGES OF CONTENT AREA READING AND WRITING

There are three special challenges of content area reading and writing: functions of literacy, structures of text materials, and aims of instruction. Students' reading and writing require serious attention during the study of the content areas. The three challenges require you to provide students with appropriate reading and writing help when they encounter subject matter information.

Functions of Literacy

Literacy involves many functions (Brice-Heath, 1980; Halliday, 1973). Three of these are:

1. Reading and writing to experience
2. Reading and writing to do
3. Reading and writing to learn.

We are reading to experience when we read adventure novels, newspaper comics, magazine short stories, and other materials that provide a pleasurable escape. Being in the middle of a good book and knowing that several chapters are still to come is surely one of life's basic enjoyments. We are writing to experience when we compose letters to our friends and family or when we produce personal diaries, journals, and creative pieces. Reading and

Figure 1.1 Students explore their feelings and reactions to classroom experiences.

Figure 1.2   Interacting with a computer program is one way students read and write to do.

writing to experience occurs when we read or write without expecting utilitarian benefits.

We also read and write to do. This purpose is met when we complete procedures that require literacy. Following directions to run an appliance, ordering or preparing a meal, and assembling something frequently require reading to do. Completing applications, acting on written memos and requests, and filling out forms are examples of reading and writing to do. On-the-job expectations often invoke this function of literacy.

Reading and writing to learn is a third function of literacy. We gather and store vast amounts of information. In fact, one of the schools' primary missions is to provide students with a common body of knowledge. This mission begins in kindergarten with lessons such as identifying the names of animals and days of the week; the process continues through twelfth grade with molecular structures, literature genres, and government practices. As students progress through school and as they become more interested in learning on their own, reading and writing become increasingly powerful tools.

The three functions of literacy presented here—experiencing, doing, and learning—tap different abilities. For instance, experiencing a joke is not the same as learning it. We all have heard a joke, laughed readily, and remembered the experience; but we might forget the details of the joke when we want to retell it. We experienced the joke superbly but learned it poorly. Thus, reading and writing to learn information is a function of literacy that

Figure 1.3   Students integrate reading and writing in order to learn content area information.

presents a special challenge because our abilities to perform that function are not necessarily as developed as are our other reading and writing abilities. This text emphasizes reading and writing to learn.

Structure of Materials

The content areas contain much information to be learned and the information has distinct structures. The phrase *structure of materials* pertains to how facts and generalizations are organized and presented. Three structures that challenge students involve differences between written and spoken language, expository and literary text structures, and one content area and another.

Written versus Spoken Language   Written language differs in substantial ways from spoken language (Kleiman & Schallert, 1978; Olson, 1977). Look at any paragraph on this page. We doubt that you have ever heard a spoken conversation in which the words are arranged in a similar way. You have heard people read aloud, but that is just written language ''wired for sound.'' In conversations people make frequent false starts, which they correct, and their word choice and grammar are often faulty. After all, writers edit out false starts and inapporpriate phrases before submitting a finished product. Written language is ordered more precisely than spoken language.

Conversation has a give-and-take quality that is missing in written language.

For example, a frown, a puzzled expression, or a request for clarification all help speakers tailor their message to fit their listeners. Listeners can interject their own thoughts and get feedback. In this way two people can jointly articulate one message. Such actions are not available to writers and readers. If you don't understand a textbook, you can back up and reread it, but you will only read the same words again. Readers can speak their thoughts while reading, but the author of the passage cannot respond like a speaker can. In addition, speakers can emphasize important points with gestures like fist pounding and with inflections like voice raising, devices that are, of course, difficult to capture in print.

These differences between the structure of written and spoken messages challenge students, and they emphasize the need to use content area materials when teaching reading and writing. Students need to become familiar with the ordered flow of words encountered in writing. Teaching students simply to pronounce and spell words is not teaching them to write. Writing is not just "talk written down." Thus, readers need to learn how to follow carefully ordered strings of words that are presented according to the unique rules of written language, and writers need to learn how to produce those strings of words.

Expository versus Literary Text Structures Exposition, which constitutes a large part of the content areas, adds to the challenge of content area reading and writing. Expository text structures set out information about the world in a distinct way (Beach & Appleman, 1984; Spiro & Taylor, 1980). In expository writing the world is analyzed through an objective, often abstract, perspective. Consider the following sentence:

Large bodies of water affect the weather of their nearby regions.

If this sentence began a passage, you would expect a detached, factual presentation. The passage probably would contain facts about water changing temperature more slowly than land and it would describe how those temperature differences affect the atmosphere. Expository writing, which generally presents facts and generalizations, tends to hold readers at a neutral, distant level.

Literary texts, on the other hand, engage readers' interest and attention at a more personal level. Writers use imaginative literary structures to present a specific view of the world. Notice the emotion of the following sentence:

His life began veering out of control last winter.

If this sentence began a passage, you would be prepared for a story that invited emotional involvement. You would expect to be drawn into the narrative and to participate vicariously in the character's life. You would expect an account of why the person's life was veering out of control. The episodes that advance the story line would connect in ways that reflect real life situations.

Thus, exposition presents facts at a remote level, and literary narration presents events at a personal level. It is difficult to read and write exposition because of its objective, frequently abstract nature. The challenge of exposition makes content area literacy instruction an essential component of schools' curriculums.

Content Area versus Content Area   Content areas such as English, science, and home economics are systematic views of the world that compartmentalize knowledge along different lines (Biglan, 1973; King & Brownell, 1966). To illustrate the differences among content areas, consider how different specialists would perceive a large boulder they might encounter during a walk in a meadow. A paleontologist would look for fossils in order to learn about the prehistoric plant and animal life of the area; an anthropologist would be interested in any pictographs that provide insight about ancient cultures; an artist might search for the inspiration to compose an original piece; and a metallurgist would analyze the rock to determine what it revealed about the surrounding metallic elements.

To further appreciate differences among the content areas, carefully read the following brief samples of subject matter:

> Cells enclose protoplasm, the substance of life. Protoplasm consists of two parts. The nucleus is the more solid central part, and the cytoplasm is the softer, more liquid part. The bulk of protoplasm is made up of carbon, hydrogen, oxygen, and nitrogen.

> In 1215 a group of barons forced King John of England to sign the Magna Carta. The barons wanted to restore their privileges; however, the Magna Carta grounded constitutional government in political institutions for all English-speaking people.

> An angle is the union of two rays that do not lie on the same line. When the sum of the measure of two angles is 90°, the angles are complementary; when the sum of the measure is 180°, the angles are supplementary.

These writing samples of science, social studies, and mathematics illustrate the challenges encountered among different content areas. For instance, technical terms such as *protoplasm* and *constitutional government* are met in specific subjects. Other terms such as *cell*, *ground*, and *ray* have meanings that are specific to each content area (e.g., "X-rays consist of electromagnetic radiations of an extremely short wavelength." "The ray at 35° is perpendicular to line CD.") In addition, the science sample describes the structure of a substance, the social studies sample lists the outcome of a human action, and the math sentence details a procedure. The first piece explores the world of nature, the second discusses human actions, and the third concerns spatial relations.

Because of the different challenges among content areas, specific literacy instruction is needed in each. Reading or writing the events of a biography differs from reading or writing the events of a natural phenomenon such as photosynthesis. Similarities exist, but so do differences. Students require guidance adapting their literacy skills to different situations.

Aims of Instruction

Content area reading and writing involves two aims of instruction. Schools are expected to impart a common body of information, and also to teach students how to acquire information on their own. Students need to know about things as well as how to accomplish things: they need to know about animals and molecules, for instance, as well as how to get information on their own about animals and molecules. Thus, content area literacy instructions has two primary aims: (1) to teach students information *about* the world and (2) to teach students *how to* learn about the world on their own.

Content area literacy instruction that focuses on teaching students about the world should help students gain the most information they can through reading and writing. For instance, effective teachers do not simply say, "Read the next 10 pages." Instead, they might say, "The next section to read is about the respiratory system. It deals specifically with asthma. Find out why asthma is not a disease itself, but a symptom of some other condition."

The other aim of content area literacy instruction, helping students inform themselves, involves teaching students how to learn independently. Strategies such as taking notes, composing questions, and keeping personal journals allow students to learn about their worlds with no outside help. Locating information, organizing it, and writing a report about it are other independent learning strategies. These strategies require instruction because most students do not pick them up automatically. Students need to be taught how to take good notes, compose thought-provoking questions, and write adequate summaries. Providing the necessary instruction for students to become independent learners is an essential teaching role. To quote a popular aphorism: "Give me a fish and I eat for a day. Teach me to fish and I eat for a lifetime."

Summary

Think back to the challenges of content area reading and writing that have been presented. Being sensitive to the challenges that students face allows you to provide effective instruction as you teach the content areas. The main challenges are (1) using reading and writing as a tool for learning, (2) understanding the structures of written, expository text materials that are encountered in each content area, and (3) learning about the world with and without a teacher's direction.

ESSENTIAL THINKING PROCESSES

Since antiquity, philosophers and learning theorists have attempted to identify the thinking processes that go into learning. Numerous books have been written on this subject and countless thinking processes have been suggested. We have concluded that the nine processes listed below account for a large share of learning. (Our conclusion was shaped by many influences; 11 sources that we believe to be especially valuable presentations of thinking processes are listed in the suggested readings at the end of this chapter.)

Essential Thinking Processes

Call Up	Monitor
Connect	Review
Predict	Evaluate
Organize	Apply
Image	

Before you read further about which thinking processes you should help your students develop, we need your cooperation. Think back to your middle teen years when you were preparing for your driver's license. You probably obtained a copy of your state's driving manual and sat down to learn the state's driving rules, regulations, and suggested operating techniques. As the nine thinking processes are described in this section, think about the processes you went through years ago to learn the manual's information.

Call Up

Most likely, you did not learn the rules of the road when you became a teenager. You probably began learning the rules when you were a young child, sitting buckled into your seat belt in the back seat of the family car. As you sat there, you absorbed a lot of information about driving a car in this country. You noticed, subconsciously perhaps, that the driver of the car sits in a particular seat and performs a set sequence of activities in order to make the car start and to keep it moving along the road safely and at a desirable speed. You also noticed that certain signs caused the driver to respond in certain ways.

As a teenager studying the driver's manual, you began to *call up* all of those bits and pieces of information about driving that you had absorbed over the years. When you read the manual, you brought to the forefront of your mind what you already knew about the topic. Without that background knowledge to build upon, learning how to drive would have been nearly impossible to accomplish in the relatively short time you took. Calling up what you already knew about road signs, for example, probably allowed you to skim through that section because the information was so familiar. When confronting any new topic, readers and writers call up what they already know so they can work with the topic as efficiently as possible. If stored information were not called up, then each reading and writing task would have to start from the very beginning.

Connect

Learning involves *connecting* information. When you receive information and you have already had some experience with it, you connect the new input with what you already know. You call up previous knowledge and either add to the information there or change the information to accommodate the new data. Connecting information is a matter of relating what is being presented to what is already known.

To illustrate the connecting process, think again about your state driver's manual. You may never have considered that each of the road signs you saw had been color-coded to convey additional information. You did know, however, that whenever you saw a stop sign you were required to brake your vehicle and come to a complete stop at the designated location. What you learned upon reading your manual was that whenever you saw a red sign, no matter what shape it was or what message it contained, the basic thought was to stop. "Do Not Enter," "Wrong Way," and "No Left Turn" signs all contain red. While studying your manual, you might have called up your prior knowledge that a red light meant to stop and related that knowledge to the new fact that any red sign means movement is prohibited. Building such a bridge between old and new information is how to connect.

Predict

When you first got your copy of the booklet and began to thumb through it, you were guessing at its contents and trying to *predict* what it had to teach you as well as what it contained that you already knew. For instance, you might have thought there would be sections on starting the car and economizing on gas. In reality, however, you would have found practically no information on those topics. Upon seeing headings in the manual about road signs, on the other hand, you probably expected to find information about their shapes and the messages they conveyed, and your examination of the manual probably verified that prediction.

Like connecting, the predict thinking process requires that you call up information you already possess. If you had no information to call up, then making predictions would be difficult. You almost never simply call up information; generally you call up information so that you can do something with it. In the case of predict, when you opened the driver's manual you anticipated what you might find there. You based those predictions upon the prior knowledge you called up about driving.

Predicting involves thinking ahead about what is to come, thus giving you a headstart on learning what is to come. Predicting also tends to motivate you to get involved with the material. Why do movie theaters show previews of coming attractions? To motivate you to come back.

Organize

To make sense of the driver's manual, you needed to *organize* the information presented there. You probably arranged that information according to some type of framework, perhaps according to the various headings that you found in the manual. Most manuals are written in chapters devoted to topics. Within each chapter, there are headings which group the topics into related subsets of information. A chapter on hazardous driving conditions might include facts about driving at night; driving in fog, rain, snow, and ice; and driving under the influence of alcohol and other drugs.

Readers and writers who organize their information generally comprehend and retain it better than disorganized readers and writers. Try a brief experiment to see how organization works. Look at the list of words below for 30 seconds. Then close your text and write down all you can remember.

Organization Exercise

deer	date	raspberry	Pennsylvania
Oregon	panda	pineapple	rooster
orange	Rhode Island	Delaware	ocelot

How many did you get correct? Now try again, but this time group the 12 words by animal, fruit, and state and by the four initial letters, D R O P, within each group.

How many were you able to recall this time? Putting some system of organization onto pieces of information helps you to recall more of the information both immediately and after a period of time. To check that out, wait until tomorrow and then make a list of as many of the same 12 words as you can remember. You will probably find yourself saying something like, "There are four animals, four fruits, and four states and the items in each category begin with four different letters, D R O P."

Image

Engaging your senses as you read and write adds to the learning experience and makes it more memorable. This process consists of forming an *image*. Visual images are used most frequently, although other sense images certainly come into play. Vicariously seeing, feeling, hearing, smelling, or tasting what is described in print can all help learning.

Think about the part of your driver's manual that discussed the appropriate distances to maintain between two vehicles in motion. Safe following distances vary according to how fast you are traveling. At 50 miles per hour, for instance, a safe following distance is 84 yards. You could easily forget these figures if there were no way to transform them. Thus, you might imagine a 100-yard football field and then mentally place a car at one goal line and your car 84 yards down the field. That visual image would help you to remember the appropriate distance to keep between two vehicles traveling at 50 miles per hour.

Driver's manuals also present information about turning at intersections. You probably studied the abstract diagrams and discussions about turning and then visualized particular instances of those procedures. In your mind's eye might have run a little motion picture of you pulling up to a multiple-lane intersection and then executing the appropriate turn.

Monitor

Throughout your study of the driver's manual you needed to *monitor* how well you were doing with the information. Internally, and probably subconsciously, you asked yourself "Am I understanding this? Am I getting what I need? Does this make sense?" Monitoring is an internal check on how well your learning is progressing.

Efficient learners continually monitor their progress. If learning breaks down, good learners stop, identify the source of their difficulty, and try to get over that difficulty. For instance, when you got to the part in your driver's manual about different kinds of licenses, you might have plunged into information about chauffeur's license expirations, the minimum age for driving mopeds, and the cost of instruction permits. Eventually you realized that you were being overwhelmed, so you stopped and thought, "Now what do I need from this section?" You might have determined that the renewal period and minimum age for a regular operator's license was all that was important to you, so you selected that information for careful study before moving on to the next section. Monitoring one's learning in this way is a crucial thinking process.

Review

Because obtaining a driver's license is so important to teenagers, no one had to tell you to *review* what you were learning from the driver's manual. You probably found yourself lying awake in bed at night rehearsing what you had read. As you walked through the hallways at school, you may have mumbled to yourself the regulations concerning speed zones. You may have gotten together with friends so that you could go over the material covered in the manual, recalling all that you could and then looking in the manual to see what you missed. Whatever you did, you probably studied the material again and again.

Why don't you stop now and review what you have learned so far about essential thinking processes? Seven of the nine processes have been presented. Close this textbook and list the seven on a piece of paper. Then write a personal example that you connect with each of the thinking processes. Provide examples of what you have done in the past in order to call up, connect, predict, etc.

Evaluate

When you *evaluate*, you judge the writing style and the information you are receiving. Judgments about writing style frequently relate to the clarity of the presentation. You want your reading materials to be user friendly. User friendly is a term that describes how understandable computers and their software are. Text materials should be user friendly, too. Was your driver's manual easy to understand, or did you find it confusing? Was the information explained clearly or not?

When you evaluate, you also judge the content of what you are learning. As you were reading your driver's manual, you may have encountered a section on safety belts under the heading *Equipment*. "What's that doing there?" may have been your response. "There are no laws requiring me to wear safety belts in my state. Why should I have to read about them?" As you read on, you may have learned some new information about the value of safety belts so you could see why that section was included in the manual.

On the other hand, you may have discovered a section in the back of your manual on recording car expenses. If you had no plans to keep track of your car expenses, you might have decided that those pages should not have been included in the manual.

Evaluating reading material is important for learning because it gets you involved. Readers and writers who make decisions about the style of writing and the value of information strengthen their grasp of the information. Those who simply accept information without examining it are at a disadvantage.

Apply

The ninth learning principle is *apply*. The only reason you plowed through the driver's manual was so you could pass the driver's test, obtain a license, and get behind the wheel of a car. Whenever you did get behind the wheel, you were required to remember all of the rules and regulations: how fast to go on various streets under various conditions, who had the right of way in different situations, and what the road signs all meant.

Applying is adapting what you have learned to actual situations. When you apply, you are also able to discover what you still need to work on. Perhaps you found that you were still a little unsure about what some signals meant. Does the flashing red light on a certain street mean "Stop" or does it mean "Slow down and proceed with caution"? When you apply information, you select the most appropriate response from all the ones you have learned. Using information appropriately is what applying is all about. When you apply knowledge, you can also tell how well you have assimilated what you have been exposed to, and you learn what you need more information on or practice with.

As was noted at the beginning of Chapter 1, this textbook is meant to help you teach students to read and write in the content areas. Our ultimate goal is for you to apply the information contained here to your classroom situations.

A Final Word

Presenting nine separately labeled essential thinking processes implies that each is isolated from the other, and listing them in order from call up to apply suggests that learners do first one, then the other, then the other in a prescribed sequence. But these thinking processes do not stand alone, and learners do not use them in a rigid order. Instead, each learner integrates the processes differently according to the demands of each situation. Learners may form images and predict upcoming information simultaneously, or they may evaluate the first few sentences of what they read or write, organize their thoughts, and then continue processing the information. Our point here is that learners combine thinking processes and use them at different times in order to learn effectively. Teachers may provide instruction in one or two processes at a time, but they should also help students learn to integrate the processes.

Students at all grade levels can benefit from instruction in the thinking processes outlined about. To paraphrase Bruner's famous quotation from *The Process of Education* (1977): "We begin with the hypothesis that any (thinking process) can be taught effectively in some intellectually honest form to any child at any stage of development" (p. 33). This means that organization, for example, can be taught in the primary as well as the high school grades. Primary-grade children might categorize pictures of animals according to those that fly, walk, or swim; high school students might classify one-celled life forms according to their kingdom, phylum, class, order, family, genus, and species. Similarly, very young children can learn to evaluate by thinking about a question like this: "Did a real boy named Jack climb a beanstalk and meet a giant?" Older students can ponder how well *The Lord of the Flies* expresses basic human nature.

School-age children seem to share the same mental processes (Donaldson, 1978). Learners from kindergarten through 12th grade call up, connect, predict, organize, image, monitor, review, evaluate, and apply information with varying degrees of sophistication. This textbook addresses K–12 reading and writing because of the fundamental similarity of these processes across the various grades.

A final point to keep in mind when considering these essential thinking processes is that motivation underlies all of them. Students who become involved with their learning and who seek information because they want to know it have a distinct learning advantage over unmotivated students. Think about how well your learning occurred when you had an intense desire to know something as opposed to your learning when you were not interested in the topic. To return to our earlier example, many adolescents who perform poorly in school perform amazingly well with the relevant, compelling demands of their state driver's manual. Teachers should remember that promoting students' motivation to learn is at least as important as developing their thinking processes.

APPROACHES TO CONTENT AREA READING AND WRITING INSTRUCTION

So far, Chapter 1 has described two aspects of content area reading and writing: the challenges that are presented and the thinking processes to be promoted. This final section focuses on teaching approaches: How do teachers approach the task of helping students read and write to learn? How are the thinking processes taught? How can teachers plan meaningful daily lessons? While there are many approaches to teaching (Broudy & Palmer, 1965; Joyce & Weil, 1972), this section presents only three: content-driven presentation of processes, fading, and personalized inquiry. These three are valuable approaches to developing readers and writers in the content areas.

Content-Driven Presentation of Processes

Literacy instruction is *content-driven*, or functional, when it occurs as needed (Herber, 1978). Teachers compare the demands of their subject matter and the proficiencies of their students in order to determine what attention needs to be devoted to reading and writing instruction. If a teacher sees that an upcoming passage presents heroes from the ancient Greek epics, for example, he or she might have students call up what they already know about modern heroes and connect that information with the text information. Helping students recall heroes from space exploration, movies, comics, and memorable local events and then connecting those heroes with Odysseus and Jason promotes essential thinking processes. Call up and connect would be emphasized here because the content of the passage readily lends itself to those two processes.

For another example of content-driven presentation of processes, think about planning writing assignments for a class. If a teacher asks students to write essays on ancient Greek government, then he or she might help establish a framework for that task. Students could be instructed to organize their essays by including information on voting procedures, form of central government, and duties of the government. The course content in this case (ancient Greek government) would drive the teacher to promote a specific thinking process (organization).

This textbook emphasizes content-driven presentation of processes, or reading and writing instruction based on the subject matter of students' courses. Content-driven presentation is an approach that helps teachers decide *when* to instruct students in specific aspects of reading and writing. The other main instructional issue is *how* to provide appropriate instruction. How do teachers develop the nine learning processes? *Fading* and *personalized inquiry* are two ways to accomplish this.

Fading

Fading calls for teachers to demonstrate the processes they want students to perform and then to gradually diminish assistance until students can perform the processes independently. Fading is used in teaching someone to ride a bicycle. Imagine that you have at your home a guest who has never seen a bicycle, much less ridden one. He spots an old bicycle in your garage and, after being told what it is, wants to learn how to ride it. What would you do? First, you would probably *demonstrate* the process: You would ride the bike in small circles around your guest, talking about how to ride it as you went. Then you'd explain, ''This is the kickstand. It needs to be up before you get started. Then grab the handlebars like this, put one foot on a pedal, and swing up to the seat.'' Your teaching here would involve demonstrating the skill as well as explaining it.

After demonstrating how to ride the bicycle, you would probably have your guest try it. Not expecting immediate success, you would stay nearby to help. You might tell your guest, ''Now it's your turn. Give it a try, and I'll be right here to help you. Believe me, it takes a while to get the hang of this.'' You would encourage your guest to keep trying, and you would point out specific things to work on as he clumsily pedaled the bike around. As he became more and more proficient, you would help him less and less. You might run alongside at first to keep him from crashing, but then you would begin staying in one spot and offering advice as he progressed. This stage of the teaching-learning process is called *guided practice*. You allow learners as much freedom with the task as their abilities allow. You begin fading out as the learner begins fading in.

Finally, after your guest becomes reasonably proficient on the bicycle, you might go out for a long ride. You might tour your neighborhood or take a long trek. Wherever you go, your purpose would be to help your guest apply his new bike riding skills. This is the stage of *independent application*. Providing opportunities for independent application of what was demonstrated and practiced allows your guest to take ownership of the new skill.

Fading in content area reading and writing takes many forms. Teachers may rarely teach houseguests how to ride a bicycle, but many do teach students to select key words in passages. First, the teacher could select a passage and identify the words that he or she considers to be key. The teacher could demonstrate this process and explain how the chosen words targeted important information. Once students were familiar with this process, the teacher could guide students' practice identifying key words. Whole-class work followed by teacher-led discussion would refine students' choices of key words. Eventually, in order to promote application, students might be directed each week to select key words and write them in notebooks.

Fading moves from demonstration to teachers guiding students' practice with a process to students applying the process independently. Teachers fade out and students fade in; teachers show students how to perform a task and then gradually move back so the students can do it on their own. The aim is to promote student independence.

Personalized Inquiry

Another approach to developing content area reading and writing processes is *personalized inquiry*. This approach calls for teachers to set the stage for learning to occur, and then help students as needs arise. Many who learned to ride a bicycle did so with practically no faded instruction. Bicycles were available, and people who wanted to learn to ride them, jumped right into it. These self-taught riders figured out the process because they were well-motivated. As they faced the problems of coordinating the two hand brakes and getting off the bike, they might have sought help. They might have watched others, or they might have simply asked questions. But mostly, they immersed themselves in riding every day and solved problems as they came up.

There are many ways to use personalized inquiry in the study of the content areas. Teachers set out various materials about the topic being studied, and students browse through them in their spare time. A topic like *outer space* is designated for a unit of study, and students investigate aspects of it on their own, obtaining information from various sources: library books, magazines, text books, encyclopedias, filmstrips, interviews, and field trips. Students generate the essential thinking processes because they are motivated to learn.

The personalized inquiry approach to instruction places teachers in a facilitative role. Teachers actively work to motivate students and provide resources that answer students' questions. Students are also given many opportunities to determine for themselves what specific topic to study and what reading and writing task they need help performing.

Summary

Think back to the teachers who helped you develop your reading and writing proficiencies in the content areas. Did they introduce learning processes as you needed them to handle certain parts of the course? Did they demonstrate how to do what they expected you to do? Did they encourage you to learn on your own about subjects that you found particularly fascinating? Teachers who blend these three approaches—content-driven presentation of skills, faded instruction, and personalized inquiry—go far in meeting the needs of learners in the content areas.

REVIEW

Chapter 1 has introduced you to many aspects of content area reading and writing instruction. This activity is included here in order to help you review what you have encountered.

Key terms from this chapter are listed below in random order. Copy each term on a separate card and categorize those cards. Note that category titles as well as category items are listed below:

Learning	Content-driven presentation of skills
Predict	Challenges of content area reading
Image	and writing
Content area versus content area	Fading
Monitor	Review

Structure of materials	Doing
Informing students	Organize
Apply	Approaches to content area reading
Personalized inquiry	and writing instruction
Written versus spoken language	Expository text versus literary text
Experiencing	Evaluate
Aims of instruction	Call up
Functions of literacy	Essential thinking processes
Helping students inform themselves	Connect

REFERENCES

Beach, R., & Appleman, D. (1984). Reading strategies for expository and literary text types. In A. C. Purves & O. Niles (Eds.), *Becoming readers in a complex society* (Eighty-third Yearbook of the National Society for the Study of Education, Pt. 1). (pp. 115–143). Chicago: University of Chicago Press.

Biglan, A. (1973). The characteristics of subject matter in different academic areas. *Journal of Applied Psychology, 57,* 195–203.

Brice-Heath, S. (1980). The functions and uses of literacy. *Journal of Communication,, 30,* 123–133.

Broudy, H. S., & Palmer, J. R. (1965). *Exemplars of teaching method.* Chicago: Rand McNally.

Bruner, J. (1977). *The process of education.* Cambridge, MA: Harvard University Press.

Donaldson, M. (1978). *Children's minds.* New York: W. W. Norton.

Halliday, M. A. K. (1973). *Explorations in the functions of language.* London: Edward Arnold.

Herber, H. L. (1978). *Teaching reading in content areas* (2nd ed.). Englewood Cliffs, NJ: Prentice-Hall.

Joyce, B., & Weil, M. (1972). *Models of teaching.* Englewood Cliffs, NJ: Prentice-Hall.

King, A., & Brownell, J. (1966). *The curriculum and the disciplines of knowledge.* New York: John Wiley and Sons.

Kleiman, G. M., & Schallert, D. L. (1978). Some things the reader needs to know that the listener doesn't. In P. D. Pearson and J. Hansen (Eds.), *Reading: Disciplined inquiry in process and practice* (Twenty-Seventh Yearbook of the National Reading Conference). Clemson, SC: The National Reading Conference.

Olson, D. B. (1977). From utterance to text: The bias of language in speech and writing. *Harvard Educational Review, 47,* 257–281.

Postman, N. (1979). *Teaching as a conserving activity.* New York: Delacorte Press.

Spiro, R. J., & Taylor, B. M. (1980). *On investigating children's transition from narrative to exposity discourse: The multidimensional nature of psychological text classification* (Tech. Rep. No. 195). Urbana: University of Illinois, Center for the Study of Reading.

SUGGESTED READINGS

The following is a review of the professional and research literature published during the first half of this century that was devoted to content area reading instruction. This review presents the intellectual milieu that promoted concerns about content area reading instruction, and provides historical perspective on key issues that confront educators today.

Moore, D. W., Readence, J. E., & Rickelman, R. (1983). An historical exploration of content area reading instruction. *Reading Research Quarterly, 18,* 419–438.

Two sources that describe ideal cases of personalized inquiry in the content areas with elementary-grade children are as follows:

McCarthy, L. P., & Braffman, E. J. (1985). Creating Victorian Philadelphia: Children reading and writing the word. *Curriculum Inquiry, 15*, 121–151.
Seaver, J. T., & Botel, M. (1983). A first-grade teacher teaches reading, writing, and oral communication across the curriculum. *The Reading Teacher, 36*, 656–664.

The following is a good methods book on reading and writing instruction in the content areas in elementary schools:

Hennings, D. G. (1982). *Teaching communication and reading skills in the content areas.* Bloomington, IN: Phi Delta Kappa.

Many methods textbooks focus on reading instruction in the content areas in secondary schools. The following three are noteworthy:

Herber, H. L. (1978). *Teaching reading in content areas* (2nd ed.). Englewood Cliffs, NJ: Prentice-Hall.
Readence, J. E., Bean, T. W., & Baldwin, R. S. (1985). *Content area reading: An integrated approach* (2nd ed.). Dubuque, IA: Kendall/Hunt.
Vacca, R. T. (1981). *Content area reading.* Boston: Little, Brown.

The first article in this group describes the role of reading in the content areas in elementary schools. The other two articles are provocative accounts that question the amount and type of reading that students actually need to do in secondary schools.

Griffin, P. (1977). How and when does reading occur in the classroom? *Theory into Practice, 16,* 376–383.
Rieck, B. J. (1977). How content teachers telegraph messages against reading. *Journal of Reading, 20,* 646–648.
Smith, F. R., & Feathers, K. M. (1983). The role of reading in content classrooms: Assumption vs. reality. *Journal of Reading, 27,* 262–267.

The following two articles extend an argument for promoting writing in the content areas. The Applebee report reviews research into the role of writing as a way to increase learning about the world. The second article investigates this role more informally.

Applebee, A. N. (1984). Writing and reasoning. *Review of Educational Research, 54,* 577–596.
Giroux, H. A. (1979). Teaching content and thinking through writing. *Social Education, 43,* 190–193.

The following are eleven sources that are helpful in specifying the thought processes that are essential for learning content area information:

Ausubel, D. P. (1968). *Educational psychology: A cognitive view.* New York: Holt, Rinehart & Winston.
Bransford, J. (1979). *Human cognition: Learning, understanding and remembering.* Belmont, CA: Wadsworth.
Brown, A. L., Bransford, J. D., Ferrara, R. A., & Campione, J. C. (1983). Learning, remembering, and understanding. In J. H. Flavell & E. M. Markman (Eds.), *Handbook of child psychology: Vol. 1. Cognitive development* (pp. 77–166). New York: Wiley.
Bruner, J., Goodnow, J. J., & Austin, G. A. (1956). *A study of thinking.* New York: Wiley.
Dewey, J. (1910). *How we think.* Boston: D. C. Heath.

Hilgard, E. R. (Ed.). (1964). *Theories of learning and instruction* (Sixty-Third Yearbook of the National Society for the Study of Education). Chicago: University of Chicago Press.

James W. (1925). *Talks to teachers on psychology, and to students on some of life's ideals*. London: Longmans.

Reigeluth, C. M. (1983). Meaningfulness and instruction: Relating what is being learned to what a student knows. *Instructional Science, 12*, 197–218.

Stroud, J. B. (1956). *Psychology in education*. New York: Longmans, Green.

Travers, R. M. W. (1977). *Essentials of learning* (4th ed.). New York: Macmillan.

Weinstein, C. E., & Mayer, R. E. (1985). The teaching of learning strategies. In M. C. Wittrock (Ed.), *Handbook of research on teaching* (3rd ed.) New York: Macmillan.

CHAPTER 2

Comprehension in the Content Areas

WHY TEACH COMPREHENSION?

Think back to your years as an elementary and secondary school student. What do you remember about reading your science, social studies, and other content area textbooks? Perhaps you remember a scene like this:

> The teacher has everyone open his or her book to the beginning of the chapter. Each student takes a turn reading part of the chapter aloud while everyone else follows along. Some students read well and fluently. Others stumble and miss words, and you think they will never get through. You look ahead instead of following along to figure out what part you might have to read so you can rehearse it before being called on.
>
> After the students take turns reading orally, the teacher spends some time firing questions at different students. The questions almost always have short answers and if a student does not answer a question right away, the teacher calls on another student to answer. For each question, the teacher continues to call on students until getting the desired answer. Finally, the students are assigned to finish reading the chapter and to write answers to the questions at the end of the chapter.

The scene just described exemplifies an ineffective way to use content textbooks. This chapter will present you with more effective ways to use textbooks.

Most of the time, we take reading comprehension for granted. We read words and automatically understand what we are reading. But comprehension does not always occur automatically. The following passage from a statistics book (Kirk, 1972) shows that comprehension is more than a matter of being able to read each word:

Fractional factorial designs have much in common with confounded factorial designs. The latter designs, through the technique of confounding, achieve a reduction in the number of treatment combinations that must be included within a block. A fractional factorial design uses confounding to reduce the number of treatment combinations in the experiment. As is always the case when confounding is used, the reduction is obtained at a price. There is considerable ambiguity in interpreting the outcome of a fractional factorial experiment, since treatments are confounded with interactions. For example, a significant mean square might be attributed to the effects of treatment A or to a BCDE interaction. (p. 256)

Did you understand what you read? Could you retell it to someone in your own words without looking back at the text? Most people who are not knowledgeable about statistics could not comprehend that paragraph, although to statisticians, the paragraph makes perfect sense. As a teacher, you are knowledgeable in all the content subjects you will teach. Elementary and secondary textbooks almost always make perfect sense to you because you already know a lot about what you are reading. You may feel as if you are learning a whole new set of facts by reading the text, but in fact, you already know much of the information presented, and are simply adding a little new information to the vast amount you already understand. Comprehension is indeed automatic when you are reading about topics for which you have adequate background, know most of the appropriate vocabulary, and know enough to sort out important from trivial information.

Unfortunately, many students are seldom in that position when reading content area textbooks. This chapter describes in detail how to plan and teach a lesson in reading comprehension. Of course, comprehension lessons are not the only means of building student comprehension; teaching word meanings, using content area literature, helping students write, and helping students conduct research are also means of developing comprehension. The next four chapters will address these other means.

Comprehension lessons are based on the principle that a primary ability of good readers is the ability to read selectively when they have a purpose for reading. This principle also applies to listening. Often, we ask students to listen to us read to them without building their background knowledge or giving them clear purposes for listening. Content listening comprehension lessons are similar to reading comprehension lessons in most aspects.

Imagine yourself holding the textbook on which you will rely to communicate much of the content of your course. How can you use this textbook effectively? Should you merely assign students to study their textbooks and then hold them accountable for the information found there? We hope that our statistics paragraph example has convinced you that for unfamiliar subjects, comprehension may not occur unless students are prepared and guided through their reading. Of course, you don't have enough time to guide students through all their reading. And the students who are already familiar with a content area can read the textbook independently. To make the best use of your textbook, then, you should select those portions which seem most important to you and least familiar to most students. Then guide your students' comprehension of those portions using a comprehension lesson plan.

DECIDING WHAT STUDENTS NEED TO COMPREHEND

Time is a teacher's most precious commodity. Using that time strategically rather than haphazardly is one key to successful teaching. Textbooks are filled with facts and terminology. Some of this information will already be known by almost all of your students; some will be known by almost none; some will be known by only part of the class; and some will be too difficult, trivial, or uninteresting to be taught regardless of who already knows it.

When teaching content early in the year, a teacher should use available information to decide what and how to teach. Except in kindergarten, a teacher begins the year knowing some things about his or her students from their test scores, grades, and reputations. Some teachers also conduct formal or informal diagnoses or testing during the first week of school. The best way to learn about your students, however, is by trying to teach them. You should soon be able to modify your teaching to meet the needs and abilities of your students as you observe them directly. By the first few weeks of school, you should evaluate your textbook to decide which portions to emphasize, given what you now know about your students. Rate each section of the textbook on the following scale:

Most important: Students' comprehension of that portion will be guided in class using a comprehension lesson.

Important: Students will be assigned to read that portion independently in class or for homework.

Least important: Students will not read that portion.

If you are unsure about the relative importance of the information in a textbook, you might consult another teacher, an expert in that content area, or a curriculum guide. But you must somehow determine a rating. You cannot effectively help students read their content area textbooks if everything in the text is considered equally important. In actual practice, rating a text is not difficult once you realize that it is your responsibility to do so.

Read a chapter of your textbook through without making any notes. Close the book and ask yourself, "What in this chapter do I really want my students to know in five years?" Jot down your response. Rate that material "most important." The facts and terms that help explain what is "most important" will be part of your comprehension lessons.

APPLY

Obtain a textbook you will or might use in your teaching. Mark the beginning of each section of that textbook with a light pencil as MI for "most important," I for "important," or LM for "least important."

Once you have classified the portions of your textbook, you can ignore the portions rated "least important." The "important" portions will be assigned reading. For the portions rated "most important," you will teach comprehension lessons. The next two sections of this chapter will explain the four steps of planning and the five steps of teaching a content comprehension lesson.

PLANNING A CONTENT COMPREHENSION LESSON

Step one: Read the text portion to be used in the lesson and identify the information to emphasize. Just as you decided which portion of the text to teach you need to decide which information within those portions deserves emphasis. Try to read the portion of the textbook that you are going to teach while imagining the student's level of learning. If you did not already know the information in the text, would you understand what you are reading?

Textbooks often are "baskets of facts." Consider how bewildering a string of facts can be when they do not seem to support any point but are simply mentioned in passing. Texts vary greatly according to their ability to organize facts coherently. In a chapter on the solar system, for example, the text might explain that planets' surface temperatures vary according to their distances from the sun; or it may present information about surface temperatures in isolation, planet by planet. When you teach generalizations, you can cover larger portions of material than when you teach only facts and details. The more information you teach through generalizations, the more material you can cover.

Once you have read the portion of the text, close the book and jot down what information you would like students to remember for many years. This is the same technique you used to decide which portion of the text to teach. For a section on the solar system, for example, you might decide that you want students to be able to list the nine planets, know their relative positions and sizes, and explain their orbits. There might be a lot more information in the section, but these three points deserve emphasis.

Step two: Choose an appropriate purpose for comprehending the selection. Without a purpose for comprehending, a lesson ceases to be a lesson and becomes a test. The purpose for comprehending is the crucial part of a comprehension lesson because of the *mathemagenic effect* (Rothkopf, 1982). The mathemagenic effect is the influence that a student's knowledge of the comprehension task has on that student's comprehension.

Imagine that a large number of students is randomly divided into two groups. The first group is given five questions and told that after they read a passage they will be asked to answer those five questions. The second group is told that after they read a passage they will be expected to remember everything they have read. All students in both groups are then given the same passage to read and the same length of time to read it. The passages are collected. Both groups are then given the same ten-question test. The first five questions on this test (Set A questions) are the same five questions that the first group of students was allowed to examine in advance; the second five questions (Set B questions) are new but equally difficult questions. Which group of students will answer more Set A questions correctly? Which group will answer more Set B questions correctly?

PREDICT

Guess which group of students will do better on Set A questions, or if there will be no difference. Guess which group will do better on Set B questions, or if there will be no difference. Jot down your guesses before reading on.

Typically, the first group will correctly answer more Set A questions than the second group, but the second group will correctly answer more Set B questions than the first group. Why? Because of the mathemagenic effects.

The first group of students used the expectation that they would be asked the Set A questions to direct their attention toward the information relevant to those questions and away from the information not relevant to them, whereas the second group directed their attention more equally toward all information.

Is reading with teacher-established purposes better than reading without such purposes? It depends on the teacher's goals. If a teacher considers that the information covered in the Set A questions is in fact the most important, the first group read better. If the teacher considers all the information equally important, the second group read better. The mathemagenic effect means that teachers who inform students in advance of the comprehension task will lead students to do better on that task than if they had not informed them in advance (Rothkopf, 1982). Setting a purpose for comprehension is the means by which teachers emphasize what is to be learned.

Why do purposes for comprehension help; i.e., why is there a mathemagenic effect? Because when reading or listening, no one can absorb all the information. Even authorities on a work of literature have to read that work again each time they develop a new hypothesis about it. Many people reread the Bible hundreds of times, claiming fresh insights with each reading.

It would be nice if students could monitor their understanding, organize information, connect what they know with what they read, form images, evaluate the message, and apply what they learn to new situations all at a high level of performance during just one reading or hearing of a text. But students cannot perform all of these functions at once when they are dealing with new material. If students read to form images, their predictions will suffer; if they listen to check on their predictions, their evaluation of content will suffer. The exceptional students who do seem to be able to perform these processes well and simultaneously only appear to do so because they already knew much of the information before reading or hearing the text.

If the purpose for comprehension is given to students in advance, they can monitor their comprehension of the targeted information while they read or listen. There must never be surprises for students when it comes time for them to demonstrate that they have accomplished the preset purpose. If students come to realize that the teacher's stated goals only mislead them, they will soon ignore those goals and the mathemagenic effect will be lost. For example, students might be directed to read in order to find out why planets maintain their identical orbits year after year. After reading, however, a teacher might begin a discussion by asking, "Well, what did you think of the passage?" Students who read to find out about the planets' orbits will be at a disadvantage compared with students who simply ignored the purpose and read to form a general impression. If the mathemagenic effect is to have its maximum influence, the after-reading task must always be the one that the purpose for comprehending led students to expect.

Choosing a purpose for comprehending requires clever thinking and careful planning. The situation is like solving an equation with one unknown variable. Three "known quantities" are given: the text selection to be comprehended, the information you want to emphasize, and the students' reading abilities. The unknown variable is the purpose for comprehending that would make maximum use of the mathemagenic effect. Unfortunately, there is no algorithm for solving this equation. Instead, we will discuss the various types of purposes and then present a list of possible ones for you to use.

A Cafeteria of Purposes

The possible purposes that we present here should be seen as being displayed in a sort of cafeteria. When you eat at a cafeteria, you realize that there are other kinds of good food besides what's available there. In other words, you may want to give students a different purpose than the ones we list, a purpose just as good as any we have given. Furthermore, when you eat at a cafeteria, you realize that you do not have to take one of every item; you can pick and choose. Even if you were to visit the cafeteria hundreds of times over the years, there would probably be items that you would never select. The same is true for our cafeteria of purposes. Select the purposes you find most appropriate and ignore the rest. Some teachers choose to use only nine or ten purposes in the course of a year; others need a greater variety.

Imagine how funny it would be to be behind someone in a cafeteria who looked up the nutritional value of each item of food, rather than simply choosing a variety of items from different sections to insure a balanced diet. Likewise, we have presented nine essential thinking processes and a teacher might take each one into consideration when setting purposes for comprehension lessons. But the same objective would be met by using a variety of purposes across different content comprehension lessons. In a functional approach to content instruction, each essential thinking process will eventually be elicited as different purposes for comprehension are used.

When you eat at a cafeteria, you make no effort to remember every item that has been offered to you. Rather, you look at the items and then make your selection. Our cafeteria of purposes is not for you to commit to memory, but rather for you to open and use when planning content comprehension lessons.

Finally, as in a cafeteria where foods are grouped together by type—salad, meat, vegetable, dessert—our purposes for comprehension are grouped together by type. Possible purposes are classified according to whether they are most appropriate for expository or literary texts. As explained in Chapter 1, expository texts consist of writings such as scientific explanations, persuasive essays, and listings of events; literary texts include writings such as novels, short stories, biographies, and plays.

A second classification for types of purposes is the kind of language that is used. Some purposes are expressed in content-specific language; i.e., they allude to specific information in the passage. For example, a teacher might say, "Listen to this section on agriculture in the South in the 1820s and 1830s so you can decide why Whitney's invention of the cotton gin helped cause the Civil War." Other purposes are stated in generic language; i.e., they label some aspect of the text with a general term. For example, a teacher might say, "Listen to this passage and pick out the causes and effects that it describes." Generic purposes for comprehension do not refer to specific information from the text, but rather to general concepts that the teacher has already explained.

Thus our cafeteria of purposes has four sections:

Content-Specific Purposes for Expository Texts
Generic Purposes for Expository Texts
Content-Specific Purposes for Literary Texts
Generic Purposes for Literary Texts.

Content-Specific Purposes
for Expository Texts

Expository writing has a different structure than does literary writing. Most textbooks consist of exposition. Thirteen methods of developing content-specific purposes for those texts are presented here in our cafeteria of purposes. The first ten methods are teacher-directed: the teacher develops the purpose for comprehending based on his or her curricular goals. The other three methods are student-centered, with students setting their own purposes through the process of prediction.

To demonstrate how you would use these methods to develop content-specific purposes, we will sometimes use Chapter 1 as an example of an expository text.

Take Two   Students are given four or more statements that are literally true. Students then read or listen to the selection to decide which two of the statements are most important. To see how this method works, call up or reread Chapter 1 to decide which two of these four statements are the most important:

1. The essential thinking processes are: Call Up, Predict, Organize, Connect, Image, Monitor, Review, Evaluate, and Apply.
2. Personalized inquiry is one approach to content area reading and writing.
3. Reading and writing to do is one of the three functions of literacy.
4. Content area reading and writing instruction should help students learn information and become independent acquirers of information.

Which did you choose? Was this a difficult task? *Take two* involves high-level thinking processes such as evaluation because it requires you to decide which two of four true statements are most important. While we believe that numbers two and three are important, we believe that numbers one and four are more important. You can determine this by looking at the page space devoted to these topics in Chapter 1. Much more space is allocated to discussing the thinking processes and to specifying the dual purposes of content area reading and writing than is devoted to the other two topics. Numbers one and four were also given more theoretical prominence than the others; they describe generalizations from the chapter rather than simply repeating specific facts.

Macro-Cloze   A major part of the selection, such as the beginning, middle, or end, is deleted or hidden from view. The students read or listen to the rest of the selection and must then infer what was left out. This is a good purpose-setting method for a text that describes steps to be followed or a sequence of events in which students can infer from the remaining steps what has been left out. For example, when using an American history text to teach secondary students about World War II, the teacher could assign the students to read the portions telling about the beginning of the war, Pearl Harbor, and the first two years of United States involvement in the war. Students might be told to skip the next portion and then read about the surrender of Germany to the Allies. Their purpose for comprehending would be to figure out what might have happened between the end of 1943 and June 1944 to result in Germany's defeat. The skipped portion of the text would be read later as one basis for evaluating their inferences.

Feature Matrix   A *feature matrix* is a figure with rows and columns. Each member of a category is written at the beginning of a row; the features that those members might have are written at the top of the columns. The students read or listen to the selection with the idea of completing the matrix by placing a plus or a minus in each box to show which features each category member possesses. Here is a feature matrix for the essential thinking processes described in Chapter 1:

	Performed Before Reading	Performed During Reading	Performed After Reading
Call Up			
Predict			
Organize			
Connect			
Image			
Monitor			
Review			
Apply			
Evaluate			

Unscramble   Students are given two or more events from the selection in random order. They read or listen so they can put the events in the right order. This content-specific purpose is useful when the text contains events whose order is important. If you were guiding your class through a unit on World War II, for example, you might provide several events from the war and have students organize them in chronological order.

Key Term   Students are given a word or phrase that is not defined in any one statement in the text and told that it is an important or *key term*. The students read or listen so they can tell what the term means. For Chapter 1, the key term, *essential thinking processes of content area reading and writing*, might have been given to you to set your purpose for reading.

Inference Sort   Students are given five or fewer statements about the content of a selection; all statements are true according to the text. Students read or listen to decide which statements are stated explicitly by the text (literal information) and which are stated indirectly (implied information). At a later stage, students may be given five or fewer statements, none of which are stated explicitly by the text. They read or listen to decide which statements are definitely true according to the text, which are only possibly true according to the text, and which cannot be true according to the text.

Here are four statements, all of which are true according to the "Structure of Materials" section of Chapter 1. Can you decide which statements were explicitly stated and which were only implied?

1. Written language is different from spoken language.
2. Most readers are more comfortable reading literature.
3. Vocabulary is important to all content areas.
4. Because different content areas require the ability to follow different kinds of text structure, each teacher should help students learn how his or her content area material is structured.

Focus   Given a subtopic, students read or listen to remember everything about that subtopic. When you use *focus* as your method for determining purpose, you are saying that the details of some subtopic in the text are important, and you want students to remember these details. This is a possible purpose only for a subtopic. You might remember everything you read in a short section, but you could not remember everything about a long section. If we were to use this method with Chapter 1, we would target the "Essential Thinking Processes" section rather than the "Challenges of Content Area Reading and Writing" section.

Cause/Effect   Given a cause, students read or listen to state the effect(s), or given an effect, students read or listen to state the cause(s). This purpose would be used when the text explained some causal relationships that you want your students to learn. For example, if a health text portion concentrates on the causes of lung cancer, you might have students read to answer this question: "How do most people with lung cancer get that disease?" Or, if a social studies text portion describes the effect of the Eighteenth Amendment to the Constitution, you might have them read to answer the question, "What happened after Prohibition became the law of the land?"

Problem/Solution   Given a problem, students read or listen to state the solution(s); given a solution, students read or listen to state the problem(s). This purpose leads students to attend to some problem and solution you believe they should understand. For example, in a physics course, you might describe Archimedes' problem of needing to tell the king whether or not the gold in his crown was pure. Students might then be told, "Read so you can tell how Archimedes figured out the purity of the gold in the crown without melting down the crown."

Compare/Contrast   Given subtopics, students read or listen to find similarities or differences among them. Referring once more to Chapter 1, we might lead you to compare various approaches to content area reading and writing by asking you to list similarities and differences between faded instruction and personalized inquiry.

The last three of our thirteen methods for developing content-specific purposes for expository text rely on student prediction. You learned in Chapter 1 that predicting is one of the essential thinking processes. In fact, predicting is the primary means you use to set your own purposes while reading or listening. In essence, prediction is the act of making one's cognitive capacity available to pursue the answer to a question. The predictions we make before or during comprehension reveal what our questions are. As we read, we predict what we will be reading; then we confirm or contradict our predictions by further reading. Teachers must require students to read purposefully, but they must also help students learn how to set their own purposes. We can help students develop their prediction skills and hence their ability to set their own comprehension purposes if we lead students to actively anticipate what they will encounter in their reading. There are three possible methods for using prediction to elicit content-specific purposes for expository texts:

Possible Sentences   Given a set of key terms from a passage, each student picks two key terms to use in constructing a sentence that is likely to be supported by the text. Individuals share their responses, which the teacher writes on the board, until there are up to five sentences on the board. Then students read or listen to decide which of the sentences are true according to the text, which are false, and which cannot be resolved using the text. If we had wanted to use *possible sentences* as a method for helping you predict what you might learn from Chapter 1, we might have given you this set of words: call up, predict, organize, connect, image, monitor, review, evaluate, and apply. By making up possible sentences that include two of these terms, you would be predicting what the text might tell you about the terms. For example, you might have written sentences like these:

When you predict, you call up what you already know.
You can predict an image.
You have to evaluate to review.

Then, using this method, you would have read Chapter 1 to decide which sentences were true. Figure 2.1 shows a teacher using this purpose for comprehending to guide students' comprehension.

Expectation Outline   Students are directed to read or listen to the title or heading of a selection, and possibly to see any illustrations or other graphic aids. Based on this limited information, students decide as a group what they expect to learn from reading or listening to the selection. The teacher puts

Figure 2.1   This teacher is recording a student's sentence.

the group expectation on the board in outline form. Students then read or listen to compare what they learned with what they expected to learn.

Preview Question   Given the title or heading of a selection, students develop questions from that heading. They then read or listen to answer those questions. Students evaluate the quality of the heading and the quality of their questions based on whether the selection answered their questions.

Generic Purposes for Expository Texts

In the previous section of the cafeteria, procedures were presented for developing purposes that are specific to the expository passage being taught. In this section of the cafeteria, we present generic purposes. These purposes focus student attention on what texts have in common. Therefore, they are not specific to any one text, though of course they are better used with some texts than with others. Here are some possible generic purposes:

   Read or listen to the selection:

   to retell it in (a number between 12 and 25) or fewer words.

   to answer the question ''What is it about?'' in (a number between 3 and 7) or fewer words.

   to list the (important) events (in order).

to choose the one sentence that best tells what the whole passage is about.

to choose the (a number between 2 and 5) most important word(s).

so you can outline it.

so you can web it. A web is an outline without numbers or letters. Figure 2.2 shows a web of the important information you have read about planning comprehension lessons for expository texts.

Content-Specific Purposes for Literary Texts

Many of the methods for developing or eliciting content-specific purposes for expository text can also be used with literature. For example, when having students read "The Legend of Sleepy Hollow," they could be given a key term and told to read so that they can fully discuss the meaning of that term as Irving used it in that story. There are, however, purposes for comprehending literature which seem unique to that genre. The following six purposes are appropriate for literary texts:

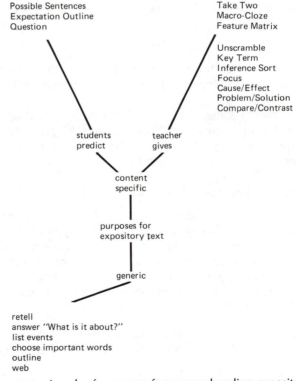

Possible Sentences
Expectation Outline
Question

Take Two
Macro-Cloze
Feature Matrix

Unscramble
Key Term
Inference Sort
Focus
Cause/Effect
Problem/Solution
Compare/Contrast

students
predict

teacher
gives

content
specific

purposes for
expository text

generic

retell
answer "What is it about?"
list events
choose important words
outline
web

Figure 2.2   A web of purposes for comprehending expository text.

Location   Given one or more settings in the literature selection, students read or listen to describe each one. You would use this purpose when you had decided that it is important for the students to have a clear image of a story's setting. Readers of *The Adventures of Huckleberry Finn* might be asked to read Chapters 8 and 9 so that they could draw a map of the island.

Event   Given an event in the narrative, students read or listen to describe the event carefully. You would use this purpose to focus student attention on a particular event that is crucial to a narrative. Readers of *Huckleberry Finn* might be asked to read Chapters 12 and 13 to tell what happened when Huck and Jim went aboard the wrecked steamboat.

Character   Students read or listen to describe the actions, feelings, reactions, etc. of an important character(s). Readers of *Huckleberry Finn* might be asked to read Chapters 19 through 31 to write a description of the actions and the psychology of "the Duke."

Relation   Given one or more pairs of characters, students read or listen to describe their relationship(s). Readers of *Huckleberry Finn* could be asked to read Chapters 1 through 3 to describe the relationship between Huck and Tom Sawyer.

Adjective Checklist   Given one or more locations, events, or characters in a literature selection, and given a list of ten or fewer adjectives, the students read or listen to tell which adjective(s) best describe the location(s), event(s), character(s), or relation(s). Readers of *Huckleberry Finn* might be given adjectives such as *true, genuine, artful, honest, natural,* and *shrewd,* and asked to read the first several chapters of the book to choose which adjective best describes Huck Finn. Additionally, students might choose the two most apt and the two least apt adjectives. Figure 2.3 shows a teacher in the midst of a comprehension lesson which has *adjective checklist* as the method of setting the purpose.

Just as we want students to use prediction to set their own purposes when reading expository texts, we also want them to learn to set their own purposes by predicting before or during their reading of literature. Here is a frequently used method for helping students predict what they will read in a literature selection:

Forecasting   Students read or listen to the title of the literature selection. They may also look at some or all of the illustrations, if there are any. Based on this limited information, individual students predict what will happen in the literature selection. Individuals share some of their predictions until there are up to five predictions on the board. Then the students read or listen to decide which of the predictions are supported by the text, which are refuted, and which are not resolved.

Figure 2.3   These students are deciding which adjective best describes a character in a story they have read.

Generic Purposes for Literary Texts

Numerous generic purposes for literary texts are possible. What follows are some possibilities to be used individually or together.

Read or listen to the literary selection:

to make up a (better) title.

to state a theme.

to dramatize the selection.

to tell where the narrative takes place.

to tell when the narrative takes place.

to tell who the main character is.

to tell what the main character's problem is.

to tell who or what caused the main character's problem.

to tell whether the main character's problem is solved.

to tell how the main character's problem is solved.

to tell what happens after the main character's problem is solved.

to tell what the main character's goal is.

to tell whether the main character's goal is achieved.

to tell how the main character's goal is achieved.

to tell what happens after the main character's goal is achieved.

to tell how the characters in the narrative get along with each other.

to tell how the characters change in the course of the narrative.

to tell why the main character does what he or she does.

to tell who is telling the narrative.

to tell why the narrative takes place where it does.

to tell why the narrative takes place when it does.

Step three: Choose one or two background concepts that students most need to know. We now return to detailing the steps for planning comprehension lessons. The first step called for you to select the information you want your students to learn; in the second step, you selected an appropriate purpose for comprehending. Step three calls for you to identify essential background information.

Students vary in the background knowledge they are able to call up about a particular topic. Students who live in Florida or California may know about oceans and oranges; Midwestern students may be more familiar with wheat and blizzards. The author of a textbook may have assumed that students can call up certain information that you know your students lack. For instance, a passage on volcanoes may assume that students are aware of the "bubbling" action of heated liquids. Thus, the passage may deal primarily with a volcano's effect on the earth's crust, while failing to explain what forces magma up through it. If students are confused about the initial thrust of the magma, they may not be able to follow the rest of the description of volcanic action. We suspect that you had difficulty understanding the paragraph on statistics at the beginning of this chapter because of your own limited background in fractional factorial designs.

If certain information seems prerequisite to students learning from a text, then you should teach this information directly, before having the students read or listen to the text. If students already know the prerequisite information, this instruction will help them call the information up. Because the initial learning or calling up of relevant information is essential for comprehension, every comprehension lesson should include attention to it.

Wait to choose the background concepts to teach in a particular comprehension lesson until you have chosen the purpose for comprehending. For any selection, there will probably be several background concepts you would want your students to know. But teaching concepts well takes time. In a single comprehension lesson you can teach only one or two concepts. By waiting until the purpose is established, you can identify what background students need to fulfill that purpose.

Step four: Plan something to do or say to teach each background concept. There are many ways to teach background concepts. Select the one that is most appropriate for your students, the text portion, and the purpose for comprehending you have chosen to give them. Chapter 3 devotes considerable attention to this topic, so it will be mentioned only briefly here.

Direct Experience

Think about how you yourself learn new concepts. How did you learn how to ride a bike or to swim? How did you learn about the Grand Canyon? Directly experiencing the phenomenon is the most effective way to learn. For the teacher, this means bringing a real object to the students or taking them on a field trip to see objects or events firsthand. It may also mean using models when the real thing is not available. For example, a model of the solar system will have to suffice! If your students are going to read about clog dancing, perhaps you, one of your students, or a guest could demonstrate. Because direct experience is such an important way to build background concepts, two strategies that focus on providing such experience are detailed in Chapter 3.

Visual Experience

Providing direct experiences is expensive, time-consuming, and frequently impossible. How could you help your class directly experience Abraham Lincoln, Mount Everest, or the New York Stock Exchange if you work, say, in Iowa? But visual experience may substitute. Photographs, movies, television shows, filmstrips, or slides should be used whenever possible.

Verbal Explanation

Of course, the teacher can explain a background concept to students by connecting what they already know to the new information. The teacher should use the simplest, most understandable language in this explanation, with examples and analogies wherever possible. To build the concept that some governments are democracies, you might refer to the democratic processes in your own classroom. If you are explaining a new food, you might say something like, ''It's like chili—but not as hot, and the beans are mushier,'' thereby using connection to clarify your explanation.

Verbal explanation can often be combined with visual experience. You might draw students' attention to a picture in the textbook or to one that you provide. When the background concept is the meaning of a term, the term should be written on the board before the teacher begins the explanation. The teacher should tell students that the concept being explained will help them understand the passage they are going to read or listen to. Following the explanation, the students should have the opportunity to ask questions.

If you believe that some of your students already understand the background concept, you may choose to have them explain it to you—and to each other. In that case, you would ask the students a question to get them to explain the concept. If no one gives an adequate answer, you are still free to explain the connections for them.

If you believe that most of your students are familiar with a background concept, you may choose to have them brainstorm about what they know while you write what they say on the board. In *brainstorming*, you ask students to tell you all they know about a given topic, and you write on the board all the terms that your students connect with the topic. For this method to be effective, you must wait until students have finished brainstorming before you correct any wrong information. After they have finished, you are free to explain anything that seems necessary.

APPLY

Obtain a copy of a textbook that you might use in your teaching. Select three portions of the text that you consider among the most important. Plan a content comprehension lesson for each portion. Remember that the steps to follow in planning a content comprehension lesson are:

1. Read the text portion to be used in the lesson and identify important information to teach.
2. Choose an appropriate purpose for comprehending the selection, one that will lead students either to important information, or to setting their purposes for comprehending.
3. Choose one or two background concepts that students most need to know before they begin reading or listening to the selection to fulfill the purpose for comprehending.
4. Plan how to teach each background concept.

Figure 2.4   This teacher is writing a content comprehension lesson on "what makes a community" in her planning book.

TEACHING A CONTENT COMPREHENSION LESSON

Once a lesson has been planned, it is ready to be taught. Knowing how to teach a lesson is a professional skill that must be learned and practiced. Here are five steps for teaching content comprehension lessons:

Step one: Teach the background knowledge that students need for the purpose you give them. Every content comprehension lesson begins by teaching the students the one or two background concepts that are most important for them to know while they read or listen to fulfill the purpose for comprehending. To teach each background concept, the teacher uses combinations of direct experience, visual experience, and verbal explanation.

CALL UP

Try to remember some time in your education when you were unable to learn from a lecture or reading assignment because the speaker or author assumed you had a background concept that in fact you lacked. Jot down you recollection and share it with others in your class. How does this experience relate to planning and teaching content comprehension lessons?

Step two: Set the purpose for comprehending. Students cannot use the purpose for comprehending unless they completely understand it. This is true whether you give them the purpose or they develop their own through prediction. It is best to write the purpose for comprehending on the board and leave it there throughout the lesson so that students can continue to keep it in mind. It is also important to ask students if they understand the purpose. If they have questions, answer them as clearly as possible without actually doing the comprehension task for them.

Step three: Have students read or listen for the established purpose. At this point, students will read or listen to the selection. Younger or less capable readers should be permitted to move their lips or "whisper read"; such behaviors simply mean that the students have not done enough successful silent reading to become good at it. It is never a good idea for the students to take turns reading aloud, unless they were given parts to practice beforehand. Students who read aloud become overly concerned with whether they pronounce words correctly, as does the teacher, and comprehension suffers.

The first few times that you teach a content comprehension lesson to a particular group of students, you will have to interrupt student comprehension early in this step. Students are used to having purposes for comprehension set and then totally ignored. For this reason, the purpose-setting step was probably not taken seriously by your students. They will learn to do so, however, if you interrupt students right after they begin reading and say, "Put your finger on the word you're reading right now and look up at me. I want to see all your eyes. Are you going to be able to (*remind them of the purpose that is still written on the board)* when you finish reading?" Ask them if they are going to be able to do the task and tell them that is all you want. Do this very early in their reading so as not to interfere with their comprehension.

Step four: Have students collectively perform a task that measures accomplishment of the established purpose. Students generally do not enjoy comprehension lessons because they are afraid to be wrong in front of the teacher or their peers. Teachers often feel compelled to call on students to answer comprehension questions, since only the bravest and brightest will volunteer. Fear of failure accounts for much of the passive aggression on the part of some students who refuse to attempt an answer, as well as for the psychological blocks of other students who cannot attempt an answer. In this difficult situation, teachers are often reluctant to deal rigorously with wrong answers for fear of hurting a student's weak self-concept, while students who fear failure often are the cruelest to others in their class ("You're stupid!").

There is a solution to these problems, but it is seldom used. Teachers should use group tasks rather than individual ones to follow up student comprehension. After the students finish reading or listening, the teacher should remind them of their purpose for comprehending. The teacher stands at the board with chalk in hand and asks if someone can start the task. "I asked you to read so that you could describe the location of the poem. Who can give us one descriptive word or phrase?" Or, "You read to complete this web, so who can tell me what to put in the middle?" The teacher waits as long as necessary for someone to begin the task, and writes down whatever that students says, whether it is right or wrong. When the student finishes, or if the student falters, the teacher asks the group whether anyone would like to add, replace, or take away anything from the first student's answer. The teacher develops the group response until there is a consensus of opinion among the students. If students cannot reach a consensus, the teacher leads the group to develop two or more competing responses. In no way is any response allowed to "belong" to one or more students. What is on the board is "our work, our response," belonging to the class as a whole. The teacher never corrects any of the responses during this step.

REVIEW/IMAGE
Look again at the cafeteria of possible purposes for comprehending that we presented earlier in this chapter. Imagine how each one would actually work as students perform a group task.

Step five: Guide students to correct their own task performance as a group. If students correct their own task performance, they will learn more than if you correct it for them. Because the task was performed by the group rather than by an individual, you can insist that the students be rigorous in the process of correction. Ask students if they think any part of the group's response is wrong. Tell each person who responds that he or she must explain why the response is wrong, or must read some evidence from the text that contradicts the response. If the students listened to the text, they can ask the teacher to reread a part that they think will correct a mistake. If a response satisfies them and you, leave it alone. If it satisfies them, but not you, tell them that you believe there is a problem, but require them to find and correct it. When the students have reached a consensus on all points with which you agree, the lesson has ended. If students reach a consensus that is in error and they seem unable to correct that error themselves, you should finally correct the error for them. When you have done so, the lesson is ended.

An Example

Remember the scene we described at the beginning of this chapter, in which everyone takes a turn reading orally and then answers questions orally or in writing. Now we would like to present you with a different scene, one which suggests what a content comprehension lesson might look like. Let's imagine that we can look in on Mr. Gunho as he plans a content comprehension lesson for a section of an American history text describing the Vietnam War. Watch for the five steps of a content comprehension lesson discussed above.

After studying the text section himself, Mr. Gunho decides that he wants students to be able to list the important events of the war in their correct order. He then considers what background information students will need. Out of the many concepts he might teach, he decides that knowing the geography of Southeast Asia and some history of the area's prewar political intrigues are most important for student comprehension. He decides to show a map of the area and have students identify important locations, and to explain the area's political history.

Teaching the lesson is easy once it is planned. Mr. Gunho spends approximately 15 minutes pointing out the important geographic locations and explaining the political history. He then tells students to read "so that you can tell the most important events of the war in the order in which they happened." After ten minutes of silent reading, Mr. Gunho has students close their books and goes to the board with chalk in hand. "I asked you to read so that you could list the important events in order. Who can give me an event?" he asks. Mr. Gunho waits until a student tells an event. He then writes that on the board. "Who can give me another one?" When a student responds with an event, Mr. Gunho writes that one on the board. As students continue to give events, Mr. Gunho records them. Once the events are recorded, Mr. Gunho asks if everyone agrees that all the events are there and that all the events are important. There is some discussion of importance, and two events are erased since the class as a whole thinks these events were minor compared to the others. Next, Mr. Gunho reminds students that they were to read so that they could list the important events in order. He asks, "Which event happened first? Next?" etc. When there are disagreements, Mr.

Gunho allows students to look back in the text for dates and other indications of the correct order. The lesson finishes with the important events listed in order. Mr. Gunho suggests that students might copy these in their notebooks because they will need to study this important information for the upcoming test.

IMAGE/APPLY

Imagine a group of students you have taught or observed someone else teach. In your imagination, teach them a comprehension lesson that you have planned. Carry out each of the five steps: (1) Teach background concepts. (2) Set the purpose. (3) Have them listen or read. (4) Guide the group to perform a task which reflects the purpose you set. (5) Guide the group to correct its task performance.

FOSTERING STUDENT INDEPENDENCE

Even kindergarten and first-grade teachers want their students to take increasing amounts of responsibility for their own learning. Of course, a teacher must always be careful not to demand more from students than they are able to do.

The content comprehension lesson allows teachers to use purposes for comprehending in a sequence that fades out teacher direction and fades in student self-direction. At first, you should teach lessons centered on content-specific purposes that match your instructional goals. These lessons provide a maximum of success for students while requiring very little of their judgments. As students' comprehension improves, they should be required to take more responsibility for choosing the information that they need to comprehend. At this point, you can use prediction to elicit content-specific purposes for comprehending from students. As students become comfortable with these kinds of purposes, you should phase in generic purposes, requiring students to take more responsibility for determining what information will fulfill a general purpose.

Teachers should help students become aware of the steps of planning a comprehension lesson, so that students can follow these steps on their own. For instance, teachers might ask, ''What is the first thing to do before reading to understand?'' A student might answer, ''Skim the passage to determine what we need to learn.'' ''Then what?'' the teacher asks. ''Choose an appropriate purpose.'' ''Next?'' ''Call up what we already know that will help accomplish the purpose.'' After your students carry out these steps, they should be encouraged to perform the task and evaluate their performances. Students should be taught to do as much as possible for themselves what you have been doing during comprehension lessons. Eventually, students will need to understand what they read without your help.

This sequence of fading should be seen as a general pattern, not a fixed progression. Any purpose is called for if it helps the students comprehend a passage and develop independence.

WHAT ABOUT . . .

What about My Students Who Won't Read Assigned Texts?

Contrary to popular belief, students will read assigned texts. But many teachers don't realize that regardless of whether purposes for reading have been given, students have learned from experience that they must read to remember everything to answer the questions they will be asked. Reading to remember everything is a very frustrating task. Students who attempt it often give up when they encounter difficult information or become overloaded. Reading for one specific purpose that is understood, however, is not so frustrating. Students generally will read much longer during the content comprehension lessons described here than when the teacher just assigns something and says, "We'll discuss it."

What about Teaching Several Comprehension Lessons on One Selection?

Many teachers say that there is no way to get students to read or listen to a textbook passage more than once. What these teachers don't realize is that students are far more willing to read or listen to a passage twice for two different specific purposes than to read or listen twice for the same purpose, particularly if that purpose is "to remember everything." In fact, the teacher's major instructional goal will more likely be accomplished if the students comprehend a passage twice. If the teacher feels that the details of a selection are most important, he or she should have students read for generalizations the first time and for facts the second time. If the teacher feels that the generalizations are more important, he or she should teach them second. Knowing generalizations helps students learn facts; knowing facts helps students form generalizations.

It is particularly important to give two or more lessons on the same selection when teaching students to apply or evaluate information. In the first lesson, the teacher insures that students understand the passage's main points; in the second lesson, students are ready to apply or evaluate that information without the problems that miscomprehension can cause.

What about Study Guides?

A study guide is a written comprehension lesson that has students perform a task during reading or listening, rather than afterwards. The major advantages of study guides are that they can be completed outside of class and that they lend themselves more to individualization than do classroom lessons. Their major disadvantages are the time they take to produce, and the degree of student independence that they require. In this book, we chose not to duplicate the several fine discussions of how to use study guides in content areas. We have included some of those in the suggested readings section at the end of this chapter.

What about Tests and Grades?

Any time a teacher records a grade, there has been a test. Tests themselves do not teach; rather, teaching prepares students to take tests. When students are tested on the ''most important'' textbook portions you have taught in class, they will do as well on the test as your lesson has prepared them to do. Thus, a test of your students' learning is also a test of your teaching. When students are tested on the ''important'' textbook portions that were merely assigned for reading on their own, only those students with sufficient help at home or sufficient ability to learn independently will do well. This discrepancy often places teachers, particularly middle and secondary school teachers, in a dilemma. Are they to test students only on what was directly taught in class and have almost everyone get good grades? Or are they to test students on everything assigned in the textbook as well, in order to encourage and reward ''excellence.''

Fortunately, there is a middle position that allows students to learn desired content for satisfactory grades while still rewarding excellence. Teachers should test both what was taught in class and what was assigned to be learned independently. Students who do well only on what was taught in class would earn the minimum satisfactory grade. To receive the highest grade, however, a student would have to do well on everything. Students who cannot learn independently would still have learned something and received satisfactory grades for it, yet excellent students are still encouraged.

REFERENCES

Kirk, R. E. (1972). Classification of ANOVA designs. In R. E. Kirk (Ed.), *Statistical issues: A reader for the behavioral sciences*. Belmont, CA: Wadsworth Publishing Co.

Rothkopf, E. Z. (1982). Adjunct aids and the control of mathemagenic activities during purposeful reading. In W. Otto & S. White (Eds.), *Reading expository material*. New York: Academic Press.

Across

5. Knowing the task before comprehending it has a _____ on task performance.
7. Use your time to teach parts of textbooks you decide are _____.
9. Reading in content textbooks should be silent, not _____.
11. After building background concepts, tell the students their _____ for reading.
14. Purposes can be content-specific _____ generic.
15. Students are more willing to participate _____ the task is a group task.
17. Students often need direction to read word problems in _____.
18. _____ is a lesson with the purpose of remembering everything about a subtopic.
20. Building background concepts by telling is _____.
21. A graphic outline without the numbers and letters is a _____.
22. When the students and teacher have evaluated their performances, the lesson comes to an _____.
24. A purpose that is not specific to one piece of text is a _____ purpose.
26. A place for learning or a group of fish is a _____.
27. Building background concepts by having everyone contribute what they know is called _____.
28. A purpose for informational text in which causal relationships are important is _____.
29. Having clear purposes for reading and listening helps students and teachers meet their _____.

30. A purpose for informational text in which students reorder events is called _____.
31. Students are given important terms with which they make _____ and then read or listen to confirm.

Down

1. Important information students must know before reading is called _____.
2. Students can listen or _____ during a content comprehension lesson.
3. When a teacher takes a grade, a _____ has been given.
4. How well your students comprehend when they have background concepts and purposes will _____ you.
6. In this chapter, you have learned to teach a _____.

8. Most content comprehension lessons have _____ purpose.
10. All responses written on the board belong to the _____.
12. Background concepts can be built by _____ real things, pictures, and models.
13. Purposes are as important when we _____ as when we read.
16. Background concepts can be built by _____ students about what they already know.
19. To develop student independence, you _____ out teacher guidance.
23. One of the nine essential thinking processes is _____.
25. You must read with some purposes in mind because no one can get it _____ in one reading.

SUGGESTED READINGS

For those who wish to know more about the preparation and use of various kinds of study guides, two excellent sources are:

Herber, H. L. (1978). *Teaching reading in content areas* (2nd ed.). Englewood Cliffs, NJ: Prentice-Hall.
Vacca, R. T. (1981). *Content area reading*. Boston: Little, Brown.

The following article is a good discussion of how teachers can help students understand how they are to go about accomplishing a particular purpose for comprehending while reading or listening:

Davey, B. (1983). Think aloud—Modeling the cognitive processes of reading comprehension. *Journal of Reading, 27,* 44–47.

Complementary instruction to that presented in this chapter is described in the following article:

Maring, G. H., & Furman, G. (1985). Seven "whole class" strategies to help mainstreamed young people read and listen better in content area classes. *Journal of Reading, 28,* 694–700.

For a thorough review of the current research on teaching reading comprehension, including increasing learning from texts, see these two articles:

Cunningham, J. W. (1985). Three recommendations to improve comprehension teaching. In J. Osborn, P. T. Wilson, & R. C. Anderson (Eds.), *Reading education: Foundations for a literate America*. Lexington, MA: Lexington Books of D. C. Heath.
Tierney, R. J., & Cunningham, J. W. (1984). Research on teaching reading comprehension. In P. D. Pearson, R. Barr, M. L. Kamil, & P. Mosenthal (Eds.), *Handbook of reading research*. White Plains, NY: Longman.

CHAPTER 3

Vocabulary in the Content Areas

THE DIFFERENCE BETWEEN WORDS AND MEANINGS

Words are used to communicate ideas. You are only able to follow an idea when you can associate the meanings with the given words. When you read words for which you have meanings, comprehension seems natural and effortless. When you read words for which you lack meanings, your comprehension is impaired. Consider some examples:

The avuncular man scratched his philtrum.

She painted all but her lunules.

These are simple sentences. You have a general idea that a "certain" man scratched "something that belonged to him," and that the woman painted all but some specific "things." Because you probably lack meanings for some key words, however, your comprehension is impaired. If you looked for a dictionary definition of *avuncular,* you found that it meant acting like an uncle. Depending on your experiences with uncles, you conjured up a meaning for the unfamiliar word, *avuncular.* You also discovered that you have both a *philtrum* (groove in the middle of the upper lip, below the nose) and *lunules* (moon-shaped white areas at the base of the fingernails which at one time were fashionable to leave white while painting the rest of the nails).

Notice that you did not lack meanings for the three words in this example. But you were unable to connect the meanings with the words. For example, you are very familiar with the groove in the middle of your upper lip, but you may not have known that it was called a philtrum. You lacked not the meaning itself, but a knowledge of the word to help you call up that meaning.

Consider some other examples:

The pharmacist needed lupulin and lupulone.

Again, you know that the pharmacist needed two "things." But which two things? Look up lupulin, and you discover that it is the glandular hairs of the hop. Lupulone is a white or yellow crystalline solid. These meanings are not very informative because you probably don't know what the meanings mean. In this example, you lack not only the word but also the meaning. Dictionaries are very helpful when we have a meaning but not the word for it, but dictionaries have limited usefulness when we lack both the meaning and the word.

As you consider how to teach word meanings to students, you constantly must keep in mind the distinction between words and meanings. If the word to be taught is one for which students already have the meaning and only lack the word, the teaching task is relatively simple. If, as is more common, students lack both the meaning and the word, the task is more difficult. Before considering how to teach students to develop meanings for words and words for meanings, it is important to understand in some detail what it takes to "know" a word.

KNOWING A WORD

Burmeister (1978) suggests that knowing a word is like knowing a person. Asking "How many words do you know?" is like asking "How many people do you know?" If we ask the latter question, you will probably look askance at us and not respond, thinking that our question could not be serious. If we persist, however, you might answer our question with a question of your own: "What do you mean by 'know'?" "What do you mean by know?" is the dilemma that has confounded educators and researchers who have attempted to study the acquisition of vocabulary. The difficulty of defining "know" is one reason why, after many decades of research, there is still no definitive answer to other questions, such as "How large is the vocabulary of the average high school student?"

There are many people whom you know only by name. There are also many words for which you have the name, but whose meaning remains vague to you. *Truffles* is a word known to many people, but perhaps the whole extent of your meaning for *truffles* consists of "I think you eat them." Our meanings for the word *potatoes,* on the other hand, could fill pages. Such meanings would not only include factual or literal meanings such as "the root of a plant" and "eaten in many forms—baked, mashed, French fried," but would also include some judgments. Some people's meanings for *potatoes* includes such ideas as "fattening" or "greasy." Thus, we see that "knowing" a word is complicated by the fact that words have not only literal, factual meanings upon which almost everyone can agree, but also personal, evaluative meanings that vary from person to person. Literal meanings are generally found in the dictionary and are referred to as *denotations.* Evaluative meanings are referred to as *connotations.* Returning to our analogy between words and people, we see that the mention of a person's name also calls to mind both connotations and denotations. Richard Nixon, for example, was born in 1913, a Republican, and the thirty-seventh president of the United States. These are all denotations for *Nixon.* If you saw Nixon's name and thought "crook" or "beleaguered," then you produced connotative meanings for *Richard Nixon.*

Recognizing that words have connotations as well as denotations is an important part of vocabulary instruction. We want students not only to understand what they read but also to evaluate it. When we say that we want our students to develop their *evaluative* thinking process, we often mean that we want them to have a sense of the connotative meanings of words.

CALL UP

Write down all the different meanings you can think of for the word *root.* Now write down all the people you have ever known or heard of who have the last name *Ford.*

Did your meanings for *root* include the following: the underground part of a plant, the part of a tooth under the jaw, the base part of a word, the number that when multiplied by itself an indicated number of times gives a specified number, and the act of encouraging a favorite team by cheering and support? Did your *Fords* include some related people, such as Gerald, Betty, and Jack, or Henry and Edsel? Perhaps you listed some unrelated Fords—Tennessee Ernie? Whitey? Phil?

Just as most names stand for many different people, some of whom are related and some of whom are not, most words stand for many different meanings, some related, some not. In the box, the first four meanings given for *root* are related. Plant roots, tooth roots, root words, and square roots all share a common concept, the idea of a basic part, often hidden, from which other parts, usually visible, emerge and grow. The related meanings of a word may be compared to related people who share the same name. Such people often share a family resemblance—physical (red hair, big bones) or behavioral (mannerisms, gestures, idiosyncrasies of speech). In some families, these resemblances are striking. In others, only the most astute observer would be able to detect family resemblances. So it is with words. The relationship among the many meanings for some words is apparent to everyone; other words reveal their kinship only to philologists. Thus most students need a teacher's help to perceive the family resemblances among words.

Now let us consider the meaning *root* has when we say, "She rooted for the Demon Deacons." This meaning may at one time have had some relationship to other meanings for *root,* but this relationship is no longer apparent. Thinking of these other meanings would hinder rather than help the reader trying to make sense of the sentence: "Does it mean she looked for the Demon Deacons under the ground?" Students must learn that while words may have related meanings, not all meanings of a word are related. The *bear* in the forest does not *bear* fruit. Coat *checkers* in restaurants might wear *checkered* jackets and play *checkers* during off hours. Words with a large number of distinctive meanings are termed *multimeaning* words. The context in which we read a word allows us to determine its appropriate meaning.

Finally, in considering how many words students know and how well they know the words' meanings, we must broaden our understanding of what words are. When we are teaching students to understand what they read in content area subjects and to write clearly in those subjects, we must be concerned with some terms not usually considered words. A few examples should illustrate this point:

> In an ANOVA design, the df is the number of items free to vary until the last item is set.
> AB = CD
> N.Z. is ESE of Australia.
> The president of ASCAP is a member of CORE.

Phrases, symbols, abbreviations, initials, and acronyms all occur in the material students read in content areas. While these terms are not technically "words," they are entities for which meaning must be built, and teachers should remember to teach meanings for any symbols that students will need to understand in order to read and write effectively.

A content teacher who is concerned about student vocabulary should keep in mind that meanings for words are not an either/or situation. Depth of word meaning and flexibility in choosing appropriate meanings for multimeaning words are important considerations. Furthermore, meaning must be developed not only for words but for those symbols and abbreviations which stand for words.

LEARNING A WORD

Learning a word is like learning a person's name. Learning the word's meaning is like learning about the person's interests, personality, and background. Keeping the person's name attached to your image of that person ("I'll never forget old 'what's-her-name.' ") is like keeping a word attached to a meaning ("Hand me that whatchamacallit."). You get to know meanings and their words in much the same way that you get to know people and their names.

Think of a person whom you know very well. Try to recall how you learned all the things you know about him or her. You may be able to remember particular instances in which you learned specific bits of information. Perhaps you recall learning that your friend was allergic to chocolate on the evening of the day you spent making chocolate mousse. You may recall learning that he or she had an identical twin after jovially greeting the look-alike on a busy street. For the most part, however, you probably don't remember how you learned all the things you know about your friend. You do realize that you got to know this person during many different encounters in various contexts over an extended period of time. Now, when did you learn this person's name? You may have learned the name the first time you were introduced—or perhaps you had several casual encounters first. Even if you heard the name when you were introduced, you may have forgotten the name but remembered a lot about the person. As time passes, you are continually adding to your understanding of the type of person your friend is. Your friend's name comes to represent your constantly expanding sense of what sort of person he or she is.

How does this apply to words and their meanings? Imagine that you are a child at a museum and see a giant telescope. You ask your friend, "What's that huge thing?" "It's a telescope," she responds. "Oh, really! How does it work?" Your friend may explain how a telescope works. At this point you have a little bit of meaning for *telescope,* as well as the word that labels that meaning. The next time you see a telescope, you will remember that you saw one before and perhaps some of what your friend told you. You may or may not remember the name *telescope.* Imagine, however, that you become an avid astronomer as a teenager. You will use various types of telescopes, read about them, and perhaps build or modify one. Soon your meaning for the word *telescope* will be an enormous network of ideas. You probably won't remember where all the meanings came from because they grew out of many different encounters, but one day, as a famous astronomer, you may reflect, "When I was ten, I had to ask someone what a telescope was!"

Most of the people whose names you know are people with whom you have interacted over a period of time. You have had firsthand, direct experience with them. Many of the words for which you have meanings are also words with which you have had direct experience. If you have actually seen a tiger in the wild or at a zoo, your meaning for the word *tiger* is based on direct experience. If you have run a marathon or played tennis or basketball, your meanings for these words are based on direct experience. When you experienced fear, love, or sorrow, your meanings for these words became based on that experience.

However, you have not directly interacted with all the people whose names you know, nor with all the meanings whose words you know. You know a lot about Ronald Reagan, Elizabeth Taylor, and George Washington, with whom you have probably not had firsthand experience. But you probably have seen them in pictures and films, and on television. You "know" these persons through visual experience. The meanings for some of the words you know are also based on visual rather than direct experience. You know what pole-vaulting is because you have seen it done, even though you may never have actually done it. There are places you have never visited but have seen pictures of; thus you have meanings for words such as *Jerusalem* or *Andes.*

Finally, you know some people whom you have neither met nor seen. These real or fictional people are ones you have read about in novels or historical literature. While you have never met these people, you use the knowledge gained from all the people you have met to understand the unknown people about whom you are reading. So it is with words. Imagine that you are reading this passage about the game of cricket:

> The batsmen were merciless against the bowlers. The bowlers placed their men in slips and covers. But to no avail. The batsmen hit one four after another along with an occasional six. Not once did a ball look like it would hit their stumps or be caught. (Tierney and Pearson, 1981, p. 56)

Now, imagine that you have never played cricket nor seen it played, but you call up what you do know to help you build meanings for the word *cricket* and other words in the passage. "Baseball is a lot like cricket," you might think. "The bowlers must be like pitchers. The batsmen are obviously the batters. Maybe the stumps are bases." You use what you know to predict meanings for words. In situations where you build meanings for words without any direct or visual experience with what the word represents, you still draw on your direct and visual experience, but you do so through comparisons: "It is like this known thing in these ways—but different in these ways." We refer to this way of learning as *learning by connection*.

CONNECT

Words and meanings, like names and people, are learned through direct experience, visual experience, and connection. List three people and three word meanings you have learned through direct experience—people and meanings with whom you have actually interacted. Then list three people and three word meanings you have acquired through visual experience—people and meanings you have not actually met or experienced, but whom you feel you know through the power of the visual media.

Finally, list three people and three words that you have learned by connection. These people and words were learned by calling up your direct and visual experience in similar situations and connecting those experiences to the new names or words to build meaning.

CHOOSING THE WORDS TO TEACH

Imagine that you have a friend moving into town and you want to introduce him to some people. Which people would you choose? You surely can't introduce him to all the people in your community. You don't even know them all. First, you think about the people you know, and consider which of these your friend would like or need to meet. You draw up a list. Carl and Carol are on the list because they share skiing and guitar interests with your friend. You put Dave and Suzanne on the list because, like your friend, they are accountants and might help your friend make some professional connections.

Once you have made up your list, you arrange the all-important first meeting. A party is planned to which you invite all the potential friends as well as the Boyds, the only people besides you whom your friend already knows. In addition to the party, at which initial introductions are made, you plan several smaller events. Lunches, football games, and bridge foursomes are all opportunities for your friend to get to know these new people better. After several months, your friend continues to interact with some of the people to whom you introduced him, without your arranging the get-togethers. He also hears about some people you know whom you hadn't thought he might want to know, so he asks you to introduce him or arrange a way for him to make their acquaintance.

You can decide which words to teach your students in much the same way that you would decide which people to introduce a newcomer to. The content area is the new community. There are many more words in this new community than anyone could possibly come to know immediately, so you select the words that the new learner might like to know because they are so interesting. You also select some words that the new learner needs to know if he or she is going to "get around" successfully in this new community. You sit down and make a list of these new words, and then plan get-togethers in which students are introduced to the words. After initial encounters, students continue to learn more about the words as they read and hear them in a variety of contexts. As students become more familiar with the new content, they might preview the materials to be read and suggest words they would like to get to know. You can then either arrange encounters for your students or suggest ways your students might independently get to know these words.

Thus, in selecting words to teach, teachers of content areas should follow these common-sense rules:

1. Consider the unit you are trying to teach the students and list all the key words. Key words are words that unlock the meaning of a passage. Be sure to include multimeaning words, such as *root,* for which the students might know a meaning that is not appropriate. Don't include words that are already known by most students. If your unit is on plants, *plants* would be a key word but would not need to be taught to most students. You would include such known words in your teaching activities, just as you invite known people in the new community to the party, but you would not spend valuable time building meaning for them.

2. The list you come up with by selecting unfamiliar key words will probably be too long. Determining how many words to teach is a difficult task, but research seems to indicate that ten new words per week is the outside limit of what we can expect students to learn. Ten words per week may not sound like much, but consider that it means 360 new words per year. Furthermore, if a student is studying five subjects and each subject includes ten new words each week, that would add up to 1800 new words per year—a considerable increase in vocabulary.

To pare your list, first select the words that are important not only to the unit of study but to the whole understanding of the content area. The word *cell* in a science unit on plants should be kept because it is crucial not only to understanding plants but also to the whole study of biology. Likewise, the word *angle* is crucial to the whole study of geometry. In addition to words crucial to the whole discipline, keep on your list words that occur repeatedly in the unit of study, and that are crucial to understanding it. A word appearing only once is probably less important than a word that occurs frequently throughout the unit.

3. Finally, include words that will be of particular interest to your students, even if such words are not crucial to the discipline or unit of study.

APPLY

Select a unit of study you might teach to a group of students. Consider what you want them to learn. Preview films, filmstrips, and other teaching aids you might use. Read the text chapters and other sources students might read. As you think, preview, and read, list all the key words. Be on the lookout for multimeaning words. These are hard to spot because when we know the appropriate meaning, we often forget that there are other, more common meanings.

Once you have listed your key words, cut the list to a reasonable number (no more than ten per week) following the guidelines given. Assume your unit will last three weeks and cut your list of words to teach down to thirty. Divide this list into words for which students have meaning but don't know the words, and words for which students have little or no meaning.

Teaching Key Words

When we are teaching words for which students already have meanings, we only have to help them attach these meanings to the new word. In content areas, however, we are more commonly trying to teach students words for which they have little or no meaning. In this case, we must build the meaning. We build meaning by providing direct experience whenever possible, by offering visual experience when direct experience is not possible, and by helping students make connections between what they already know and the new concept.

Students need initial encounters with new words, along with some additional chances to interact with the words, adding meaning and strengthening the association between a word and its meaning. Teachers need to plan introductory lessons as well as activities for review and practice. Additionally, for students to become independent learners, they must learn how to select and learn new words and meanings on their own. The remainder of this chapter will discuss how to teach lessons in which you (1) build meanings for words, (2) teach words to go with the meanings that students already have, (3) review words and meanings, and (4) promote student independence in selecting and learning words and meanings.

BUILDING MEANINGS FOR WORDS

Building meaning is necessary when you are teaching words for which students have little or no meaning. To build meaning, you must engage students in firsthand or visual experiences with the concept represented by the word. When firsthand or visual experience is impossible to provide, help students make connections by showing them how to compare the new concept with concepts they already have.

PREDICT

Call up what you already know and predict the content of the five strategies we suggest for building meaning, listed below. Write a sentence or two describing what each strategy might involve. Decide for each strategy whether it will provide firsthand experience, visual experience, or help in making connections.

The Real Thing

Skits

A Picture Is Worth a Thousand Words

Scavenger Hunts

Analogizing

The Real Thing

The Real Thing is exactly what it sounds like. You want the students to develop a meaning for a word, so you put them in direct contact with the thing that the word represents. Field trips are often good ways to show students the real thing. If you have ever taken a field trip to a state capitol to watch the legislative process, your teacher was providing you with real experience for a number of words: capitol, legislature, gavel, quorum, debate, adjourn. Field trips are one of the best ways of providing students with direct experience on which to base meaning for new words, but they are expensive and time-consuming, and often the things you need to show students are not available at a reasonable distance from the school. Figure 3.1 shows students learning stitchery as real experience for a social studies unit on U.S. Colonial life.

When you can't take the students to the real thing, the next best option is

Figure 3.1   Stitchery provides direct experience during a unit on Colonial life.

to bring something to the students. Learners at all levels learn something best when they have actually seen it, touched it, smelled it, listened to it, even tasted it. Sometimes the actual subject of study could never be available for students to interact with, but a model could. Models of the human heart, a pyramid, or a DNA molecule, while differing in size and other features from the real thing, are still three-dimensional representations that can be explored by the senses. For our purposes, we will consider such models as "real things."

Teachers sometimes think that they can only provide students with direct experience when the word for which they are building meaning represents an actual "thing." That is simply not true. You can provide students real experience with verbs like *cringe, catapult,* or *pontificate* by demonstrating these actions, then letting students act them out. You provide students with real experience with concepts such as *assembly line* or *electoral process* by simulations in which each student takes part as the class manufactures something assembly-line style or participates in a mock election. Because of time and other constraints, not all meanings can be developed through this method. But the time and effort involved in providing the real thing must be weighed against the depth and the permanence of the learning and excitement that this method generates.

In field trips and classroom events, such as special guests or simulations, the meanings for many words are being developed. Consequently, preparation and follow-up are required. In order to make the most of providing the real thing, follow these guidelines:

1. Help students figure out what they already know as a group about the

trip to be taken or the classroom event. Conduct a "What do you know?" discussion in which you make a list of what students know, based on their responses to questions such as the following: "What things will we probably see happening when we visit the legislature?" "What do you think Dr. Horsey will tell us about what a veterinarian does?" "How do you think an assembly line works?"

2. Help students figure out what they would like to know and prepare a list of questions to be sure to try to answer. You may want different students to write down or be responsible for certain questions to make sure they all get answered.

3. Make a list of all the words for which you want to develop meanings. Have students write down these words. As you see and hear things that develop meanings for these words, be sure the students understand how to match words with meanings. You may want students to make notes next to the word, or at least check off each word as meaning for it is developed. Younger children can each be responsible for a word or two.

4. As soon as possible, have a discussion in which the answer to each student question is discussed. If some questions are not fully or satisfactorily answered, this is an excellent time to have students turn to resource books to get more information.

5. Discuss what students saw happening for each of the words. Formulate definitions that are based in this experience, rather than in dictionary style. For example, "the *quorum* was when they called the roll and saw that there were enough senators there. The quorum had to be at least two-thirds of the senators." You may want to write these experience-derived definitions on a piece of chart paper or have students write them in their notebooks.

CALL UP

What field trips or classroom events do you remember from your own education? List these and whatever you remember about them. Were you prepared ahead of time for the questions you wanted answered and the new word meanings you would learn? Do you remember following up on these questions and words after the trip or event?

Skits

Skits are actually a special version of the real thing. Because they require special preparation, we have chosen to give them a separate name and discuss them separately. A *skit* is a short drama. Generally, the teacher writes a short description of the skit, including the number of actors needed, a sentence containing the word whose meaning is to be acted out, a short description of what the actors should try to get across, and questions the actors should ask the audience after completing the skit. In Figure 3.2, you see two girls doing a skit for the word *conciliation*.

Figure 3.2   Two students complete a skit on the new word, *conciliation*.

Here is an example of a skit lesson plan to teach the word and meaning of *controversy*:

Example sentence: All parties had something to say in the *controversy* about whether or not athletes deserve special privileges.

Skit: (Actors needed: 3) Two students are standing in the cafeteria line when the star football player goes to the head of the line, gets his plate filled with specially prepared food, and takes his tray over to the "athletes' table." "I just don't think it's right," says the first student. "Athletes in this school get all kinds of special treatment." "Well," says the second student, "I don't see what the controversy is all about. Athletes are special people. They need more and better food. After all, they earn their special privileges." The two students continue to discuss the pros and cons of the controversy while the football player eats his lunch, oblivious to the discussion.

Questions to ask audience: What did *controversy* mean in our skit? Have you ever been involved in a *controversy*?

The teacher prepares for the lesson by writing out a skit card similar to that shown above and giving the card to the actors so that they have time to prepare. A teacher might have a skit day and divide the whole class into teams of two to four members, giving each team a skit card and allowing five minutes for each team to prepare. As each group of actors comes up, one of them writes the target word on the board and pronounces it. They then do their skit, trying to sneak in the target word as often as possible. If the actors have done a good job, the watchers should be able to answer the question, "What did the word mean in our skit?" The second question, "Have you ever . . . ?" is intended to help the watchers access any experience they might have had with the target word, and to attach the word to the experiences.

Skits are especially valuable when you are trying to teach an unfamiliar meaning for a multimeaning word. Most students know what *fog* is, but many don't know what it means to be *in a fog*. A skit in which this use of the word *fog* was demonstrated would help students to learn the new meaning.

APPLY

Create a skit card for the word *fog* used in the sense of "She was in a fog." Be sure to include the number of actors needed, a short description of the skit, and the two questions that help students clarify and access meaning.

Skits are strategies for building meaning because watching the skit provides the watchers with visual experience of a concept. For students who have not had the experience represented by a particular word, the skit is the basis of their new understanding. Other students may have experienced controversies but did not know the word that stood for what they had experienced. These students did not actually need the experience of the skit, but only needed the appropriate meaning to be accessed and attached to the new word. For these students, the question, "Have you ever . . . ?" helps them find the appropriate experience to connect with the new word. Classes always contain a wide variation of ability and experiences. Thus, our original breakdown—words for which students need the meaning developed, and words that are themselves new—is a little simpler to describe in theory than in reality. As a general rule, if you can't decide whether most of your students are familiar with a word's meaning, go ahead and build meaning for that word. Then your activity will build meaning for those who need it, while offering additional review and practice for others.

A Picture Is Worth a Thousand Words

Visuals provide us with "the next best thing to being there." All of us have numerous words for meanings that we have not experienced directly, but have developed through movies, television, still photographs, paintings, diagrams, or maps. Imagine trying to explain the Grand Canyon to someone who has never seen it. Describe with words the color *teal*, what *fencing* looks like, or life at the bottom of the ocean. Your words are meaningful only to those who have seen what the word represents.

Fortunately, we are surrounded by visual stimuli. Television programs offer great possibilities for content teachers. Most school system media centers contain many films, filmstrips, and other visual aids which suffer from underuse. As you consider how to build meaning for words, ask yourself, "Where could I find a picture of this?" Often, the answer is as close as your textbook.

When you have your list of words for which you must build meaning, look at the textbooks and other books you have available. Note page numbers where various concepts are portrayed visually. You can introduce these concepts by writing the word on the board, pronouncing it and having students pronounce it with you, and directing their attention to the appropriate text visual.

APPLY

Take the list of words for which you need to build meanings and look in the textbook or other available books. Note the page numbers for each appropriate visual. Note particular parts of the visual on which you would want to focus student attention.

In addition to visuals found in books, look for appropriate prints, slides, and filmstrips. Filmstrips, especially, often are an overlooked source; although most teachers think of showing filmstrips only as a whole, they often contain several frames that vividly portray the concept you want to develop. In this case, you should show these frames only. Use filmstrip titles to save yourself time. If you are looking for a picture of a camel, a filmstrip called "The Desert" is probably a good place to start.

Finally, consider films and videotapes. While you might want to show just a portion of a film or tape to develop meaning for one word, you might also want to show the whole thing to develop many new words and meanings. In that case, follow the guidelines given above for field trips and classroom events. Students who have listed what they know and which questions they want answered, and who have been alerted to words whose meanings they're looking for will get more than just enjoyment (or boredom!) out of watching a film. When you have many concepts to develop, you will probably want to show the film more than once. The second time around, consider stopping the film at points where it answers questions or develops meanings. Record answers and definitions on a chart, or have students record them in their notebooks. After pausing for students to think and record, resume the film.

In the case of visuals, one is good, and two is twice as good. Remember that a meaning is not a matter of "one time—now you've got it." Your meaning for mountains is not based on having seen just one picture of one mountain. If your students see several visuals, the depth of their meaning for the word will be much greater than if they see only one. In addition to broadening their concepts, each visual provides review of the meaning represented by the word.

APPLY

Begin a picture file. Collect pictures of things wherever you find them. Magazines, advertisements, calendars, and newspapers are good places to begin. Be sure the pictures are large enough for a group to see, and that they clearly depict the concept you want to teach.

Establish ten to twelve categories to sort your pictures, plus the all-important "miscellaneous" file. Your categories should reflect the grade level and subject areas you teach or plan to teach. If you are unsure about the grade level, use general categories, such as places, famous people, or holidays. If you have access to a laminating machine, laminate your pictures so they will last longer.

Scavenger Hunts

Have you ever had actual firsthand experience with a scavenger hunt? Have you actually gone to gather assorted items, competing to be the team that found the most in a limited time? If you have not had firsthand experience with a scavenger hunt, perhaps you have had visual experience, watching others go on one. Scavenger hunts are fun because they develop both competition and a sense of team spirit. For a scavenger hunt that helps your students build word meanings by collecting real things and pictures, follow these steps:

1. Make a list of the items you want students to scavenge for. Include anything for which students might be able to find a real object, model, or picture, but make sure to include items represented by those words for which you need to build meaning. Be sure to add some well-known, easy-to-collect words so that some of the finds will be easy and immediately satisfying. Here is a list used for a scavenger hunt before beginning a unit on the desert:

sand	woodpecker	cactus	vulture
skunk	dune	fox	kangaroo rat
mesquite	dates	oasis	nomads
roadrunner	coyote	yucca	arid

2. Divide your class into teams of three or four students. Ask your students to share experiences with scavenger hunts. If necessary, explain how scavenger hunts work. Be sure students understand that they must bring in objects and pictures by a certain date, and that each team should keep secret which items were collected and where the items came from.

3. Give each team your list. Tell the team that they get two points for each object or model and one point for each picture. Pictures include drawings and tracings (you may want to make tracing paper available). Only one object

and one picture can be counted for each word. Let the team choose a leader, or appoint one yourself. Have the leader read the list and lead the group in a discussion of who thinks they can find what and where. Set a date for students to bring objects and pictures to school. One week is a reasonable amount of time. Do not allow objects and pictures to be displayed before the due date.

4. Allow the teams to meet briefly once or twice more to check things off their lists and see what is still needed. Be sure to promote an atmosphere of secrecy and suspense. If students protest that "No one could find a . . . ," assure them that "no one could possibly get objects or pictures for everything. The goal is to collect as much as you can." This will generally result in some students making sure that they have a picture, if not an object, for everything, just to prove you wrong!

5. On the culminating day, let teams meet to go over their findings and tally up their points. Double-check the teams' figures. Count drawings and tracings only when they actually represent the thing and are not merely "thrown together." The winner is the team with the most points. Reward the winners by allowing them to display the findings. Cards on which each word is printed might be attached to a bulletin board and all the pictures representing that object arranged in collage fashion around the word. Objects which are not alive, dangerous, or valuable can be labeled and placed on a table near the bulletin board. Be sure to include the names of all the winners next to the display.

Scavenger hunts are fun and, more importantly, they involve students in the preparation for the unit. These hunts are best done a week or two before you actually begin the unit for which the objects are being collected. That way, by the time you are ready to explore the topic with your students, they already have a lot of information about and interest in the subject. In addition to learning what the words on the list mean, students often pick up incidental information as they peruse magazines looking for pictures, or talk to people whom they hope will have objects to loan. In one class where Mexico was the scavenger hunt topic, a student had an uncle in California who had been to Mexico often. He called his uncle, who sent a box containing many of the objects on the list as well as some other objects. In addition, the uncle wrote a long letter describing Mexico and comparing it to the United States, and he sent along many photos he had taken. A scavenger hunt on the weather once included the word *meteorologist*. A student who lived next door to the local television meteorologist brought the woman along as one of the "objects." The meteorologist, of course, brought many of the objects on the list as well as other weather-related paraphernalia and talked to the class about forecasting the weather. You can imagine how interested the students in those two classes became in their units! While these two instances are somewhat unusual, students do become good at digging up objects and pictures. They develop some sense of ownership in the unit to be studied and generally begin the unit with more enthusiasm.

One final benefit of scavenger hunts is the ratio of teacher work to student work. For a scavenger hunt, the teacher makes the list, forms the teams, arranges for them to meet a few times, and checks their tallies of the points. The students do the rest—including the often onerous and neglected task of making a bulletin board!

Analogizing

Analogizing is the process of making up an analogy, or connection, to help students develop a concept for a word that you can't represent with firsthand or visual experience. You think of something students know that is like the unknown thing you wish to teach them. The idea that cricket is a lot like baseball is an analogy. (*Analogy* is sometimes used narrowly to denote statements such as "summer is to hot as _____ is to cold"; we use the word in a broader sense.)

To analogize something, you first think of something your students are apt to know that is like the thing they don't know. It is very important that students be familiar with the concept being used to teach the unknown concept. Telling you that cricket is a lot like rounders is not helpful if you don't know rounders either. Once you have decided which analogy to make, consider the similarities and differences between the familiar and unfamiliar concepts.

To present the analogy to the students, first ask them what they know about the familiar concept. Highlight the relevant traits, adding to the information they give you as necessary. Next, tell them that this familiar concept is a lot like another, unfamiliar concept and point out the similarities. Finally, tell students how the new concept is different from their known concept. Here is an analogizing example from the social studies:

> Imagine you want to teach the students about taxation without representation and its relationship to the Revolutionary War. You decide to analogize this concept with the idea of belonging to a club to which you have to pay dues. You don't mind paying the dues, even though the club founders meet each year and decide how the dues are to be spent. After a while, it occurs to some club members who are not founders that since the dues are partly theirs, they should have some say in how the dues are spent. The founding members will have no part of this and insist that the power to spend dues is theirs, as is written in the club's bylaws. Once you have gotten from students what they know about clubs and dues, you may have to interject the notion that founding members could have control of the dues since this may not be in the experience of most students. Then, explain that taxation is like dues and that representation, in this case, means the power to decide how something is spent. A difference that should be pointed out is that you as a club member

always have the right to quit the club and stop paying dues. When the colonists quit and stopped paying taxes, a war ensued.

IMAGE

Pick one of the five meaning-building strategies: The Real Thing, Skits, A Picture Is Worth a Thousand Words, Scavenger Hunt, or Analogizing. Try to picture yourself preparing to teach and actually teaching this lesson to a class of students. What grade are the students in? What subject are you teaching? Imagine the steps you would lead the class through. What questions might they ask? What would you answer? Create a movie in your mind with you in the starring role teaching your chosen strategy. Imagining how the actual process will look will help you to be clear about what you will do and to anticipate possible problems.

TEACHING WORDS
FOR MEANINGS

Often when we are teaching a new word, we realize that the students have had experiences from which meaning was built for that word, but that they have never attached a word to this meaning. Remember that you had lunules and a philtrum for years without knowing what they were called. There is a wonderful children's book called *Hugh and Fitzhugh* (Goodspeed, n.d.) that revolves around Hugh using unfamiliar words to describe his dog, Fitzhugh. No one understands the words, even though they all have meanings for the words. For instance, Hugh tells a boy his dog is indefatigable, and the boy responds, "He doesn't tire out easily either." Hugh tells a girl that his dog is inscrutable, and the girl responds, "You sure can't tell that from looking at his face." In this section, we describe five strategies to use when you want to teach words for which students already have meanings.

PREDICT

Use what you already know to predict what our five strategies might involve. Write a sentence or two for each:

Remember When?

Capsule Vocabulary

Context Power

Multimeaning Luck

Morpheme Power

Remember When?

Remember When? is a simple two-step strategy that requires no preparation and can be used whenever you discover that students don't know what a word means, but suspect that they have experienced the meaning that the word represents. The first step is for you to recall an experience you had with the word. Then ask students to recall an experience they have had, and put the new word with the old experience. Here is a scenario of this method for the word *squeamish*. The assumption is that everyone has felt squeamish about something but may not have the word to describe that feeling.

TEACHER: (Writes *squeamish* on the board.) Many years ago, I was teaching first grade for the first time. I loved it and everything about it—well, almost everything! One day, as the little angels were getting their lunch, Veronica Baines started to reach for her tray and then quickly pulled away. "I can't eat from that tray," she exclaimed. "It has peas on it!" "Well, you don't have to eat the peas if you don't like them," I responded. "Just leave them on your tray." "But I can't even be near peas or I get sick," she protested. "Don't be ridiculous," I ordered as I handed her the tray. "But you don't know what you're doing," she began and then she threw up all over the tray, the peas, and me! Whenever I think of that day, I get a squeamish feeling in my stomach—and I can't stand the sight of peas! In fact, sometimes I get squeamish just hearing about people throwing up. If you teach first graders and you are squeamish about people throwing up, you are going to have some squeamish days! Are any of you squeamish about anything? What are you squeamish about? When do you feel squeamish? (Let children share experiences with squeamish. Be sure to use the word squeamish to describe how they feel.)

STUDENT: I hate when my little brother throws up. My mother always gets mad because when he gets sick, half the time she has to clean up after both of us and I'm not really sick. I just feel like throwing up when he does.

TEACHER: So you get squeamish just like I do when people throw up. Are there other things people feel squeamish about besides throwing up? Does anyone get squeamish about anything else?

STUDENT: I can't stand the sight of blood—especially mine.

STUDENT: Snakes, worms, and other creepy, crawly things.

STUDENT: Liver! (Other students agree and pretend to be sick.)

TEACHER: (Decides this is a good time to end the discussion since they all seem to know what squeamish means.) Today we have talked about many different things that make us feel squeamish. As you read today, you will notice the word *squeamish* in your story (points to the word on the board and has pupils pronounce it). After you read, we will talk about what made the main character in today's story squeamish.

The only trick to this method is having an interesting experience with the word that you can relate to your class. If you do not have an interesting experience, make one up and tell it as a story.

CONNECT
Do you have any interesting experiences you could relate to a class for the words *predicament, obnoxious, mortified,* and *procrastinated?* If not, use your imagination!

Capsule Vocabulary

Capsule Vocabulary (Crist, 1975) is a strategy in which students listen to, speak, write, and read words related to a particular topic. These topically related words (using approximately six works best) are presented one at a time by the teacher, who writes each word on the board, briefly tells the students of an experience with the word, and lets students share their own experiences. The first part of the lesson is similar to remember when, except that many topic-related words are introduced. In addition to words for which students have meaning but not the word, include some words already well known to students, and perhaps some for which you have already built meaning in previous lessons. After all the words have been introduced and all the experiences shared by teacher and students, have each student copy the words from the board onto a sheet of paper. Pair the students and give each pair a limited time (3 to 5 minutes) to try to use the words in a conversation about the topic. Students should check off the words as they are able to sneak them into the conversation. (Use a timer or appoint an official clock-watcher to announce when the time is up.) Finally, have students write a paragraph about the topic in which they use as many of the capsule words as possible. (This step can be eliminated for kindergartners or first graders.) Form children into groups of four or five and let them share their paragraphs. Then collect the paragraphs and select several to read to the entire class.

Context Power

Often the surrounding words, or *context,* help us access known meaning and put it with a new word. Do you know what a jingo is? Imagine that you are reading and you come across the unknown word *jingo* in this context:

> All he ever talked about was war. His country was the best country, and anyone who disagreed should be ready to fight in battle. He was really quite a jingo!

You could now infer that a jingo must be a militaristic person ready to defend his or her country (or have someone else defend it) at the drop of a hat. The word *jingo* may have been unfamiliar, but if you have had experience with nationalistic, militaristic people, the meaning wasn't. The context helped you associate your old meaning with a new word. Context is a valuable tool for associating meaning with words, because once you learn how to use context, you can do so independently without a teacher's help. Many students, however, do not make use of contexts. They do not know that the surrounding words often give clues to an unfamiliar word, and sometimes do not understand how our language gives these clues.

To prepare for a lesson in which you teach students to use context clues, select some words for which students have the meaning but not the word and use them in a few sentences (or select sentences from your text) that give clues to their meaning. There are a variety of context clues and you should try to use all the common types so that students become familiar with them. Common types of context clues include explanatory sentences, as in the *jingo* example above; synonyms ("mean, cruel, and truculent"); antonyms ("Some things are easy, others are arduous."); similes and metaphors ("as fervid as a stove"); and appositives ("the pandowdy, a pudding made with apples"). Once you have chosen the words and written the sentences with their context clues, the steps of the lesson are as follows:

1. Write the words on the board without the context clues. Pronounce each word and have students pronounce it with you. Have students write down a meaning for each word. If there are more than two words, let each student pick two, or assign two words to each student. If students actually know a meaning, they can write it down. If they don't know the meaning, they should make something up! They can also make something up if they know the meaning but want to fool everyone. Once everyone has written something down for two words, call on volunteers to tell you what they have written. Ask them to give their answers as if they are absolutely convinced that they are right. Often students will make up a definition that sounds like the word. For the word *manticore,* for example, students have made such guesses as: the pit of the manti fruit, a manicure for an apple, and the heart of a mantelope! The guesses are fun, but more importantly, they help students see that they don't know the meaning for the word. Often when word's context helps us to access meaning, we grasp the meaning so quickly that we think we knew the word all along. Students will see how helpful a context is only if they realize that they didn't know the word until they saw it in context.

2. Display the word in its context. Then have students guess a second time what the word might mean. Emphasize that context only gives us clues to words and sometimes these clues can lead us astray. Our ideas about what a word means when we see it in context should be considered tentative. Our context-based guesses, however, are more likely to be right than the guesses we make without any context.

3. As students guess what words mean based on context, have them explain how the context clues helped. Don't settle for "*It* said so." Students who do not understand how context clues are contained in language do not see what is obvious to those of us who do know how our language system gives clues. Through your questions, get students to explain the obvious: "Mean and cruel mean almost the same, so truculent probably does too." "Stoves are hot; if something is as fervid as a stove, it must be hot too." "The commas around 'a pudding made with apples' tell you that it is the same as pandowdy."

4. As each word is guessed from context and the reasoning behind the guess is explained, have a volunteer look up the word in the dictionary and read the appropriate definition to the class. This reinforces the notion that minimal context gives only clues, not certain answers, and it models for students using the dictionary to check hunches and gain more precise information.

APPLY/IMAGE

Choose five words for which students are likely to have meanings but not the words and make up context sentences illustrating the various types of context clues. Then picture yourself teaching this lesson to a class. What definitions might students come up with when faced with the word out of context? How will they explain how the context helped them make more probable guesses? What happens when a volunteer finds the appropriate dictionary definition and reads it to the class?

Multimeaning Luck

Multimeaning luck is a particular type of context activity in which you want students to use the context to choose the appropriate meaning for a multimeaning word. Imagine that for a unit on plants you want to teach students the plant-related meanings of the words *plants, roots, cells,* and *stems.* Prepare for the lesson by writing down each word, with one plant-related and one non-plant-related definition next to each word. Overhead transparencies work best for this lesson, but you can also write the words on the board. On the bottom of the transparency or on a part of the board you can cover temporarily, write one sentence for each word. Be sure to include in these sentences both related and unrelated definitions, as students will have to guess which definition your sentence uses. If you use only related definitions, they will easily figure out the system.

Begin the lesson by displaying the words and their two definitions:

Plants   1. living things including trees and grass
            2. factories for manufacturing things
Roots   1. words from which other words are made
            2. underground parts of plants
Cells   1. parts of jails where prisoners sleep
            2. microscopic structures which make up plants
Stems   1. stalks of plants
            2. makes headway against, as in "stems the tide."

PREDICT

Try your luck. Which definitions do you think our context sentences used?

As you read each word and its two definitions, have each student write the word and a ''1'' or ''2'' to indicate a guess of which definition you have used in the covered sentences. Be sure to tell students that doing well on this part of the lesson is simply a matter of luck. You may want to tell students this is a way to find out how their luck is running today.

When all students have made their guesses, display the sentences one at a time. Have students give themselves five points for every lucky guess and deduct five points for every unlucky guess. The person with the most points is the lucky person for the day. Once lucky and unlucky persons have been applauded or commiserated with, tell the class that they will be reading and talking about plants today and have volunteers point out the four plant-related definitions.

Are you curious as to how you did with your guesses? If so, you will see one of the advantages of this method. Once you have made a guess, you want to know how you did. You care about which definitions the sentences used. Here they are:

The plants are shut down because of the strike.

The storm was so violent it pulled the tree from the ground by its roots.

Prisons have terrible problems because of overcrowded cells.

Some stems are edible.

Give yourself five points for every lucky guess and subtract five for every unlucky guess. Are you having a lucky day? Did you pick only the plant-related definitions even though we told you to include others?

Morpheme Power

Many of you remember being taught to figure out a word's meaning by examining the word for familiar parts. Prefixes, suffixes, and roots can be helpful as we try to determine the meaning of an unfamiliar word. However, caution must be used when teaching students about these meaningful word parts. Students are often turned off to vocabulary instruction by being taught obscure Latin and Greek derivatives which have few examples in common use today, and by meeting a word with a known part which has no relationship to other words with that known part. In order to identify word parts that are appropriate to teach, use the *Five Test*. Imagine that one of your new words is *malnutrition*. You wonder if helping students see that the prefix *mal*, meaning "bad or evil," will help them remember the meaning for *malnutrition* and will be useful in figuring out other words they meet. If you are using the five test, you will alert students to the meaning of a word part only when you can think of five other common words in which this word part has the same meaning. Can you think of five other words? Don't run to your dictionary. If you can't think of five, the part with this meaning can't be very common. Did you think of *malpractice, malice, malignant, malfunction,* and *malcontent* or similar words? If so, the prefix *mal* passes the five test. Once you determine that your word part is worth teaching, use this procedure:

1. Write two familiar words containing the word part on the board and have students tell what the words mean. Most students know that doctors are sued for malpractice when it is alleged they have done something wrong, and that a malignant tumor is a bad or cancerous one.

2. Underline the word part and point out to students its common meaning in the two familiar words.

3. Write the word you wish to teach on the board in a sentence. Underline the word and pronounce it for students. Ask students to use their knowledge of the word part to try to figure out the meaning of the word. "If *mal* means something like 'bad,' *malnutrition* must be bad or 'not good' nutrition." Have the word read in the sentence to see if the meaning makes sense. You may want a volunteer to find the word in the dictionary and check the dictionary definition since morphemes, like context, give clues but are not always completely reliable.

4. Write at least one example of a word students know in which the word part does not have the meaning just taught. *Mallet* and *mallard* are unrelated to the "evil" meaning of *mal*. Tell them the following: "This method won't work all the time and you shouldn't expect it to, but if your derived definition works in the context of the sentence, you have a good probability of being right."

REVIEWING WORDS
AND MEANINGS

The teaching strategies suggested so far are all good ways to introduce a word, but a good introduction to a word, like a good introduction to a person, is only the beginning. More encounters with the word and its meaning are generally needed before a student can really use a word. You have already built some review into your vocabulary teaching by the way in which you selected the words. By choosing both words that were important to the whole unit, and words that were important to the whole discipline, you assured that students would be hearing, reading, speaking, and writing these words in many different contexts as the unit and year continued. You can also preview words by using them in lessons intended to introduce other words. If you introduced some words, say, through a filmstrip or scavenger hunt, you might also include them in a context power lesson or multimeaning luck activity.

Word Sorts

Organizing and classifying words so that relationships among words can be seen is the goal of *Word Sorts*. A word sort activity requires students to categorize words. In open sort activities, the way of sorting words is not given ahead of time. Rather, students are given words to write on cards and told to group the words together in some way. Then they discuss the different ways they grouped the words and the reasons behind their groupings.

In closed word sorts, students are told how to group the words. You might say, ''Sort the words according to whether they are important places, people, or discoveries,'' or ''Group the animals according to whether they are mammals, fish, reptiles, or birds.'' Figure 3.3 shows a student grouping together words with the same root. Word sorts can be done with the children working individually, in pairs, or in small groups.

Word Books

Many teachers like to have students make word books—vocabulary notebooks in which to record the words they are learning. Students may use a notebook or sheets of paper stapled together and decorated with an interesting cover. Words are then usually entered according to their first letter, but in the sequence in which they are introduced, alphabetical by first letter only. Depending on the age of the children and the type of word being studied, different information can be included with each word. Many teachers like children to write a personal example for each word (''Frigid is a February day when the thermometer hits 20°F.'') as well as a definitional sentence (''Frigid means very, very cold.''). Although children may consult the dictionary for help, it is best not to let them copy dictionary definitions, since this requires little thought or understanding. In addition to the example and definitional

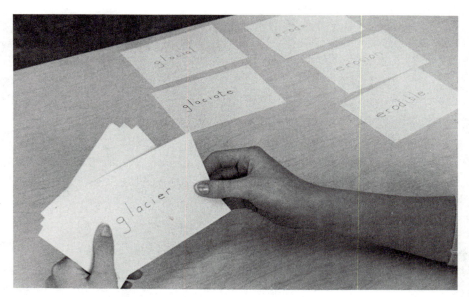

Figure 3.3   A student sorts cards by looking for the words with the same root.

sentence, other information may be included when it is helpful. A phonetic respelling may help students remember the spelling of irregular words. Sometimes, a common opposite is helpful in remembering the word. If the word has a common prefix, root, or suffix that will jog students' memory of its meaning, this can be noted. For some words, pictures, diagrams, or cartoons are helpful reminders.

Word Wall

You should provide as much additional review as your students seem to need and as you have time for. A *Word Wall* is an excellent device to insure that the key words are kept in the front of all your minds. Although a word wall lends itself to many good review strategies, it should actually be started when you introduced your first words, and you add to it each time new words are introduced. Many teachers reserve one bulletin board for words printed on colored construction paper or large index cards. The space above the chalkboard is another possibility. A word wall above the chalkboard in a primary classroom can be seen in Figure 3.4. With older students, teachers often write new words on a large sheet of butcher paper and have the students write them on a word wall page of their notebook.

Regardless of how you display the words, the important principle is that words should be added gradually and remain easily visible to all students. Once you have your word wall started, many *sponge activities* are possible.

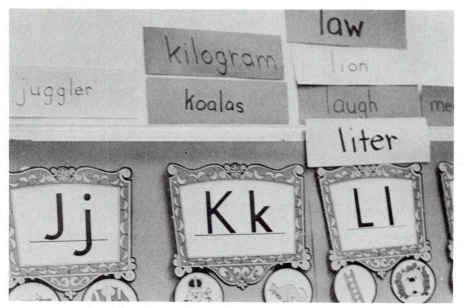

Figure 3.4 A word wall in a primary classroom is displayed above the chalkboard.

A sponge activity "wipes up spilled minutes." Such an activity can be done with little or no preparation, taking as little time as thirty seconds or as much as ten minutes. Two minutes at the end of a class or when lunch is delayed can be spent having students make up sentences, leaving a blank where a word wall word fits. The student who makes up the sentence then calls on a volunteer to repeat the sentence filling in the missing word. That student then gets to make up a sentence for another student. Students may likewise define a word and then call on a volunteer to tell which word was defined. Teachers can use word walls to devise more sponge activities than we have room to describe, but here are a few of our favorites:

Possible Sentences   *Possible Sentences* was described in Chapter 2. When it is used as a vocabulary review strategy, students try to make true sentences using as many of the words on the wall as possible. These sentences can be spoken or written down.

Feature Matrix   Imagine that your word wall contains a number of nouns from the same category, such as the animals from the desert. To review features of these animals, students can construct a *Feature Matrix* (see Chapter 2) by listing all the animals down the side of a sheet of notebook paper. Volunteers then suggest a feature that is true of one or more animals. Everyone writes this feature at the top of a column and then puts pluses and minuses to indicate which animals they believe have the feature. Disagreements should be resolved by appointing researchers to check out the controversies in library resources and report back their findings.

Webs   Have students create *Webs* (see Chapter 2) by writing all the words from the wall on small pieces of scrap paper, sorting them into categories like a word sort, and then arranging these words to show their relationships. Students need not use all the wall words, and may add words as they need them. This is a good small group activity.

Be A Mind Reader   For the class to play *Be A Mind Reader,* the teacher thinks of one of the wall words and writes it on a slip of paper that is not shown to the students. Students number sheets of scrap paper from one to five. The teacher gives clues, the first of which is always, "It's one of the words on our wall." Successive clues narrow the choices until, by clue number five, everyone should have the correct word. Students write next to each number what they think the word is. If a subsequent clue forces them to change their minds, they write something different. If a subsequent clue does not contradict what they have, they write the same word again. Imagine that the word wall contains the names of all 50 states. Here are the mind reader clues, and what a student might have guessed for each clue:

FIRST CLUE: "It's one of the states," which is the same as saying, "It's one of the words on the wall!" Students moan, good-naturedly. One student writes a guess:

   1. North Carolina

SECOND CLUE: "It has a coast." The student, realizing that North Carolina has a coast, writes:

   2. North Carolina

THIRD CLUE: "The coast is on the Pacific Ocean." The student groans and writes:

   3. California

FOURTH CLUE: "It does not border Canada." Student writes:

   4. California

FIFTH CLUE: "Its capital is Sacramento." Student triumphantly writes:

   5. California

The teacher then has students indicate if they have written *California* next to number five. Let us hope that all hands are raised. Now, the teacher asks, "Let's see who read my mind. Keep your hand up if you have *California* next to number four . . . number three . . . number two . . . number one." The teacher then unfolds the slip of paper on which *California* is written to prove that the teacher did not trick the students by changing his or her mind in midstream.

Be a mind reader is a review activity that students love. Often, someone gets the word on the first clue and that student is always amazed by his or her good luck. Once the students catch on to the game, let them take turns thinking of the word and giving the clues.

PROMOTING STUDENT INDEPENDENCE

So far, this chapter has stressed teacher-directed vocabulary instruction. The teacher selects words. The teacher finds films and filmstrips. The teacher creates context sentences. Some of you may have wondered why the teacher seemed to be doing all the students' work! Be assured that we believe students should work also. Indeed, as the year goes on, at every grade level, in every subject area, students should be assuming more of the responsibility for their own learning. But you can't start out simply hoping that students will learn something; you must teach in such a way that by the end of the year, more of them can direct their own learning. Here are some suggestions for helping students become independent learners of words:

   1. Let students help select the new words to be taught. Haggard (1982) suggests a vocabulary self-collection strategy in which students preview materials to be read with the purpose of listing two words they consider impor-

tant and relatively unknown. Help students to define "important" as occurring many times in the material to be read. Help them also to consider whether the word is unknown not by their ability or inability to pronounce it but by their "I wonder what that word means" reaction. The list of words that students suggest should be modified by the teacher to fit the criteria for choosing which words to teach offered earlier in this chapter. Of course, the teacher should add words not suggested by students if these words are crucial to the discipline or the unit.

2. Let students plan a lesson to teach some of the words. After the teacher has directed the students' lessons, students should know that we can build meanings for words by providing direct experience, visual experience, or an analogy. Students can work individually or in pairs to prepare their lessons, which might include bringing in the real thing or a model; finding a picture, including films, filmstrips, and slides; creating a skit for a word; and creating an analogy. Students will, of course, need some initial help with this work, but as time goes on, they should become more independent. As students teach their lessons, the teacher should remind them that they can perform some of these activities whenever they meet a word for which they don't have meaning. "Where could I find a picture? I wonder if there is one in my text." "Is this like anything I already know?" are models for how students should think when faced with an unknown, important word.

3. Move students toward independence in the lessons you teach. For example, in analogizing, the teacher presents an analogy to the students. That strategy can be modified so that instead of presenting an analogy, the teacher asks students to think of one as they read. "Today, you will be reading about circuits and how electrons move only through a complete circuit. As you read, try to think of how open and closed circuits are a lot like something you already know. When you have finished, we will share all our ideas for what circuits are like." When students finish reading, the teacher should accept all reasonable analogies, helping students to state how their analogies are similar to and different from the new concept. As the teacher, you can of course share your own analogy with students, but be sure not to give them the idea that there is only one right analogy.

This process of moving students toward independence can be applied to all teaching strategies. For example, in context power, students guess word meanings first without, then with context sentences. To move students toward independence, ask them to use the context provided in the textbook rather than sentences you write. In that case, students would guess without context, then be directed to a specific part of a page that contains the new word. Students figuring out meanings from the context in their books are moving toward greater independence. Ultimately, students could be alerted to several words before they begin reading, and then asked to use the text's context clues to figure out meanings. After completing the reading, various students could suggest meanings, and show where and how the text gave them clues.

WHAT ABOUT . . .

What about Pronunciation?

How important to learning word meanings is being able to pronounce the word? While being able to pronounce the word does not in any way insure that students know its meaning, it is nevertheless difficult for students to recall meaning for a word they can't pronounce. Storing information in memory seems to have a sound or acoustic component—and students won't use words they are uncomfortable pronouncing. Therefore, you will want to help students learn to pronounce words as you teach them about meaning.

Throughout this chapter, we have suggested that you introduce words by writing them, pronouncing them, and having students pronounce them. If a word's pronunciation is a little unusual, have students say the word several times. If there is something distinctive about the pronunciation that would help students remember it, point this out. The *ch* in *chasm*, for example, is pronounced like the *ch* in *Christmas* and *character*.

One way that we become proficient in pronouncing unfamiliar words is by doing it. A good sponge activity is *Timed List Reading*. A student volunteer reads the words on the word wall aloud while the teacher times him or her using a stopwatch. (You, a student, or the teacher next door will probably have a digital watch with a stopwatch on it.) There is only one rule: If the student does not mispronounce any word, the time taken to read the words will be written by the initials of that student in the corner of the chalkboard. If the student mispronounces any words, each word missed is pronounced for the student and he or she is told that there may be another chance later. As you proceed through the unit, you will see a remarkable decrease in the amount of time students take to read the list. You will have to limit this activity, since students will want to do it all the time.

What about Spelling?

Again, meaning is more important than spelling, but knowing how to spell a word helps students remember it and recognize it in reading. Spelling key words correctly is also important for students learning to write well about the content they are learning. Many activities in this chapter have had students writing the key words. To make a feature matrix, they copy from the wall the nouns to be compared. In being mind readers, they write down words as you give clues. Having students write words as an incidental part of an activity helps them to learn to spell. You may also want to do a sponge spelling activity in which you have students write down numbers from one to five, and then write down five wall words as you call them out. This open book spelling test gives them practice in spelling words correctly. You may want them to correct each other's papers. Students might get a bonus point for spelling all the words correctly. This encourages them to look at each word and take care with its spelling. Some teachers lead the class, or have a student lead it, in chanting the spelling of the words as they check. This rhythmic chanting helps students get an auditory handle on how to spell the word.

What about the Dictionary?

As you began this chapter on vocabulary, did you expect to find a chapter full of dictionary activities? That expectation is reasonable when you consider the experience you have probably had with vocabulary activities throughout your schooling. The most common vocabulary activity in classrooms at all levels is to assign students to look up words and write down their definitions. This frustrating practice is like expecting that you could get to know some new people by looking them up in *Who's Who* and writing down their distinguishing characteristics. Such an activity is helpful only if you already know something about the people and want to find out more. In the same way, dictionaries are wonderful resources for adding to or clarifying a word's meaning. Keep dictionaries handy in your classroom and have students use them in the way they were intended—to add meaning, check meaning guessed from context, and clarify meaning. Do not waste your students' time, as yours was probably wasted, in having students passively look up words, copy the first or the shortest definition, memorize the definition until Friday's test, and then promptly forget it.

What about Testing and Evaluation?

Once you have gone to all the effort of teaching words and word meanings, how will you know if students have actually learned them? Your observations of students as they read and write in your content area should give you the best indication of how well they are learning. If you want a more formal measure, you might give a *limited-cloze test*. To construct a limited-cloze, write several paragraphs in which you summarize what students have learned. Include in these paragraphs as many key vocabulary terms as possible. Once the summary is written, delete from it as many of the key words as you wish and replace each of these with a blank of uniform length. Have students complete the cloze passage by selecting from a list of the key vocabulary. If you have a word wall, you might be sure that all deleted words are on your word wall and let students choose words from the wall to complete the exercise. Before students begin the test, read the limited-cloze passage aloud to them, saying "blank" when appropriate. Here is a limited-cloze passage for you to complete to review your knowledge of key terms from this chapter.

REVIEW

analogizing

a picture is worth a thousand words

direct

independence

key words

morpheme power

read

review

skits

unit

words

context power

connection

capsule vocabulary

discipline

interesting

meanings

multimeaning luck

remember when?

scavenger hunts

the real thing

visual

write

Teaching _____ and _____ for meanings is essential if you want students to learn information as they _____ and _____. The question of which words to teach is easy to answer if you consider which words are crucial to the whole _____, which words are crucial to the _____ being taught, and which words would be particularly _____ to your students. Once you have your list of _____, divide it into words for which students have no meaning and words for which students have meaning but not the word. To build meaning for words, use _____ or _____ experience, or make a _____. _____ brings the students to the experience or the experience to them. _____ is a strategy to provide visual experience. Students enjoy acting out new words and meaning in _____. Students are working to find objects and pictures when you arrange _____. _____ is a strategy that helps students build a concept for which you cannot provide direct or visual experience.

When students have meaning but don't know the word that represents that meaning, there are many strategies to use. These include: _____, _____ , _____ , _____ , and _____ . Since using a word just once is never enough for vocabulary, teachers must provide _____ . Because students will not always have you to direct them, you must also provide for _____ .

REFERENCES

Burmeister, L. (1978). *Reading strategies for middle and secondary school teachers* (2nd ed.). Reading, MA: Addison-Wesley.

Crist, B. I. (1975). One capsule a week—a painless remedy for vocabulary ills. *Journal of Reading, 19,* 147–149.

Goodspeed, P. (n.d.). *Hugh and Fitzhugh.* New York: Platt & Munk.

Haggard, M. R. (1982). The vocabulary self-collection strategy: An active approach to word learning. *Journal of Reading, 26,* 203–207.

Tierney, R. J., & Pearson, P. D. (1981). Learning to learn from text: A framework for improving classroom practice. In E. K. Dishner, T. W. Bean, & J. E. Readence (Eds.), *Reading in the content areas.* Dubuque, IA: Kendall/Hunt.

SUGGESTED READINGS

Approaches to developing vocabulary in general with a special chapter for content area vocabulary can be found in this recent book:

Johnson, D. D., & Pearson, P. D. (1984). *Teaching reading vocabulary.* New York: Holt, Rinehart & Winston.

Many activities for categorizing and word sorts can be found in the following article:

Gillet, J. W., & Kita, M. J. (1979). Words, kids and categories. *The Reading Teacher, 32,* 538–542.

Research on the use of analogy to develop unfamiliar concepts in a health textbook are reported in the following article. The methods described are applicable to any content area.

Vosniadou, S., & Ortony, A. (1982). The influence of analogy in children's acquisition of new information from text: An exploratory study. In J. Niles (Ed.), *Searches for meaning in reading/language processing and instruction* (Thirty-First Yearbook of the National Reading Conference). Rochester, NY: 1982, pp. 71–79.

Practical approaches to vocabulary instruction that could be used in any content area are included in the following articles:

Blachowicz, C. L. (1985). Vocabulary development and reading: From research to instruction. *The Reading Teacher, 38,* 876–881.

Carr, E. M. (1985). The vocabulary overview guide: A metacognitive strategy to improve vocabulary comprehension and retention. *Journal of Reading, 28,* 684–689.

Marzano, R. J. (1984). A cluster approach to vocabulary instruction: A new direction from the research literature. *The Reading Teacher, 37,* 168–173.

CHAPTER 4
Content Area Literature

GOING BEYOND THE TEXTBOOK

If you wanted to experience a new place, you might go there by car, traveling over different types of roads. Controlled-access freeways, divided and undivided highways, residential streets, and unpaved roads are among the choices you might have. You likewise have many choices in how to learn about content area information. If you are learning through reading, then you could go by routes such as textbooks, library books, encyclopedias, newspapers, and magazines. Content area reading materials are generally broken down into two broad areas—textbooks and literature. This chapter introduces you to the variety and uses of content area literature. *Literature* is defined broadly here to include library materials, such as books and encyclopedias, and outside materials, such as pamphlets and brochures.

Think of traveling through your state via different types of roads. Freeways get you through the territory quickly and efficiently. Freeway planners did not design routes to show off the surroundings, but to move people through the area with maximum speed. Freeways traverse only a small part of the territory within your state; if you want to get to a special area of interest such as a small town, a lake, a state park, or an historical site, you most likely would use a freeway for only part of your trip. A freeway might speed your journey to a certain point, but freeways rarely take you directly to where you want to go. Even when you arrive at a major city, freeways whisk you around on a perimeter belt loop, or they shoot you through the city (unless it's rush hour!), revealing only a few outstanding landmarks. In order to genuinely know an area, you need to get off the freeway and travel the connecting roads.

Traditional content area textbooks are like freeways. They may get you through a lot of territory, but they move you so quickly that you are unable to obtain close, personal insights about the area. Think of how a typical middle-school social studies textbook presents the ancient Greeks. The textbook probably devotes 10 to 20 pages to topics such as Greek mythology, government, social order, culture, art, architecture, warfare, and overall influence on modern life. The text most likely gives passing mention to "landmarks" such as Zeus, Aesop, Homer, Plato, and Alexander, to Athens, Sparta, and Macedonia, and to city-states, democracies, and republics. That's quite a lot of ground to cover in only 10 pages, but the Roman Empire comes next, and it too has several noteworthy features that must be covered.

But now think of all the library books and magazine articles on ancient Greece. For instance, *Gods, Men and Monsters from the Greek Myths* (1982) takes 152 pages to describe only one aspect of ancient Greek life, mythology. This book contains a full account of the exploits of the mythical characters, memorable graphics depicting scenes from the various myths, a chart depicting the relationships and roles of the gods, and an index. Prometheus, Apollo, Jason, Helios, and others come alive in this book. Such a carefully detailed, well-crafted treatment of a topic is not possible in a textbook because textbooks must cover too many topics.

ADVANTAGES OF CONTENT AREA LITERATURE

This section presents some of the major reasons why students profit from content area literature. Two major advantages of this literature are the fact that it is usually better written and more interesting than most textbooks, and it offers greater variety than textbooks.

Content Area Literature: Better Written, More Interesting

Textbook writers have a captive audience once their book is adopted in a classroom. These writers realize that a teacher will be available to explain confusing points and fill in missing information. Textbook writers also know that adults, not students, select the books. Thus, the composition of textbooks is designed to impress adults who look for extensive coverage of information.

Writers of content area literature, on the other hand, realize that their readers will be working mostly on their own. Writers and publishers know that teachers tend to explain what is presented in textbooks, but won't have time to explain the material in most library books. Writers and publishers also know that young readers select and stay only with books that are interesting to read. Therefore, writers of content area literature know that they must present their information in as clear and interesting a way as possible.

To appreciate the differences between traditional textbooks and well-written content area literature, think back to what you learned in this text about the organize and connect thinking processes. Remember that good readers arrange information into categories, and good readers also form connections between what they already know and what a passage contains. Likewise, proficient writers compose passages that are well organized and that provide familiar examples to help the reader make connections. Good writers make organizing and connecting seem effortless. Let's consider how writers have organized and connected information for their readers when presenting ancient Greek mythology.

Organizing Material   A typical middle-school social studies textbook might mention myths in a paragraph on festivals in ancient Greece. The text might point out that Herodotus, the first historian, shared his knowledge through public speaking; that many theaters were dedicated to Dionysius, the god of festivals; and that in these theaters myths were occasionally acted out. The next paragraph might then shift to a discussion of the early Greek thinkers, Socrates, Plato, and Aristotle. Such a treatment of mythology is not coherent, logical, or well organized. The fact that the ancient Greeks retold myths could just as easily have been inserted into the presentation of the Acropolis and the Parthenon. Students thus face a basket of isolated facts that need to be organized into some type of system that the author did not provide.

On the other hand, the writer of a book that might be found in a school library has many opportunities to include background information and to point out the relationships among ideas. Two books of myths, *The Warrior Goddess: Athena* (1972) and *Lord of the Sky: Zeus* (1972), exemplify solid organization. These books include only the myths that center on each main character, Athena and Zeus. Thus, one personality ties together the numerous stories in each book. Mythology can appear fragmented and disconnected, but Doris Gates, the author of the two books, imposed order by using single main characters as unifying elements. She arranged the information in such a way that her readers did not need to impose an organizational scheme of their own.

APPLY

Doris Gates organized her books of myths according to dominant personalities. Of course, many other types of organization are possible. List five additional ways that a writer might group various myths for his or her audience.

Connecting Material   As you know, learners who connect information tie together already-learned information with the new information being presented. Learners link what they already know to what they are trying to learn. Writers help readers make connections by reminding their audience of what they already know, then comparing that knowledge with new facts and generalizations.

Textbook writers rarely are able to suggest connections for readers, whereas writers of content area literature usually have enough space to make analogies. They can call up direct experiences for readers: the concept of untied balloons flying through a room might be compared to jet propulsion in science; families voting on where to go out for dinner could be linked to democracy in social studies; and dividing a chocolate cream pie among friends might be connected to fractions in math.

Michael Gibson, the writer of *Gods, Men and Monsters from the Greek Myths*, presented a connection for his readers that was quite effective. In one chapter of Gibson's book, Hades, the ancient Greek concept of the underworld, is compared to modern notions of Hell. The author points out that Hades, like Hell, was a place for the dead where sinners suffered eternal damnation. However, Gibson explains, Hades differed from Hell because all the dead—good and bad—first traveled to Hades to have their fates decided. Those who had led commendable lives then continued on to an afterlife of great happiness. Young readers who encounter this concept of Hades for the first time will probably have little difficulty understanding and remembering it, thanks to the author's connecting it to a familiar concept.

The Variety in Content Area Literature

If you took students out on a football field and had them run 100 yards, individuals would finish at different times, and some would enjoy the exercise more than others no matter which place they came in. In fact, the differences among students' running abilities and among their running interests probably would get bigger as students got older. The same holds true for reading. When you give your class a reading assignment, you can count on students finishing at different times, with different amounts of understanding and different degrees of interest. Thus, content area literature is useful because the variety of materials that is available can be matched with the variety of students that you have in your classes. Incorporating many different library books, periodicals, encyclopedias, newspapers, brochures, and other reading materials into the study of subject matter allows you to match students with what they can and want to handle. The variety of content area materials allows students to conduct personalized inquiry, promoting better attitudes toward learning and supporting the monitor thinking process.

Attitudes toward Learning
Let's face it! Students don't always appreciate teachers telling them what to learn. Sometimes students like to figure things out for themselves. Substituting content area literature for the single all-powerful textbook allows students to read for the purposes that they find personally satisfying, seeking the answers to their own questions. Instead of reading a chapter because it was assigned, students read a book or article because it captures their attention. And because interesting, readable materials tend to hold readers' attention, students may spend even more time actively engaged in reading and learning from content area literature than from textbooks.

One finding that has consistently emerged from classroom research is that students who spend time on tasks they can do well learn the most (Cunningham, 1985). Students do best when the assigned reading and writing tasks are well within their limits. In addition, students' behavior on a task is related to the task's level of difficulty. Understandably, students tend to avoid frustrating assignments and search for something else to do. Making available a variety of reading materials allows more students to succeed.

Students have the opportunity to develop positive attitudes toward reading while involved with content area literature because such literature can present a distinctive point of view on a topic, whereas textbooks tend to present no specific viewpoint or only a traditional perspective. For instance, *The Roots of Crime* (1981), an adolescent-level book, argues that children who learn to hate themselves frequently grow into lawbreakers. The roots of criminal behavior are said to be found in problems such as child abuse, uncaring families, and unemployment. This argument offers a clear contrast to neutral presentations of crime-related facts and to fervid appeals for strong-armed law and order. Such a contrasting view might interest an otherwise apathetic student. Content area literature can likewise present alternative, interesting points of view on issues such as genetic engineering, UFOs, nuclear power, sex roles, and treatment of the mentally handicapped.

Monitoring the Learning Process   As you know from Chapter 1, monitoring is an internal check on how learning is progressing. Efficient learners continually check themselves to see if they are getting what they need from their learning materials. If learning breaks down, then efficient learners stop, identify the problem, and do what they can to get back on track. When students are given frustrating materials, they miss the opportunity to monitor their learning. Few things make sense to them, and little can be done about it. Allowing students to find content area literature that they can and will read is an important part of teaching students to monitor their learning.

Many students who consistently work with materials that are too difficult for them don't know how to tell if they're getting what they need because they've never had that full feeling of thoroughly understanding a passage. It's like water skiing. Once you have gotten up on your skis even a single time, then you know what getting up feels like and you can do considerably better the next time. Providing students materials that they can fully understand allows them to know what understanding feels like so they can better monitor their progress in the future.

Benefits of Textbooks

By now you probably are convinced that we are totally in favor of the use of content area literature and totally opposed to the use of textbooks. Not so! After all, we wrote the textbook that you currently are reading. Textbooks do play a needed role in education. They systematically introduce readers to a body of knowledge. They save teachers time by outlining learning sequences for students. They specify content beforehand so that teachers know how to plan. Textbooks provide the glue that holds together a wide assortment of facts and generalizations. Indeed, we expect that you will use textbooks when you teach, but we hope that you will also use library books and other reading materials. Such content area literature gives students a chance at getting something meaningful from their reading; it at least meets students halfway. We suggest that some of the time you might spend helping students understand their textbooks would be better spent getting literature into the hands of your students. The remainder of this chapter clarifies what is available in content area literature and presents ways to employ it.

AN OVERVIEW OF CONTENT AREA LITERATURE

Authors

Authors of content area literature have an enormous responsibility. Not only must they present accurate information, but they must present it in an interesting, entertaining manner in order for the work to sell. These authors must master the subject matter as well as the writer's craft. Certain authors and illustrators have contributed a significant number of interesting and useful books:

Elementary School	*Middle School*	*High School*
Irving Adler	Franklyn Branley	Isaac Asimov
Aliki	Leonard Everett Fisher	James Haskins
Byron Barton	Genevieve Foster	James Herriot
Jean Bendick	Jean Craighead George	Elisabeth Kübler-Ross
Tomie DePaola	Shirley Glubok	Eda LeShan
Muriel Feelings	David Macaulay	Peter Mayle
Jean Fritz	Laurence Pringle	Robert McClung
Roma Gans	Miroslav Sasek	John McPhee
Gail Gibbons	Jack Denton Scott	Milton Meltzer
Alice E. Goudey	Seymour Simon	James Michener
Tana Hoban	Alvin Tresselt	Farley Mowat
John J. Reiss	Edwin Tunis	Carl Sagan
Millicent Selsam	Harvey Weiss	Gary Trudeau
Margot and	Herbert Zim	Eliot Wigginton
Harve Zemach		

When you come to evaluate content area literature, remember that accuracy of information and style of writing are your two main criteria. Consider the following aspects of a book:

Is the information accurate?

Is the information up to date?

Is the information presented in a logical, well organized manner?

Are familiar examples provided when introducing unfamiliar concepts?

Will the material be interesting to its intended audience?

Are controversial issues identified as such and other viewpoints acknowledged?

Are illustrations provided to clarify text information rather than just to decorate the page?

Is a complete table of contents or an index available to help readers locate specific information?

Are directions and supplies lists in how-to books complete enough to allow the intended audience to succeed without outside help?

APPLY

Investigate the materials produced by at least five of the authors and illustrators in the list we provided. Make bibliographic cards for specific books you may want in your future teaching. Include pertinent bibliographic information (title, author, illustrator, publisher, and date of publication) so that you can easily locate the sources later. Annotate the cards with a few sentences about the content and special features of the book.

Next, choose one author and carefully study about three of his or her books. Bring the books to class and share your impressions of them using the criteria listed above.

Content

At the elementary level, content area literature ranges from titles such as *Benny Bear Gets Ready for Winter* to *Bears: Preparation for Hibernation*. The second book is clearly identifiable as a piece of content area reading material. From the title you can guess that the author has identified the steps bears go through in order to prepare themselves for months of deep sleep without food. The book evidently presents information in objective fashion about bears finding safe, relatively warm places to sleep and about bears eating heavily before winter in order to survive on stored-up fat. The first title, however, may leave you uncertain. Benny Bear could be a ''cutesy'' story about a bear who wears clothes, lives in a human-style house, and shops at the local mini-mart. On the other hand, Benny Bear might behave like a real bear, to whom the author gave a name in order to make the material easier for children.

Some educators and librarians refer to content area literature only as expository, or nonfiction, books. But that designation leaves out a whole realm of materials that present facts in the context of a story. The Benny Bear example indicates how a story might present a wealth of information. For instance, books that follow a story line while presenting extremely valuable information to older readers include *Watership Down* (1975), *Sounder* (1972), *Across Five Aprils* (1964), *Fantastic Voyage* (1966), *On the Beach* (1957), *Johnny*

Tremain (1943), and *Julie of the Wolves* (1972). Consequently, we include in our definition of content area literature straightforward *expository materials* as well as *literary materials* that provide factual information through a story line.

Content area literature comes in a wide range of types for pre-school-age children through adults. The suggested reading section at the end of this chapter contains book selection guides appropriate for the content areas. There are far too many non-textbook materials for us to list them all here. But we can describe the major categories of content area literature likely to be found in elementary and secondary schools.

Concept Books   Concept books are primarily appropriate for very young children. Generally speaking, *concept books* cover basic information that young children will need in order to understand school tasks later on. These books introduce concepts such as size, shape, color, spatial relations, the alphabet, and numbers. For instance, *Push, Pull, Empty, Full* (1972) depicts fifteen pairs of opposites. *In* and *out* are represented by a turtle whose head is pulled inside and then extended outside the shell; *whole* and *broken* are represented by two intact eggs and two eggs smashed on the floor; and so on.

The focus of concept books should be on clearly presenting the content. Many concept books are written more for adult consumption (''Oh, isn't that cute!'') than for children's learning. When searching for books to teach basic concepts to children, carefully scrutinize them to make sure that the books do in fact teach what they claim to teach. Some materials about shapes, for example, present distortions such as squares shown at an angle so that they resemble diamonds, circles that are really ovals, and circles that are bisected. As with all content area literature, the information in concept books should be unambiguous.

Reference Books   Students are frequently intimidated by *reference books* because the information in them is presented differently than the information in other books. Reference materials usually have extremely dense text summarizing a great deal of information in very little space. Nonetheless, some materials are better than others. Some publications contain striking visuals, accurate information, and accessible writing. In one book's presentation of the atmosphere, an illustration shows the sea, the world's tallest building, an eagle flying, Mt. Everest, and an airborne jumbo jet in order to depict how high birds and airplanes can fly.

While the majority of reference materials are aimed at good readers in the intermediate grades and above, there are some excellent materials for primary-grade students. When searching for reference materials, keep student reading abilities in mind and examine the composition of the materials. Are they well organized? Are examples provided? If the material is too sparse, students will not be informed and may even go away from the material confused because information was missing.

Topical Books   *Topical books*, frequently called informational books, present information about a specific subject in expository fashion. *The Day Lincoln Was Shot* (1955), *Silent Spring* (1962), *Bury My Heart at Wounded Knee* (1971), and *Megatrends* (1982) are some well-known examples of topical books for older students; *Bones* (1969), *How Kittens Grow* (1973), and *The Doctors* (1968) are popular with younger students. Some topical books cover a wide range of information, while others detail a specific aspect of a phenomenon. The information in these books is often surprisingly up to date. For example, students and adults alike generally are fascinated with ancient Egypt and the construction of the pyramids. A new thesis being proposed about the construction of the pyramids is that the massive stones used in construction were created from liquid which hardened in the hot sun. This explanation makes far more sense than the prevailing one, which contends that 14-ton blocks were transported across many miles on sledges and then carted to the top of the pyramid. We can expect a book on this particular topic written for the young in the near future.

Many books that present straightforward, factual information are available for all subject areas. One can find books about birds or about a specific bird. There are books about the water cycle, the life cycle, and the bicycle. The best of these books are illustrated with high-quality drawings or photographs which enhance the textual information.

How-to Books   *How-to books* describe a process. These books explain how to perform activities such as playing chess, conducting science experiments, folding paper artistically, cooking, repairing cars, and making music. This category has somewhat limited usefulness because it applies to only a few content areas. Numerous how-to books exist to support the sciences, mathematics, and vocational skills; such books are rare in the social sciences and the humanities.

Biography   Books about people who have made contributions to the content areas are numerous. *Biographies* are available about people prominent in reform movements, politics, sports, medicine, war, and entertainment, to name only a few fields. Abraham Lincoln, Jim Thorpe, Marie Curie, Anne Frank, and Bill Cosby are only a small sampling of those whose life histories have been written. Young readers often appreciate biographies as they search for heroes and heroines to emulate. Unfortunately, some biographers let their own infatuation with the subject interfere with the honest depiction of a multifaceted human being. Students need to be on the alert for folklore that passes for truth from one book to another. For instance, the story about George Washington and the cherry tree is not substantiated. Some myths are easily spotted; others pass into the general culture as truths. Though more biographies exist for people in the content areas of the arts, humanities, and social sciences, biographies have been written about important figures associated with all major curricular areas.

Fiction   We venture to say that a great deal of your knowledge about the climate, language, flora, fauna, and ethnic groups in certain parts of the world came from reading fiction by authors such as James A. Michener. There are two basic types of fiction suitable for content area classrooms: contemporary realistic fiction and historical fiction. Contemporary realistic fiction portrays current events and people who seem to be involved in the recognizable trials and uncertainties of life. Young-adult books such as *I'll Get There, It Better Be Worth the Trip* (1969) and *A Day No Pigs Would Die* (1972) are becoming classic statements of young adults' changes from dependent children to independent adults. Many books now are available that deal with issues such as divorce, developing sexuality, mental and physical handicaps, and death and dying. For instance, *Johnny Got His Gun* (1939) is a compelling piece of antiwar fiction that has a place in an English or social studies class along with a traditional text. Likewise, *My Side of the Mountain* (1959) or *Hook a Fish, Catch a Mountain* (1975) could easily be used in a science classroom when dealing with ecological issues.

Historical fiction attempts to re-create a believable past. Authors of such works often create fictional characters who interact with people who actually shaped events in history. Through these imagined and real characters, the past can be interpreted. After reading *Across Five Aprils* (1964), *Rifles for Watie* (1957), or *Zoar Blue* (1978), students begin to understand much better why the Civil War was so devastating on a personal as well as national scale.

Figure 4.1   Students enjoy opportunities to browse through a variety of reading materials.

While reading fiction tied to history, art, or music helps to enliven the content being studied, teachers should be cautious. Fiction's goal, first and foremost, is to tell a good story. Trying to grasp the entire Civil War era through novels is inefficient, if not impossible. Some periods and personalities make better stories and are therefore written about frequently; other important events hardly figure in novels at all. In any case, you would have to read a great many novels to get all the important facts.

Periodicals   A wide range of published material is available by subscription. *Periodicals* are an excellent supplement to content area materials both because they are timely and because they include short, lively, well-illustrated articles on interesting topics. Periodicals can provide students with an introduction to a new subject, pique student interest in a subject not considered interesting, and summarize information after students have done other extensive research. Periodicals from *Ranger Rick's Nature Magazine* to *Popular Mechanics* to *Junior Scholastic* are available for class or individual subscriptions.

USING CONTENT AREA LITERATURE IN THE CLASSROOM

For years teachers have used non-textbook materials to extend students' knowledge of a unit being studied. Nevertheless, even though materials might be made available, teachers frequently have difficulty providing students with the time and the guidance to learn from them. We now present three major considerations in planning students' use of content area literature: (1) selection of materials, (2) reading time, and (3) book projects.

Selection of Materials

Providing students with a wide range of reading materials is crucial. Materials should include articles from periodicals, captioned or labeled illustrations, captioned filmstrips, materials prepared by students from previous classes, and appropriate books from the types discussed above. The materials should vary in length, reading level, depth of information, and point of view. Experienced teachers generally collect such materials over time. When a classroom magazine contains a good article about a topic, teachers save that issue. They might maintain picture files for topics they teach. Library books and audiovisual materials are located and requested each year when the appropriate unit of study comes up. Since materials are brought into the classroom, rules about taking materials home must be established.

A good way to organize the selection of materials for a unit of study is through curriculum webbing. As you know, a web can be constructed of the relationships among words; these are called *semantic* webs. *Curriculum* webs are useful for organizing activities and materials for upcoming units.

To construct a curriculum web, write the general topic of your unit in the center of a large piece of paper. Then branch off to list subtopics. Finally, brainstorm materials and activities in reading, writing, listening, and speaking for each subtopic. Curriculum webs allow you to generate many possible ideas for a unit of study; once formulated, these webs provide a structured view of the entire unit, which might aid your day-to-day planning. Figures 4.2 and 4.3 depict sample curriculum webs for content area topics in middle school.

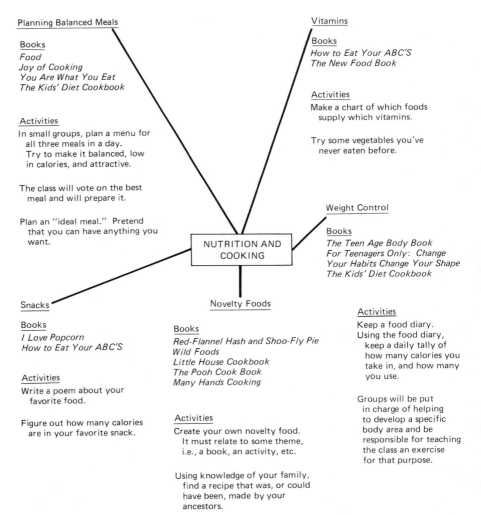

Figure 4.2   Curriculum web on nutrition and cooking.

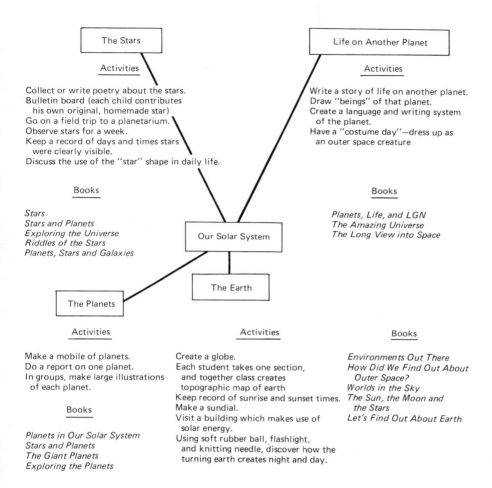

The Stars

Activities

Collect or write poetry about the stars.
Bulletin board (each child contributes
  his own original, homemade star)
Go on a field trip to a planetarium.
Observe stars for a week.
Keep a record of days and times stars
  were clearly visible.
Discuss the use of the "star" shape in daily life.

Books

Stars
Stars and Planets
Exploring the Universe
Riddles of the Stars
Planets, Stars and Galaxies

Our Solar System

The Planets

Activities

Make a mobile of planets.
Do a report on one planet.
In groups, make large illustrations
  of each planet.

Books

Planets in Our Solar System
Stars and Planets
The Giant Planets
Exploring the Planets

Life on Another Planet

Activities

Write a story of life on another planet.
Draw "beings" of that planet.
Create a language and writing system
  of the planet.
Have a "costume day"—dress up as
  an outer space creature

Books

Planets, Life, and LGN
The Amazing Universe
The Long View into Space

The Earth

Activities

Create a globe.
Each student takes one section,
  and together class creates
  topographic map of earth
Keep record of sunrise and sunset times.
Make a sundial.
Visit a building which makes use of
  solar energy.
Using soft rubber ball, flashlight,
  and knitting needle, discover how the
  turning earth creates night and day.

Books

Environments Out There
*How Did We Find Out About
  Outer Space?*
Worlds in the Sky
*The Sun, the Moon and
  the Stars*
Let's Find Out About Earth

Reading Time

There are various ways to provide students with class time for reading content
area literature. One way is simply to allow students who finish assigned tasks
to browse through a classroom collection of materials. However, many teachers plan for this browsing time by setting aside a certain time of the day for
sustained silent reading (SSR). SSR calls for students and teachers to do nothing
but read. Students may not work on assignments, and teachers may not grade
papers. Instead, students and teachers begin an SSR period by locating reading materials, and then spend a specific amount of time reading them. If some
form of accountability is required, teachers may record the amount of time
spent reading rather than books completed or projects submitted.

SSR time frequently is scheduled immediately after breaks in the day, such as lunch or class changes, because it tends to calm young people. As Figure 4.4a shows, students might remain in their seats during free reading time; however, Figure 4.4b shows how students also might go in pairs to an attractive designated free reading area. A specific time is set, from 5 to 20 minutes, and students are held to it. No formal book report projects are assigned with SSR materials because continued attention is the desired response. Remember, students share their responses to what they experience all the time. If the material they are reading is worthwhile, they will share responses to it, too. These shared responses may be just as valuable to students as formal book reports.

Book Projects

When students participate in SSR, they are not expected to produce reports about what they read. But in many other situations such reports are appropriate. The content area literature students read should be regularly incorporated in the other content you are presenting. If students see that you do not include information from reading materials in your discussion of a unit, they will quickly decide that there is no need to attend seriously to the variety of materials you have made available. Therefore, when you present information on a unit, be sure to refer to specific pieces of literature. When you evaluate students' learning of the topic being studied, include information presented in the literature. It may be necessary to give extra credit to students

Figure 4.4a   Older students will make valuable use of SSR time.

who read beyond the textbook. Students eventually will see that the textbook is merely the road map for their journey through the content, whereas content area literature is the AAA Guidebook to more detailed information.

You no doubt have experienced the every-nine-week-assignment of reading a book and then summarizing what you read in a report. You probably have some negative feelings about producing all those summaries. Because of the limited and negative connotations of the term *book report*, we use the term *book project*. Book projects go beyond mere summaries, and can be valuable teaching strategies.

Ideally, book projects should lead students to deeper insights about what they have read. Students activate essential thinking processes while participating in meaningful book projects. In fact, meaningful assignments can lead students to all nine of the thought processes we have described. When left

Figure 4.4b Younger students also enjoy time to read a good book.

alone, students can easily slip into passive reading habits, barely attending to a book's message. Books become a sort of mental chewing gum; they feel good for a while, but have no long-lasting benefit. As we argued earlier, students require opportunities to read freely and to experience well-written prose, but they also benefit from sharpening and extending their understanding of what they read by expressing their reactions through various projects.

Perhaps the greatest contribution of book projects is the criteria they provide for students to independently monitor their comprehension. In order to produce some tangible reaction to a book, students need to step back mentally and collect their thoughts. If students find portions of their understanding to be unclear, they can reread and rethink the passage that contains the confusing information. Without book projects, students can remain at superficial leveis of understanding.

A common reason for assigning book projects is to have students demonstrate that they actually read what they claim to have read. That is, the project was assigned for purposes of assessment. We would emphasize instructional purposes rather than assessments. Book projects should lead students to increased understanding; they should not just allow the teacher to assess what was understood.

Once a piece of content area literature is selected for a student's book project, the exact nature of the project needs to be specified. Some students understand what they read, but have difficulty understanding the teacher's assignment. When you assign projects, or have students select their own, make certain that the students know exactly what they are supposed to do. Having them explain to you in their own words what they intend to do frequently helps to clear up any misconceptions about the assignment.

Book projects can take many forms. Visuals, realia and models, dramatizations, and written and oral compositions are some possible forms, besides the numerous forms within each of these categories. When you help students plan the project they intend to construct in response to a book, you should maintain a balance of project types over the school year. Following are some types of book projects that we have found to be effective.

Visuals   As we said earlier, a picture is worth a thousand words. Students benefit from viewing visuals in order to learn information, and they also benefit from producing visuals in reaction to what they read. If the purpose of a book project is, "Identify three pieces of new information that you learned," the best way to represent the new learning may be visually.

Illustrations. Illustrations and photographs are good substitutes for the real thing. Students often draw pictures, collect photographs, or take their own photographs in order to depict what was encountered in a passage. They may also make posters or bulletin boards. Such visuals graphically depict what words can only suggest. For example, the Grand Canyon, cell division, parts of the body, and geometric figures are natural candidates for illustrated book projects.

Time Lines and Murals. The key events of a phenomenon are frequently displayed on a *time line.* Any number of illustrations, or none at all, may be on a time line. The essential feature is that events are labelled and represented in sequence on a linear chart. *Murals* are similar to time lines in that they represent a sequence of events; the difference, of course, is that murals consist solely of pictures.

Maps. Representing an area graphically requires careful reading and composing. Students need to decide what locations to represent, and must then produce that representation. Illustrations can be added to maps for greater detail. Maps can depict locations on many scales. For instance, locations within a building, neighborhood, community, state, nation, the world, or the universe can be mapped.

Collages. Collages are groups of pictures and various other materials glued to a surface. These artistic compositions generally symbolize a topic. Making a collage of an area of study such as ethnic and racial groups, geographic locations, inventions, and animal groups is a good project for students of all ages.

Homemade Transparencies. Older students can make their own overhead transparencies. Have your students take thin-line, permanent-ink, felt-tip markers and either draw or trace pictures on a sheet of acetate. Give the pictures a few minutes to dry and then cover them with clear adhesive plastic. If appropriate, cut the pictures apart so they can be reassembled when the report is presented. Homemade transparencies made up of separate parts are especially useful when presenting development, such as the growth of the United States; components, such as the parts of a plant or animal; and processes, such as photosynthesis and weather changes.

Realia and Models   Realia and models are objects that represent the phenomenon being studied as closely as possible. *Realia* are actual objects; *models* represent objects (such as buildings) and processes (such as radiation). Actual objects, models, and simulations can be displayed in the classroom in order to approximate direct, firsthand experiences. The teaching strategy entitled the real thing, presented in Chapter 3, is based on realia and models. Figure 4.5 shows a table of books and realia that students prepared for a unit of study in American History.

Students can buy, borrow, or make realia as part of their book projects. For instance, young students reacting to Frontier Living might collect objects that represent life on the western frontier in the 1800s. Weapons, farm tools, kitchen implements, clothing, and assorted household items can be brought into class in order to depict concretely aspects of a bygone way of life. Students who read *Birth of an Island* (1975) could fashion a clay and water representation of geologic actions to show the formation of islands. Older students who read *Man Kind? Our Incredible War on Wildlife* (1974) could bring in representative traps, guns, and other means of destruction that are used to kill animals. Students who read about scientific processes such as evapora-

Figure 4.5 Assembling a display of objects and related reading materials is an effective book project.

tion, covalent bonding, and friction cannot bring in the actual "thing," but they can demonstrate the outcomes that result from those intangible forces. Indeed, science fairs, which are traditional parts of many schools' curriculums, are excellent examples of students producing realia and models.

Dramatizations   Many students like to stage short skits in reaction to what they have read. They simulate certain phenomena through action and dialogue. For example, older students might read *On Death and Dying* (1974) and then present different skits that portray the stages people exhibit when facing their own imminent deaths. Other students might take Studs Terkel's *Working* (1981) and present selected scenes wherein people talk about the emotional side of their jobs and how their jobs affect their whole lives. Young students who read about collecting rocks could go through a series of scenes that illustrate the rules described in such a book for gathering a personal collection.

Written and Oral Compositions   Visuals, realia, and models can include composition, although they do not emphasize it, and dramatizations are a special form of composition. The compositions described in this section emphasize instead somewhat lengthy written or oral responses to books. As we mentioned earlier, traditional book projects mostly consist of written or oral summaries. However, students have available other types of compositions for responding to what they read.

Literary Book Compositions may require a special format. Teachers of older students frequently distribute composition guides to help students structure their reactions to novels and short stories. The guides should include generic questions grouped according to literary elements such as character, plot, setting, and theme. Figure 4.6 displays a sample guide that contains two tasks under each literary element; other tasks certainly might be included. Some teachers assign different maximum numbers of points that can be earned for the various tasks and allow students to choose the ones they wish to perform.

LITERARY BOOK PROJECT COMPOSITION GUIDE

Directions: Complete one task that is listed under each literary element.

Character
1. Write a letter to a friend, a member of your family, or an actor or actress that describes how he or she is like a character in your book.
2. Pretend that you are one of the characters in your book. Write a letter to Ann Landers to get her advice on coping with the main problem you faced. Write her response.

Plot
1. Produce a calendar of events that reflects the story line. (The calendar can be divided among hours, days, weeks, months, or years.)
2. Produce a diary that one of the characters might have kept in order to chronicle the events of his or her life.

Setting
1. Pretend that the book is being turned into a one-hour special or a mini-series on television. Describe at least five locations where five different scenes should be filmed.
2. You are responsible for obtaining the props for a stage production of your book. List five props that are essential for the production, and justify their use.

Theme
1. Describe at least one insight that the main character gained by the end of the story.
2. Describe how another story that you know makes the same point as the story you read.

Figure 4.6   Sample literary book project composition guide.

Additionally, tasks that do not fall neatly under a specific literary element (e.g., "Write a different story that parallels the original one." "Write a new ending for the story.") can be included under an *Other* category. Of course, teachers should demonstrate how to perform the tasks before expecting students to perform them independently. Primary-grade teachers would not provide composition guides in the form shown here, although young children could accomplish many of the tasks that are listed.

Expository Book Composition guides should be content-specific rather than generic. Such guides are often more difficult to produce than those for literary books. For instance, the task of comparing friends with story characters can be done in response to practically any literary passage, and this task elicits much thinking. However, this task is not appropriate for an expository book. Indeed, few generic tasks fit the great variety of topics covered in expository writing.

Composition tasks for expository book projects seem therefore to function best when they are designed for individual books. Teachers need to help students structure their own responses. If a student chooses to produce a written or oral composition in response to, say, *Megatrends* (1982), then the teacher should help decide which questions about the book need to be addressed. Should the student explain the ten new forces transforming modern lives? Should the most important new trend be selected and reasons for the selection described? Should the actual, foreseeable impact of one trend on the student producing the composition be predicted? You can see how each expository book requires a separate assignment from the teacher.

WHAT ABOUT . . .

What about Obtaining Content Area Literature?

There are many ways to obtain content area literature for your students without spending any money. Obviously, you can check materials out of the public library to use in your classroom. While this is a bit time-consuming, the number of books and magazines available makes this method very worthwhile. You can also have students produce reading materials for their peers. In only a few years, you will have collected a veritable cornucopia of resources. What else can you do to obtain reading materials?

Talk with your public librarian as well as the school librarian. Ask them to contact you when they are ready to discard content area books. Typically, books are discarded when they have become too worn for continued use by the public. Sometimes they have even gone through one re-binding process. But that won't matter to you. Look through the books. Is the content useful to you? Are the passages you would like to use in good condition? If so, collect the books, find a razor blade, and settle in front of the TV for your favorite program while you slice the passages you want from each book. Using book binding techniques described in Huck (1979) or Coody (1980), create a series of little books, one for each of the passages you want to use.

Magazine distribution centers (you can get the address of the one closest to you from your local magazine vendor) collect unsold magazines, rip off the covers, and mail the covers back to the publisher so that an accurate tally of sales can be maintained. The magazines themselves are destroyed. Ask for those magazines that you would like to have. You can frequently obtain class-size sets of magazines rather than just single copies.

Students may be willing to bring their copies of magazines or books to school to share, though they are rarely willing to donate them. A week or two before you begin a unit, request that students who are willing to share related materials bring them to school on the Friday before the unit will begin. This gives you a weekend to go through what is available and organize it for the students. Remind them to mark their materials with a name before bringing them to school. Also tell them that you cannot guarantee the safety of anything, so if a particular issue of a magazine is a prized one that they couldn't bear to lose, they ought not to bring it to school.

Two other sources for content area materials do require the expenditure of money, though not yours. Go to your school's parent-teacher organization and request a specific amount of money for a list of books and magazines which you have compiled. It's often wise to ask for a lot more than you think you will be able to get. If you show that you have a really great need for a large number of special materials, then you are more likely to get at least some of those materials. Another source of supplies is the paperback book clubs that continually send order forms to teachers. Distribute the forms to your students. When they return their order forms and money for books they want, you will discover that your class has earned a number of bonus points that you can apply toward the purchase of free books or other content area materials such as maps or filmstrips.

What about Censorship?

Many teachers have had to deal with censorship issues during the last several years. In response to the concern over academic freedom, the National Council of Teachers of English formed a committee which, among other tasks, formulated a set of guidelines for school districts to follow prior to censorship action (Donelson, 1972). By having a school board-approved plan that deals with questions about the appropriateness of reading material, the school district and the teacher will be in a far better position to discuss the issue—if it ever arises—without having to take a defensive stance.

What triggers an objection from parents or community groups? Sensitive issues dealing with people's value systems, prejudices, and fears are likely to cause concern when the school attempts to teach about them. These include racial, sexual, and religious concerns. If you are teaching a course in family living, you can anticipate that there will be some concerns about how you plan to deal with the topic of reproduction. Objections might be raised if you study death. Groups in many areas of the country have gone to court over the issue of evolution versus creationism as a way to explain the origin of the earth.

In order to be prepared for potential dissension, be aware of the community values where you teach. Make sure that your school district has a ready plan that delineates a course of action both to prevent issues from arising and to deal with those that might arise.

REVIEW

Call up what you learned about webbing relationships among words earlier in this book. In order to review what you have learned in this chapter, try to reconstruct the web we used when planning this chapter. Take out a blank sheet of paper and write *Content Area Literature* in a box at the center. Draw lines out from the center box, writing one of these headings at the end of each line: *Going Beyond the Textbook, Advantages of Content Area Literature, An Overview of Content Area Literature, Using Content Area Literature in the Classroom,* and *What About?* Complete the web by filling in subtopics under each heading. Be brief with these entries; they should only be reminders.

REFERENCES

Professional Sources

Coody, B. (1980). *Using literature with young children.* Dubuque, IA: W. C. Brown.

Cunningham, J. (1985). Three recommendations to improve comprehension teaching. In J. Osborn, P. T. Wilson, & R. C. Anderson (Eds.), *Reading education: Foundations for a literate America.* Lexington, MA: Lexington Books of D. C. Heath.

Donelson, K. L. (1972). *The students' right to read.* Urbana, IL: National Council of Teachers of English.

Huck, C. S. (1979). *Children's literature in the elementary school* (3rd ed., updated). New York: Holt, Rinehart & Winston.

Content Area Literature

Adams, R. (1975). *Watership down.* New York: Alfred A. Knopf.

Amory, C. (1974). *Man kind? Our incredible war on wildlife.* New York: Harper & Row.

Armstrong, W. (1972). *Sounder.* New York: Harper & Row.

Asimov, I. (1966). *Fantastic voyage.* Boston: Houghton Mifflin.

Bishop, J. A. (1955). *The day Lincoln was shot.* New York: Harper & Row.

Brown, D. (1971). *Bury my heart at Wounded Knee.* New York: Holt, Rinehart & Winston.

Carson, R. (1962). *Silent spring.* Boston: Houghton Mifflin.

Clement, F. (1975). *Birth of an island.* New York: Simon & Schuster.

Donovan, J. (1969). *I'll get there, it better be worth the trip.* New York: Harper & Row.

Fisher, L. E. (1968). *The doctors*. New York: F. Watts.

Forbes, E. (1943). *Johnny Tremain*. Boston: Houghton Mifflin.

Gates, D. (1972). *Lord of the sky: Zeus*. New York: Viking.

Gates, D. (1972). *The warrior goddess: Athena*. New York: Viking.

George, J. C. (1975). *Hook a fish, catch a mountain*. New York: E. P. Dutton.

George, J. (1972). *Julie of the wolves*. New York: Harper & Row.

George, J. (1959). *My side of the mountain*. New York: E. P. Dutton.

Gibson, M. (1982). *Gods, men and monsters from the Greek myths*. New York: Schocken.

Hickman, J. (1978). *Zoar blue*. New York: Macmillan.

Hoban, T. (1972). *Push, pull, empty, full*. New York: Macmillan.

Hunt, I. (1964). *Across five Aprils*. Chicago: Follett.

Keith, H. (1957). *Rifles for Watie*. New York: T. Cromell.

Kübler-Ross, E. (1974). *On death and dying*. New York: Macmillan.

LeShan, E. (1981). *The roots of crime*. New York: Scholastic.

Naisbitt, J. (1982). *Megatrends*. New York: Warner Books.

Peck, R. N. (1972). *A day no pigs would die*. New York: Dell.

Selsam, M. (1973). *How kittens grow*. New York: Four Winds.

Shute, N. (1957). *On the beach*. New York: Morrow.

Terkel, S. (1981). *Working*. New York: Simon & Schuster.

Trumbo, D. (1939). *Johnny got his gun*. Philadelphia: J. B. Lippincott.

Zim, H. (1969). *Bones*. New York: Morrow.

SUGGESTED READINGS

Several textbooks focus on literature for the young. The following three books treat content area literature quite well. The first text addresses young adults' literature; the next two address children's literature.

Donelson, K. L., & Nielsen, A. P. (1980). *Literature for today's young adults*. Glenview, IL: Scott, Foresman.

Huck, C. S. (1979). *Children's literature in the elementary school* (3rd ed., updated). New York: Holt, Rinehart & Winston.

Sutherland, Z., Monson, D. L., & Arbuthnot, M. H. (1981). *Children and books* (6th ed.). Glenview, IL: Scott, Foresman.

The following collection of articles on the characteristics of well-crafted exposition deserves the attention of those who are serious about teaching students through this form of writing.

Carr, J. (Compiler) (1981). *The literature of fact*. Chicago: American Library Association.

An update on exemplary content area literature for elementary school children is available through *The Kobrin Letter*, which is published monthly except July and August. Subscription correspondence should be addressed to the following:

The Kobrin Letter
732 Greer Road
Palo Alto, CA 94303

Providing time for reading is something that teachers sometimes have difficulty justifying as well as managing. The following sources might help alleviate some of the difficulties:

Allington, R. L. (1983). Fluency: The neglected reading goal. *The Reading Teacher, 36*, 556–561.

Bishop, D. M. (1981). Motivating adolescent readers via starter shelves in content area classes. In A. J. Ciani (Ed.), *Motivating reluctant readers*. Newark, DE: International Reading Association.

Berglund, R. L., & Johns, J. L. (1983). A primer on uninterrupted sustained silent reading. *The Reading Teacher, 36*, 534–539.

Fader, D., Duggins, J., Finn, T., & McNeil, E. (1976). *The new hooked on books*. New York: Berkley.

LaRocque, G. E. (1979). You gotta kiss a lotta frogs before you find Prince Charming. *English Journal, 68*, 31–35.

Book projects are time-honored instructional activities. Additional ideas for projects beyond the ones presented in this chapter might be found in these sources:

Carlson, R. K. (1976). *Enrichment ideas* (2nd ed.). Dubuque, IA: William C. Brown.

Fisher, C. J. (1979). 55 ways to respond to a book. *Instructor, 88*, 94–96.

Mavrogenes, N. A. (1977). 101 ways to react to books. *English Journal, 66*, 64–66.

Monson, D. L., & McClenathan, D. K. (Eds.). (1979). *Developing active readers*. Newark, DE: International Reading Association.

Whisler, N.C. (1975). Book reporting comes alive. *Journal of Reading, 16*, 383–387.

Censorship issues can drain teachers' time and energy from the actual job of teaching. As with most debilitating conditions, prevention is better than cure. The following publication offers guidelines for preventing censorship from interfering with teaching.

Donelson, K. L. (1972). *The students' right to read*. Urbana, IL: National Council of Teachers of English.

Some people contend that books will become obsolete in the future. A good discussion of this issue is presented in the following:

Moskin, J. R. (1983). The future of books in the electronic era. *Visible Language, 17*, 399–407.

BOOK SELECTION GUIDES

General

Montebello, M. (1972). *Children's literature in the curriculum*. Dubuque, IA: W. C. Brown.

Concept Books

Lima, C. A. (1982). *A to zoo: Subject access to children's picture books*. New York: Bowker.

Reference Books

Peterson, C. S., & Fenton, A. D. (1981). *Reference books for children*. Metuchen, NJ: Scarecrow Press.

Sheehy, E. P. (1976). *Guide to reference books* (9th ed.). Chicago: American Library Association. (*Supplement* published, 1980).

Topical Books

Art.

Bunch, C. (1978). *Art education: A guide to information sources*. Detroit: Gale Research.

Health.

Ayarnoff, P. (1982). *Best books on health for children*. New York: Bowker.

Mathematics.

Matthias, M., & Thiessen, D. (1979). *Children's mathematics books, a critical bibliography*. Chicago: American Library Association.

Schaaf, W. L. (1982). *The high school mathematics library*. Reston, VA: National Council of Teachers of Mathematics.

Wheeler, M. M., & Hardgrove, C. E. (1978). *Mathematics library—Elementary and junior high school*. Reston, VA: National Council of Teachers of Mathematics.

Science.

Wolff, K., et al. (1983). *Best science books for children: Selected and annotated*. Washington, DC: American Association for the Advancement of Science.

Social Studies.

Czarra, F. (Ed.). (1983). *A guide to historical reading: Nonfiction*. Washington, DC: Heldref Publications.

Metzner, S. (1973). *World history in juvenile books*. New York: H. W. Wilson.

Wiltz, J. E., & Cridland, N. C. (1981). *Books in American history: A basic list for high schools and junior colleges*. Bloomington: Indiana State University.

How-to Books.

Gallivan, M. F. (1981). *Fun for kids: An index to children's craft books*. Metuchen, NJ: Scarecrow Press.

Biography.

Hotchkiss, J. (Compiler) (1973). *American historical fiction and biography for children and young people*. Metuchen, NJ: Scarecrow Press.

Nicholsen, M. E. (1969). *People in books*. New York: H. W. Wilson. (Supplement published, 1977).

Silverman, J. (1979). *Index to collective biographies for young readers* (3rd ed.). New York: Bowker.

Stanius, E. J. (1971). *Index to short biographies for elementary and junior high grades*. Metuchen, NJ: Scarecrow Press.

Periodicals

Matthews, J., & Drag, L. (1974). *Guide to children's magazines, newspapers, reference books*. Washington, DC: Association for Childhood Education International.

Richardson, S. K. (1978). *Periodicals for school media programs* (rev. ed.). Chicago: American Library Association.

Richardson, S. K. (1983). *Magazines for children*. Chicago: American Library Association.

Richardson, S. K. (1984). *Magazines for young adults*. Chicago: American Library Association.

CHAPTER 5

Composition in the Content Areas

THE NEED TO TEACH COMPOSITION

Several national studies reported in the early 1980s analyzed how well public school students performed in the basic skill areas (Education Commission of the States, 1983). Writing was tested, and the reports concluded that students lacked the ability to compose effective communications. These reports alarmed the U.S. public. Our society—a nation with one of the highest literacy rates in the world—expects its students to be able to articulate their thoughts in writing.

In his discussion of one of the reports, Petrosky (1982) stated that students had great difficulty producing written compositions that adequately defended or supported ideas. Students' writings were said to be "generally superficial and abstract" (p. 15). Petrosky suggested that one reason for this inability to write well was the predominance of multiple choice assignments in schools. Students rarely have the opportunity to respond to open-ended questions. In other words, students receive much practice selecting correct answers, but relatively little instruction in developing their own answers.

Students' writing abilities deserve emphasis in the content areas because students acquire information effectively by writing about it (Emig, 1977; Newell, 1984). Additionally, writing researchers, theorists, and practitioners generally agree that as students improve their writing skills, they develop a deeper understanding of the subjects they write about.

Four types of regular writing activities we recommend are translation writing, journal writing, guided writing lessons, and research reports. Chapter 6 deals specifically with research reports; this chapter presents the first three types of writing activities.

TRANSLATION WRITING

Summarizing passages, producing class notes, recording observations in a laboratory, and completing essay test items are examples of *translation writing*. The common feature of these tasks is that the facts and ideas are provided, so students' primary responsibility is to convert that information into their own reworded message. Teachers assume that the class is familiar with the targeted information, so translation writing tasks are assigned as a way to help students articulate the experience in their own terms, to help them save the experience for future reference, and frequently to check students' understanding of the assigned content. These tasks generally are rather brief. Five translation writing activities are presented here—Written Answers, Content Language Experience, Group Summary Writing, Sustained Summary Writing, and Review Sentences.

Written Answers

Written answers requires students to respond to a question in writing before responding orally. When you ask, "Why were the Northern states opposed to slavery?" or "Who was President during World War II?" ask students to jot down their responses to the question. After allowing them time to do so, you call upon students as usual. Although this approach takes more time than the traditional oral question-answer method, using written responses means that all students compose a response, not just the one called upon, and that all students are given adequate time to think through what they want to say.

Content Language Experience

Language experience as a means of teaching young children reading and writing skills has been discussed in the professional literature since the end of the last century. Very simply, the *language experience approach* (LEA) calls for students to describe orally an event and for teachers to transcribe that event for students to read later. For descriptions of various ways to use LEA, consult Stauffer (1970); Allen and Allen (1966); and Cunningham, Moore, Cunningham, and Moore (1983). While LEA is frequently used in elementary classrooms during formal reading instruction, the method is certainly appropriate in the content areas as well. A sample content language experience passage obtained from a group of second-grade children follows:

Magnets

Magnets are metal things that pick up stuff (Karl).

They pick up metal, but they don't pick up anything else (Susan).

Magnets don't pick up all metal things like aluminum (Paul).

They for sure can't pick up plastic and wood! (Jim).

Magnets can be in any shape, but ours are circles and horseshoes (Kay).

Magnets make a design with little tiny pieces of iron (Lee).

This passage summarizes information about magnets. It includes what the children observed earlier when they manipulated several magnets. Providing an experience and then eliciting children's language about it leads many to rename LEA the "experience-language approach."

Placing children's names after each entry, as shown in the sample above and in Figure 5.1, helps young students to identify their own contributions. Seeing their names beside a sentence motivates them to read what they dictated and helps them remember what was said. With older students it may

Figure 5.1   Children dictate expository passages to be used in later reading activities.

not be necessary to label each entry with a name or to record the sentences in list form.

After the passage is dictated, the teacher duplicates it for all students or, if the passage is recorded on a large sheet of chart paper as in Figure 5.1, puts the dictation in a prominent place in the classroom. The passage is reread periodically, with children encouraged to make changes as they learn more about the topic. The dictated passage can be used as another piece of reading material, albeit one that can be changed at will.

Group Summary Writing

Group summary writing is based upon students' understanding and recall of textbook information that has been read to them. This translation writing activity requires that students listen to a section of their textbook and state the important points of what they have heard. The points are listed by the teacher for all to see in the form of notes. The notes then are used, along with students' memories, to produce a piece of text at the students' reading level that parallels the information in the textbook. Students may need to listen to the text material several times to become familiar with the information. The more familiar they become with the information, the more comfortably they can manipulate it to create a parallel text. The following two passages represent, first, a piece of textbook material and, second, the student-translated version of the information.

Textbook Passage: "What Is Fat"

Everybody today is so weight-conscious, and so many people are on diets, that you could probably say fat is something nobody wants. Yet fat, of course, is very necessary to the body. It accumulates in this way: At certain points, the connective-tissue cells become filled with fat. First tiny droplets appear inside the cells. They increase in size, run together into a large drop, and finally fill the cell and swell it out like a balloon. Eventually, the cell is changed into a large drop of fat surrounded by a thin envelope of tissue.

This takes place only in certain parts of the body. The ears, nose, forehead, and joints of the body normally have no fat tissue. Usually, the female body stores more fat than the male body. For example, the normal male body contains about 10 percent fat, but a normal female has about 25 percent. This means that a young man may have about 13 pounds of fat in his body and a young woman about 35 pounds of fat in hers.

Translated Passage: "What Is Fat?"

Even though lots of people want to get rid of it, we need fat. Fat gets together in our bodies sort of like raindrops running down a window. A little raindrop runs into another raindrop and gets bigger, and that bigger drop runs into another raindrop and gets even bigger. After a while the little raindrop has become a big one. Fat does that, too. Little drops get together and make a big one.

Only some parts of our bodies have fat tissue. Women have more fat tissue than men do. Men have about 10 percent fat and women have 25 percent fat.

EVALUATE

Compare the translated passage on fat with the original text. What was done well in the translation? What do you think could be improved upon? Are all the key points included?

Time is a major concern when using group summary writing. Though the original text material can be tape-recorded, someone still needs to sit with students the first time or two they listen to the material, so that they can be guided in obtaining accurate information. Someone also needs to tape-record the dictated translation so that students can recopy the translated material into their notebooks for future reference. Translating a text is not only time-consuming, but, because so much student energy is going into such a small amount of text material, translation keeps the students from covering as many concepts as the rest of the class.

Although time limitations are real and do cause difficulties, they can be over-come. For the student who is plowing through text material that is too difficult, translation writing represents a chance to learn a small portion of the material well, rather than missing it all. Of course, the teacher must identify those few concepts from each unit that are considered essential, so that the translation writing can focus on them. Other students or parent volunteers might save the teacher time by helping with various stages. And keep in mind that tutors typically learn more than their tutees in such situations.

Sustained Summary Writing

Another translation writing strategy is *sustained summary writing* (Cunningham and Cunningham, 1976). This strategy requires students to summarize what they remember from listening or reading by recording their ideas without reference to notes. The writing is timed to last for a very short period, depending upon the age level of the students and their writing capabilities.

Students write their summaries of the material as best they can, capturing the most important points from the material. We suggest that the students take a few moments as they begin the exercise to jot down a brief listing of the main topics they want to include. Then students write, for perhaps five minutes, what they remember about the topics. A student summarizing the "What Is Fat?" material might write a list like the following:

Fat fills cells.
Men have less body fat than women.
We don't have fat tissue everywhere in our bodies.
We have fat tissue on our feet, hands, face, and bottoms.

After compiling this kind of list, students then construct a paragraph or two that summarizes the information from the passage. Many teachers let students simply compile a list of important ideas. Later, as students' composition skills increase, teachers show students how to weave those ideas into connected discourse.

Review Sentences

Review sentences summarize a passage previously read or a lesson just completed. This strategy parallels the possible sentences strategy described in Chapter 2; however, review sentences are produced only after information is presented.

The teacher lists key vocabulary on the chalkboard or on chart paper. After reviewing the meanings of the words, the teacher calls for sentences containing at least two words from the list to be dictated about the passage. The words may be used in more than one sentence. Students are not allowed at this point to interrupt the dictation with corrections because corroboration of information comes later. Additionally, information can be contributed in any order; the sequence of dictated sentences need not parallel the sequence in which the information was presented originally. To illustrate, after finishing a unit on the ocean, a teacher might list the following key vocabulary words:

evaporation   continental shelf
sodium chloride   continental slope
abyssal plain   continental rise
echo sounder   earth's crust
water vapor   earth's mantle

The students then dictate the following set of sentences:

Water vapor evaporates from the ocean.

The *continental shelf*, *rise*, and *slope* are features on the ocean floor that were explored and charted by the *echo sounder*.

The *echo sounder* also mapped canyons and the *abyssal plain* on the ocean floor.

The oceans were formed from *water vapor* and minerals such as *sodium chloride*.

Water vapor and other gases came from the *earth's crust* and *mantle*.

After the dictation is complete, the students turn to their texts or notes in order to check the accuracy of the statements. Inconsistencies and errors are corrected, and crucial missing information is added. Students and the teacher can then arrange the sentences so that related pieces of information are grouped together. Finally, the completed summary is duplicated for all students, or they copy it into their content notebooks.

CONTENT JOURNALS

The second type of regular writing activity appropriate for the content areas is keeping *content journals* (Fulwiler, 1980; Yinger & Clark, 1981), in which students record in a notebook their personal insights about the topics being treated in class. Students write for themselves primarily to review information, to make explicit what is known and not known about a topic, and to evaluate the information being presented. Having students keep journals also is a way to encourage smooth and rapid writing.

Content journals may have a geat deal of structure or very little. When there is little structure, students choose what to write about. One student might write a diary-style account of what went on in school while another might write a letter to the teacher, complete with visuals, explaining his or her reaction to what is being studied. When students have control over the specific content they are writing about, the journals are said to have *low structure.*

With *high-structure* content journals, the teacher requires students to react to specific ideas they are exploring in class. Students may be asked to explore some controversial issue associated with the content. For instance, if westward expansion were the unit of study in American history, students might be asked to record their impressions of the similarities between nineteenth century movement by U.S. citizens into Texas and twentieth century movement by Mexican citizens into Texas. Students could be asked to call up impressions they had before beginning the class and compare them to their current impressions. They might be asked to summarize chapters or articles they are reading. The structure is high because the teacher assigns the writing task; students have little say about what they are to write about. It seems useful for the teacher to use high-structure journals initially, identifying specific questions for the students to address. Students can then be faded from high-structure to low-structure content journals.

Typically, students should be expected to write in their journals from 5 to 10 minutes each day. Most teachers using journals allow in-class time for writing some of the entries. With all content journal entries, students are required to date and list the time for each entry, which makes it easier for the teacher to refer to specific pieces of writing. A table of contents also is maintained. When class time is given for journal writing, all students must be writing for the entire time period. If they can't think of anything to write, they should be asked to discuss in writing why they are having trouble writing about this topic, switching over to information about the topic whenever they are able. Students should be told not to be unnecessarily concerned with spelling or other mechanical factors as they write. They should just try to get their ideas flowing.

Many teachers have students produce journals that combine high and low structure. This calls for students to keep translation writing tasks and totally personal entries together. Additionally, visuals can be maintained in the same

Figure 5.2   Students of all ages and abilities use content journals to review and react to information.

place. Such teachers help students produce a combination scrapbook-note-book-diary that becomes a valuable momento of each student's school year.

Journals are collected several times a term in order to do a "body count" (to make sure that students have been regularly writing) and in order to determine whether students are learning course content and reacting thoughtfully to the ideas they are encountering. While reading the journals, the teacher writes comments to the students, creating a written dialogue, about how well students are learning the course material and how clearly they express what they have learned. Students' attitudes and efforts regarding journal writing seem to be directly related to the frequency and quality of a teacher's comments in the journals. Weekly reactions are ideal, although biweekly and triweekly input is generally more feasible. Grades can be assigned for keeping the journal if the teacher so desires.

GUIDED WRITING LESSONS

Guided writing lessons are a third type of writing activity. As with all writing activities, guided writing lessons should be tied into the content of the course, with teacher direction gradually faded out. Guided writing lessons focus on the three stages of the writing process: planning, drafting, and revising. Teachers must intervene to help students at each stage.

Stages of the Writing Process

Each stage of the writing process calls for a different type of decision. The following section presents a brief summary of the three stages, with the sections after that describing how to plan lessons that focus on each stage.

Planning   Writers who have clear compelling plans for their work generally produce better writing than those who begin haphazardly. Before good writers begin a paper, they first engage in several *planning* activities. They call up information they already have about the topic. They might make a list of the different approaches they can take. They might begin to organize their thoughts by constructing an outline, list, or web. Sometimes they discuss the topic with friends, either to elicit information or to clarify their own thinking. Writers in the planning stage frequently go off to work on other tasks and let their ideas incubate.

Drafting   In the *drafting* stage, the pencil meets the paper, fingers touch the keys, or a voice hits the airwaves. When writers draft, they try to give a definite shape to the ideas they mulled over in planning. Writers frequently return to planning in order to change their organization or to produce new ideas. Writers also move into the third stage, *revising*, as they correct spelling errors, change words, and rearrange sentences. Mostly, however, the drafting stage should focus on stating ideas in any form possible.

Revising   *Revising* is the stage in which ideas and the language used to convey those ideas are modified. In this stage, writers examine their output to identify the strengths and weaknesses of their drafts. Depending upon the goal set for a particular session, the revising writer may focus on word choice, organization of ideas, spelling, punctuation, or some other aspect of the work. Beginning writers should probably attend to no more than one or two aspects of their writing at a time when revising, since it can be overwhelming to consider all possibilities simultaneously.

Interaction of Writing Stages   The term *stages of composition* is troublesome because it implies discrete steps being managed in a particular sequence. However, the composition process is actually not *linear* (going along in a straight line, one step following another without repetition) but *recursive* (doubling back on itself until a task is finished). The composing process requires writers to plan, begin drafting, circle back to plan some more, revise, continue drafting, and so on. Figure 5.3 displays a model of writing stages that emphasizes the recursive nature of the process. The circular design indicates that writers continually move among the three stages as part of a cycle; the two-way arrows indicate that writers move from one stage to another in a flexible sequence.

CALL UP

Call up your high school writing assignments. What were your compositions about? What were the topics you wrote about, and how were the assignments worded for you? Get together in groups of four to six and brainstorm a list of ten writing assignments your group can recall.

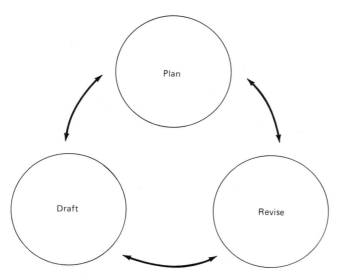

Figure 5.3   Recursive stages of writing.

GUIDING THE PLANNING PROCESS

If you intend to teach children in kindergarten and first grade, you may find that the following information on producing lesson plans is most helpful if you make one change: substitute *oral composition* or *dictated passage* for the term *writing*. This substitution recognizes the fact that young children talk more fluently and effectively than they write. Oral compositions typically precede written compositions. The following guidelines pertain to both written and oral compositions for students of all ages.

In the planning stage, a topic is isolated, and information about the topic is developed. Teachers focusing on this stage should have students get together in small groups to brainstorm lists of ideas. Students can discuss their ideas and some possible ways to present them, while teachers can help students organize the information from their discussions so that it can be systematically and clearly presented. Teachers should encourage students to predict potential problems and ways to address them.

Also at this stage, students should connect what they already know with the topic under consideration, while teachers demonstrate how to use examples to strengthen statements. These activities can be grouped into four categories: designing the task, building background and motivation, modeling the process, and generating and organizing information.

Designing the Task

Three elements—purpose, form, and audience—need to be considered when designing composition tasks. Each can be discussed in isolation; however, the three aspects of designing tasks interact and cannot exist apart from one another.

Purpose   *Purposes* provide direction to writing tasks. A purpose defines the information you wish to convey and the topic of the composition. For example, teachers frequently set the following type of purpose: "Now that we have finished studying a number of different animals, choose the one most interesting to you and write about that animal's life cycle." With their topic clearly defined, students know how to focus their attention. Isolating a clear topic is the first step in designing useful composition tasks for your students.

Along with the topic, *intent* determines the purpose of a composition. The intent, or reason, for writing typically falls into one of the three functions of literacy presented in Chapter 1: to experience, to do, or to learn.

Writing to experience is personal writing in which you explore feelings and motivations, as in a diary or a novel. Sometimes when you write to experience, you are trying to escape from your own world to examine a world you have created. *Writing to do*, as explained in Chapter 1, accomplishes pragmatic tasks, such as filling out applications, responding briefly to memos, completing school worksheets, or recording recipes. In *writing to learn*, you are clarifying information. The learning might be for yourself, for others, or for both—when composing research reports, for example, you frequently gain insights while sharing information with others. Yet another reason for writing, not yet discussed, is *to persuade*. Writers who challenge a traffic fine, request the restoration of goods damaged in the mail, or complain about an inadequate service are composing pieces intended to persuade.

Thus, the purpose for writing or speaking helps direct the composition. Purposes define both the topic and the intent of a composition. Topics depend largely on the unit being investigated in class, with intentions depending on whether the writer wants to experience, to do, to learn, or to persuade. If the teacher helps students to define clear purposes, then he or she will help students produce clear compositions.

Form   The *form* of a composition is the medium through which information is presented. Is the content to be presented as a poem, a letter, an essay, a play, a mathematical theorem, class notes, a journal entry, or the steps in a scientific experiment? The list below contains assorted forms of writing appropriate for the content areas. Even in a math class, the students could use any of these forms. Though most writing in math takes the form of succinct statements ("A gram is a metric unit of mass and weight equal to about one cubic centimeter of water at its maximum density"), a math student might also write a humorous piece about how misunderstanding metric measures resulted in an inedible recipe.

Selected Writing Forms

ads (for magazines, newspapers, yellow pages)
allegories
announcements
autobiographies
awards
bedtime stories
billboards
biographies
book jackets
book reviews
brochures
bulletins
bumper stickers
campaign speeches
captions
cartoons

certificates
character sketches
comic strips
contracts
conversations
critiques
definitions
diaries
directions
directories
dramas
editorials
epitaphs
encyclopedia entries
essays
fables
game rules
graffiti

good news-bad news
grocery lists
headlines
how-to-do-it speeches
impromptu speeches
interviews
job applications
journals
laboratory notes
letters
lists
lyrics
magazines
menus
mysteries
myths
newscasts

newspapers
obituaries
observational notes
pamphlets
parodies
persuasive letters
plays
poems
posters
propaganda sheets
product descriptions
puppet shows
puzzles
questionnaires
questions
quizzes

quotations	requisitions	sequels	travel folders
real estate	resumes	serialized stories	tributes
notices	reviews	slogans	vignettes
recipes	sales pitches	speeches	want ads
remedies	schedules	TV commercials	wanted posters
reports	self descriptions	telegrams	wills
requests			

Specifying the form of a passage includes setting its length. Teachers should not avoid this issue by telling students, "I'm more interested in quality than in quantity." Specifying the approximate length of a composition helps students understand how much information to include. For instance, describing the metric system might be the purpose you assign for students' writing. Assigning a 2-page paper tells your students one thing, and assigning a 10-page paper tells them another. Assigning approximate lengths for writing leads writers to clarify the depth of discussion they need ("I'd better provide many examples of the metric measures."). Think about it, when you write a letter about your past week to your family or a friend, don't you have some notion of the length you intend to produce and shape your letter accordingly?

In closing, return to the example unit on animals' life cycles. The teacher of such a unit might set the life cycle of a butterfly as the topic of composition. The intent of the piece would be to learn. With that purpose—topic and intent—a teacher might choose a thousand-word essay as the composition's form. But the composition could also take the form of a four-page illustrated pamphlet; or of a short fantasy story written from the butterfly's point of view, explaining how difficult it is to get through life when you never know whether you're going to be crawling, sleeping, or flying. Much writing done in schools is unnecessarily limited in form, whereas actual writing contains a large number of forms. People write letters, lists, and journal entries; they fill out applications and devise petitions. Teachers need to introduce students to many varied forms in order to prepare their students for the demands of life outside the classroom.

Audience   The *audience* of a composition is the individual or group the writer conceived of as the listener or reader. The audience is not necessarily those who actually listen to or read a piece. When we began this textbook, we envisioned an audience of college and university students like the ones we have taught in our classes. We imagined the questions that might occur to such readers by calling up the types of questions we have encountered from such students. But perhaps our relatives might also read this book. Our relatives would be readers of this material, but they are not the intended audience. This book is not designed for their level of understanding, and they will undoubtedly have many questions that we do not address. By the same token, we did not write to inform our professional colleagues. If we had, then we would have taken a different tone, including more research citations and fewer examples of how to implement our suggestions.

Figure 5.4 Students collaborate to construct timelines in order to display information they have organized.

Helping students to specify an audience for their writing is crucial for effective communication. Meaningful audiences might include pen pals, parents, peers, school personnel, or agencies that provide free materials. To return again to the butterfly life cycle example, knowing that you are producing a children's book about the life cycle of the butterfly helps you to choose the words, illustrations, and analogies you will use to describe the transformations of the butterfly. On the other hand, if you were describing the butterfly's life cycle in a book for professional entomologists, you would include far different material.

APPLY

Imagine this vignette: It was a dark and foggy night, and you were driving home from class. You didn't stop at a stop sign that had only recently been installed at a familiar intersection. Fortunately, there were no other cars in the intersection and you got through safely. Unfortunately, a police officer was parked along the curb ahead and saw your error. The police officer stopped you and gave you a ticket for running the stop sign.

Form groups of three in your class. Each person in the group is to write a letter describing the event to a different audience. One person should write to a 4-year-old sibling or cousin, one should write to a best friend, and one should write to Father, since the car is registered in his name. Each person should write as if he or she were the one who had been cited.

After five minutes, share the three pieces of writing, which have the same purpose and form but which have different audiences. Compare how the compositions present facts and how they use language. How are the pieces similar, and how are they different?

The Composition Starter   The two types of writing presented earlier, translation writing and content journals, deemphasize the planning stage of composition, although they do not altogether ignore it. But in guided writing lessons, planning is of paramount importance. Students seem to come alive for writing that they view as an actual attempt to communicate rather than as a chance to display their knowledge in order to win a good grade.

The *Composition Starter* helps to demonstrate possible purposes, forms, and audiences for your composition tasks. Table 5.1 contains a composition starter for a unit in middle-school social studies. Note that the purposes for writing combine topics and intentions into one statement. The composition starter allows you to design numerous writing tasks for a single general subject by combining various items from each column. Consider the following possibilities that come from the composition starter in Table 5.1:

Describe the Santa Maria through a poem to a teacher.

Describe the New World in a letter to Marco Polo.

Present the voyages in timeline form for a college professor.

Present the voyages in essay form for a travel club.

Write background information on Columbus in news article form for a third-grade audience.

Write background information on Columbus in news article form for a tenth-grade audience.

Table 5.1 Composition Starter: Christopher Columbus

Purpose	Form	Audience
Describe the ocean voyages.	letter	younger sibling
Explain why Columbus sailed West.	poem	sick friend
	play	travel club
Portray the Santa Maria.	timeline	pen pal
Describe the New World.	obituary	sailor's family
Persuade someone of the value of the trip(s).	outline	Ferdinand and Isabella
	journal	Marco Polo
Explain ancient navigational procedures.	news article	college professor
	essay	your teacher
Provide background on Columbus.		other students

APPLY

Select a unit from a content area. Then identify various purposes, audiences, and forms that would be appropriate for writing about information from that unit. Use the format in Table 5.1 to produce your own composition starter.

In order to further clarify how compositions vary when purposes, forms, and audiences are manipulated, we present here four illustrative types of content area compositions: one-paragraph essays, brochures, news articles, and reviews.

One-Paragraph Essays. With *one-paragraph essays,* teachers show students how to present information succinctly. The intent of a piece using this form is generally to provide information for others to learn. The form is highly structured. It is an essay that consists of a topic sentence followed by a specified number of supporting details. Teachers frequently have students write topic sentences stating explicitly what the paragraph is about, then they ask students to write a certain number of sentences. The audience for such a piece is typically the teacher. Here is an example from a unit on mathematics; the topic is angles. As can be seen, the writing is narrowed to a single sentence about each item.

Types of Angles

There are four kinds of angles. Acute angles are less than 90°. Right angles equal 90°. Obtuse angles are between 90° and 180°. Straight angles are equal to 180°.

Another example of one-paragraph essays comes from a government unit and may be more appropriate for older students. Note that this essay contains several sentences about each subtopic within the paragraph.

The Congress

The United States Congress consists of two houses. The House of Representatives has one representative for every 450,000 people in the United States. The number of representatives from each state depends upon the state's population. Because of this, California has more representatives in the House than does Nevada. The Senate consists of two senators for each state. The states have equal representation in the Senate.

Brochures. Having students produce small informational booklets can be an interesting alternative to traditional writing assignments. *Brochures* typically promote specific information, with the intent of persuading people. The form can include illustrations, creative lettering, isolated sentences and captions, and short paragraphs. For example, a brochure written in response to a book on Greek myths could have sections on the major mythical characters, with appropriate illustrations, genealogy, and descriptions for each. Teachers should make sample brochures available for students to see typical layouts. Naturally, the audience for a brochure will substantially affect the content. A brochure about the state of Iowa produced for primary-grade children certainly would differ from one produced for business executives.

News Articles. The inverted triangle style of writing *news articles* is another good writing project. With news articles, as with one-paragraph essays, the form is clearly defined. An all-encompassing title comes first, followed by a topic paragraph. The succeeding paragraphs move from general to specific information. Students should study selected news articles from local newspapers to become familiar with this form of writing.

Reviews. Reviews include information about a book, movie, play, television program, or sporting event while also evaluating the work or event. Reviewers should also decide whether they recommend future similar events and give reasons for their recommendation. Teachers frequently have students place their reviews in a central location for classmates to read. As with news articles, students benefit from studying model reviews from newspapers and periodicals before producing their own.

Building Background and Motivation

As with reading comprehension, students don't get very far with composition if they don't have adequate background knowledge and interest. When planning composition tasks, teachers must decide how to increase their students' understanding while motivating their interest. Effective teachers covering, say, the life cycle of the butterfly typically present actual mounted butterflies, show movies, photographs, and illustrations, and perhaps have students act out a butterfly's metamorphosis or recall various personal experiences with butterflies. In short, teachers of writing must first engage students in concept development activities such as those presented in Chapter 3. Before students write, they need to have something to write about.

Modeling the Writing Process

As we have emphasized, designing clear relevant tasks and building background and motivation are essential features of planning effective compositions. But students also need specific models that demonstrate how to implement their ideas.

Teachers frequently *model* the process of writing by presenting finished compositions completed by professionals, by the teacher, or by previous students. For instance, if your students are writing brochures, you might gather several for your students' inspection. Be sure to point out noteworthy features of the brochures to guide your students. Point out that most brochures contain numerous illustrations that are explained in the text; call students' attention to the somewhat sparse writing contained in brochures; and note that most brochures contain a table of contents.

For large-scale projects such as term papers, teachers frequently walk students through the writing process one step at a time. Teachers might first help students to generate appropriate questions about their topics, then to locate suitable references, then to organize the information, and finally to report it. Chapter 6 covers these steps in much greater detail.

Generating and Organizing Information

The final step in the planning stage is when students organize the information that they want to include in their drafts. *Word Gathering* is a good way to generate information. Students who are gathering words for food groups might call up a list of 20 to 50 different foods ranging from pizza to banana to abalone. The words are recorded somewhere (perhaps on a word wall, as described in Chapter 3) both to remind students of the possible content, and to help with spelling. Students can generate words individually, in small groups, or as a class. Students who jot down key words as they prepare to answer essay questions on exams exemplify one type of word gathering.

Additionally, students might organize words in a *List, Group, and Label* lesson. In this type of lesson, words are grouped into subcategories which then are labeled. For instance, fruits, pastries, meats, and cereals might be separated and labeled accordingly.

Teachers' main role during this stage of planning is to show students what to do. Some students require a great deal of help generating information ("I can't think of anything to say!"); others generate so much that they can't categorize it neatly ("I don't know where to begin with all this!"). As a general rule, make sure that your students understand what they are supposed to produce and how they are supposed to go about doing it.

ORGANIZE

Key terms from our discussion of guiding the planning stage are listed below in random order. Copy each term on a card and organize those cards by category. Note that category titles as well as category items are listed here; also, be aware that some titles cover many items, while others cover only a few.

Topic	Model the process
News articles	List, group, and label
Composition starter	Brochures
Word gathering	Form
Design the task	Reviews
Purpose	One-paragraph essays
Audience	Generate and organize information
Build background and motivation	Intent

GUIDING THE DRAFTING PROCESS

The major help that teachers can provide students in the drafting stage is to make time for uninterrupted writing. Teachers might also make available resources such as lists of information and spelling aids. During drafting, students should write their ideas without being overly concerned with accurate spelling or word usage. Those features can be dealt with during revision. If students or teachers are not comfortable postponing these concerns, we suggest that you use *checkers,* or spelling aids. Checkers might be dictionaries, brainstormed word lists, a word wall, or the classroom teacher who wanders around the room and writes spelling requests on a sheet of paper at each student's desk. In any case, encourage students to write words as best they can, perhaps writing a blank for missing letters and using an asterisk in the margin to signal places where spelling must be checked.

During and after initial drafting, students need to check over their piece and make changes before sharing it with anyone else. Students should not expect to come to a revision session with a perfect piece, but they should try to identify at least some problems on their own. They might even identify questions to take to the group: "I really had trouble describing what a cocoon is made of. How can I fix that part?"

After the group or teacher makes suggestions for the writer, he or she needs a session to revise the composition and make decisions about others' comments. This interaction among planning, drafting, and revising can occur several times.

GUIDING THE REVISING PROCESS

Students should be given a variety of opportunities to obtain others' reactions to their compositions. Typically, well-ordered reactions help the writer to revise the piece, resulting in a better composition. Three strategies to direct students' revising are described in this section: peer response teams, peer editing teams, and writing conferences.

Peer Response Teams

Peer response teams consist of two to five students responsible for helping the writer. Although teams of five are valuable for providing various viewpoints, such large groups sometimes become difficult to manage. Many teachers have teams of two students work collaboratively. We have successfully used peer response teams with students as young as first grade and as old as college seniors. Figure 5.5 shows two fifth-grade students engaged with one piece of

Figure 5.5   Peer response teams evaluate what has been written.

writing. These teams focus on the ideas being developed and the organizational structures being used.

Four main guidelines for peer response teams are (1) initial reactions to the piece must focus on what was done well, (2) all negative reactions to the piece should be stated as questions, (3) reactions may be either oral or written, and (4) the writer may not respond immediately to reactions. Positive initial reactions are important because it is easier for students to accept suggestions after hearing about their strengths. By identifying what was done well and why, students learn to monitor their writing. They learn how to write well by doing so and being praised for it. Getting such positive reinforcement means that they will probably want to use their successful approach again.

It is helpful to provide students with some generic positive statements that apply to every piece. For example, "I thought the most interesting part of your paper was . . ." or "You gave the most complete information about . . ." are statements that help students monitor and evaluate their own and others' writing.

Students should state negative reactions as questions to help the writer develop the piece. A good generic negative question is, "Can you tell me more about . . . ?" The teacher needs to teach students how to apply that question. For example, rather than saying, "I don't understand what you're getting at here," a student might learn to ask the writer, "Can you tell me more about how pulleys help people lift heavy objects?" Instead of saying to the writer of a story, "The girl in your story would never say that to her friend," a student might ask, "Can you tell me more about why the girl in your story would say that to her friend?" By stating negative reactions as questions, they do not seem so negative, and writers can generally deal with them far less emotionally.

Peer response team members may express reactions either orally or in writing. In the latter case, students write directly on the composition, bracketing sections for the writer to consider. One advantage of this method is that student anonymity can be maintained. Thus, students might put an identification number, rather than their name, on their paper. This helps maintain objectivity in both the responses and the writer's reception of them.

Although it is natural to do so, the writer is asked not to respond immediately to his or her peers' reactions. Delaying the response helps to keep the group from becoming argumentative, or from becoming overly involved with one point and failing to cover the rest of the piece. The writer's chance to respond comes with the revision of the piece. Likewise, you should not let your peer response teams go on for very long—perhaps five minutes for younger students and up to fifteen minutes for older ones. Three ten-minute sessions are probably more effective in helping students improve compositions than one thirty-minute session.

How Peer Response Teams Work   The following is an abbreviated version of a peer response session. Marcus, a third-grade child, has written a piece trying to convince others that his state is a good one to live in. With young children's peer response teams, we usually have students read their compositions aloud so that students can find and correct many of their own errors as they hear themselves read. Marcus, with pencil in hand, reads the following piece to his peers:

> Georgia is a good place to live. But the gass is to higth. The cars are giong up. The close are to much. The people are nice The schools are nice. The teachers are very nice. I just like Georgia.
>
> The End

Aside from the obvious mechanical errors, which will be dealt with later in peer editing teams, it is clear to the group that Marcus's composition doesn't focus on one area and develop its ideas. However, the students begin with positive statements: "You have a good first sentence." "I wanted to know why Georgia is so good." "You tried to make your first sentence and last sentence go together."

Then students ask questions: "Can you tell me more about why Georgia is a good place? You already told all the bad stuff like the gas being too high and how much clothes are." "Can you tell me more about the people being nice? Can you tell something about when and how people are nice?" "How are the schools 'nice'? Is there anything else you can say about the schools?" "Are there any other reasons Georgia is a good place to live?"

Marcus goes away to revise his paper with his peers' comments in mind. Here's what the next draft looks like:

> Georgia is a good place to live. The people are real frenly and helpful like when you go in to stores and stuff. They smile at you to. The schools are fun to go to becus they teach us a lot. The teachers are frenly and very helpful. We have pretty good wether to. We have lots of warm days. Now you can see why I like Georgia. It has everything I like.

Though Marcus's composition still has several limitations, you can see how much he has been helped by peer team comments.

IMAGE

Chris writes the following piece in response to an assignment in science. You are the teacher. Picture yourself formulating the positive and negative reactions to the piece as described above and then presenting them in a peer response team.

> Animals are either vertebrates or invertebrates. They can live in the ocean or on land. Some animals are called simple animals. We use animals in many ways, and some animals depend on humans for their growth. There are many kinds of animals in the world.

It is also appropriate to give specific directions to peer teams. For instance, if students are writing about states, then you might distribute a *response sheet* with the following questions: "What part of the paper dealing with climate did you like best?" "What more would you like to know about the state's climate?" "What did you like best about the state map?" "What else would you like included on the state map?" Response sheets direct student attention to specific aspects of their peers' compositions.

Peer Editing Teams

Peer editing teams help the writer monitor features of writing mechanics. As with peer response teams, editing teams can consist of either a small group or a pair of students. These teams can discuss spelling, punctuation, word usage, and word choices, pointing out any overuse of certain words, the use of clichés, or simply inappropriate word choices. Whereas peer response deals with the composition as a whole, peer editing focuses on how each sentence is written.

Conducting peer editing teams is relatively simple for both students and teachers, possibly because response to student compositions has for so many years focused on mechanics. But these teams are also easier to handle because they deal so frequently with objective matters. There are only so many acceptable ways to spell words; therefore, when an unacceptable version is found, students readily submit to making the change.

During peer editing, everyone looks at a copy of the written piece. Depending on the purpose of the session, students may or may not have to formulate their reactions as questions. If the group is giving a final once-over to a piece, looking for mechanical errors, then group members can just point out the errors. If, on the other hand, group members are helping with word choice, then they may need to ask questions that cause the author to think about the number of times the word "nice" is used or whether the author really meant to call an argument "plausible."

Writing Conferences

Writing conferences may deal with either the contents or the mechanics of a composition, as the writer meets individually with the teacher. These confer-

Figure 5.6   Writing conferences can focus on the content or mechanics of a passage.

ences help the student not only to become a better writer, but also to learn what to look for when reading or listening to someone else's work.

Students may choose to sign up for writing conferences themselves, indicating on the sign-up sheet what they would like to discuss. Or the teacher may initiate the conference to insure periodic checks on student compositions. If a conference lasts approximately five minutes, during which time a great deal can be accomplished, the teacher in a self-contained elementary classroom can reasonably see three students a day. Thus all students can be met individually every two weeks. In departmentalized content area classrooms, the teacher should turn the class over to peer response and peer editing teams several times during the term. The more frequently the teams are used, the sooner will results be seen in students' writing. Students can be called out of their peer response or editing teams for a five-minute writing conference, so that in a typical 50-minute period, the teacher could reasonably meet with six students.

MONITOR

Do you understand the differences among peer response teams, peer editing teams, and writing conferences? Write "peer response," "peer editing," and "writing conference" on each of three file cards. Call up and make notes of everything you can remember about each. Check your notes against the information in this chapter.

PROMOTING STUDENT INDEPENDENCE IN WRITING

As do the chapters on comprehension and vocabulary, this chapter on composition stresses the importance of student independence. Students need to be taught how to produce their own compositions in the same way that they need to be taught how to independently understand passages and words.

The three steps in fading instruction—demonstration, guided practice, and independent application—are appropriate for developing independent writers. Guided writing lessons allow the teacher to fade out as students fade in. To illustrate, teachers frequently demonstrate how to plan compositions by doing it for students. The teacher specifies the purpose, audience, and form of the task; the teacher develops student background and motivation; the teacher provides sample compositions and helps to generate information. After a while, teachers can begin gradually releasing the responsibility for these actions to the students. Teachers might specify the purpose for writing, but ask students to specify their own form and audience. Eventually teachers might have students specify all three aspects of the writing task. Teachers might have students gather their own background information as well as find their own models for writing. Teachers also might have students generate and organize their own information, first with close supervision, later with almost no supervision. With regard to revising, teachers should eventually have students inspect their own first drafts, with students answering for themselves what they like best, what they want to know more about, and what mechanical aspects need work. In short, teachers first demonstrate and explain how to plan, draft, and revise; teachers then gradually diminish their assistance with the stages of the writing process in order for the students to take over for themselves.

Journal writing falls into another category of instruction, the personalized inquiry approach that we presented in Chapter 1. That is, journals emphasize student-centered exploration of a topic. Teachers may set the stage for learning to occur by providing students with direct experiences, visuals, models, and materials to read, but student journal-writers respond to the information in their own idiosyncratic ways. If plants were being studied, one student might use the journal to illustrate and label parts of various leaves, one might write a poem about a flower, and another might simply reproduce everything that he or she could remember about trees. Journals don't require teachers to fade out because they begin as student-centered activities. They promote personal reactions to what is being studied, which goes far in developing independent writing abilities.

WHAT ABOUT . . .

What about the Paper Load?

One reason teachers do not require more writing from students is their concern that they will be overwhelmed by the amount of work that students turn in. We see several ways to address this concern. First, we believe that investing a little bit of time at the beginning of the year to teach students how to revise their own compositions and those of their peers soon pays off. Peer response and editing teams take some of the burden off the teacher besides teaching students more about writing.

Second, having students collaborate further reduces the teachers' workload. If two students submit one paper, the total number of class papers is cut in half. Not only does collaboration reduce the teacher's workload, it frequently improves the quality of student writing. Writers who plan, draft, and revise as a team can benefit from alternate viewpoints throughout the writing process.

A third approach is not to evaluate everything that your students write. Teachers might have students write each day, but only evaluate papers occasionally. Students should be encouraged to keep a file of their drafts so that they can see their own progress and so that they can go to the file to find pieces that need more work. There should be many more pieces in students' writing folders than ever are seen by other eyes. If needed, you can check the quantity of students' writing frequently by simply noting how much is in their folders, reacting only occasionally to the quality of their work.

Finally, the pieces that you do evaluate can be judged in different ways. Unlike more traditional evaluations, in which the teacher judges every paper on content, writing mechanics, and organization, the teacher may respond to only one of these concerns at a time.

What about the Mechanics of Writing?

We believe very strongly that students need to produce acceptable punctuation, spelling, and word usage in their final drafts. These conventions of print were not devised as torture devices to harass generations of students. Rather, the writer's control of these mechanics aids the reader's understanding. The less a reader has to puzzle over the use of words or the meaning of the punctuation, the more he or she can attend to the concepts in a piece. Likewise, conventional spelling makes reading easier and less ambiguous.

The best way for students to improve their control of spelling, punctuation, capitalization, word usage, and handwriting is for them to produce compositions in the content areas. Writing workbook sentences in isolation does not really help students learn the mechanics of writing. Those who could complete the exercise on *was-were and saw-seen* probably already knew how to use those words; those who failed probably did not learn the distinction. Adding peer editing groups to your teaching repertoire allows students to learn about language mechanics as they need to do so. This is functional instruction. After all, we all mastered the mechanics of speaking through functional instruction; our parents hardly sat us down for daily lessons on word usage and sentence structure. Rather, when we encountered a new object or when we were trying to refine our use of the words we already knew, we got help in the context where we were working, at the time when we were ready to use the help.

Teachers must certainly attend to the mechanics of writing, but they should keep in mind a few points. The mechanics are only the surface features of writing, and can be learned more easily than you might imagine. After all, the students learned the nonstandard forms. It is much harder to teach the thinking that goes into a composition. Students learn to control the mechanics of writing when their own compositions are the stimulus for instruction and when those compositions are shared with real audiences.

What about Word Processing?

The new microcomputer technology available to students and teachers has vastly improved the opportunities we have for composition instruction. Students who compose at the computer keyboard and can revise and edit on the computer not only create longer pieces, but also stay with the revision process longer than if they were composing with pencil and paper.

Why is it that students seem to work longer and more intensely on compositions written at a computer? One reason may well be the novelty factor. But there are surely other factors to be considered. For example, we have noticed that many students at all levels become discouraged by the apparent impossibility of turning out a neat, errorless paper. No matter how hard they tried, they seemed unable to produce a product of whose appearance they could be proud. With the computer, a neatly typed paper appears from the printer, with no trace of the messy stages whereby it was produced.

Furthermore, even the simplest of the word processing programs allows students to experiment with alternative placements of text passages before being committed to a particular one. Knowing that a whole page must be recopied discourages many students from editing; with word processing, a sentence can be moved at the touch of a key. Another reason why students may feel more successful, and therefore work harder at a computer-composed piece, is that spelling checkers are now readily available, allowing students to produce pieces free of spelling mistakes. These spelling checkers speed up the editing process greatly since one doesn't have to read every word in the piece to locate spelling mistakes: the program will either correct or identify every error. We believe that computers herald a major improvement in the composition skills of U.S. students.

REVIEW
Complete the crossword puzzle using the words you have learned in this chapter.

REFERENCES

Allen, R. V., & Allen, C. (1966). *Language experiences in reading.* Chicago: Encyclopaedia Brittanica Press.

Cunningham, P. M., & Cunningham, J. W. (1976). SSW, better content-writing. *The Clearinghouse, 49,* 237–238.

Cunningham, P. M., Moore, S. A., Cunningham, J. W., & Moore, D. W. (1983). *Reading in elementary classrooms.* New York: Longman.

Education Commission of the States. (1983). *A summary of major reports on education.* Denver, CO: Education Commission of the States.

Emig, J. (1977). Writing as a mode of learning. *College Composition and Communication, 28,* 122–127.

Fulwiler, T. (1980). Journals across the disciplines. *English Journal, 69,* 14–19.

Newell, G. E. (1984). Learning from writing in two content areas: A case study/protocol analysis. *Research in the Teaching of English, 18,* 265–287.

Petrosky, A. R. (1982). Reading achievement. In A. Berger & H. A. Robinson (Eds.), *Secondary school reading.* Urbana, IL: National Conference on Research in English/ERIC Clearinghouse on Reading and Communication Skills.

Stauffer, R. G. (1970). *The language experience approach to the teaching of reading.* New York: Harper & Row.

Yinger, R. J., & Clark, C. M. (1981). *Reflective journal writing: Theory and practice* (Report No. 50). East Lansing, MI: The Institute for Research on Teaching.

Across

3. Give structure to
4. Label for a concept
5. Ability to read and write
8. Portraying thoughts with sentences and paragraphs
11. For example, abbrev.
13. A process that doubles back on itself to reach completion
15. Teachers in self-contained classrooms who conduct writing conferences meet with _____ students each day.
16. Medium used for a composition
18. The intent and topic of a composition
20. Revising session with teacher: a writing _____.
23. Unidirectional
24. Spoken
25. Prepares for writing

Down

1. Attend to progress in learning
2. Ordering activities to promote student independence
4. To set down language on paper
6. Go over what is known
7. Represent a situation through one of the senses
9. The stage of writing for making changes
10. Who composed for
12. Spoken or written product
13. Reactions to the content of a composition
14. Teaching with student-dictated compositions based on subject matter
17. Usage, spelling, and punctuation
19. One's equal
21. Groups reacting to the surface features of a composition
22. _____ up, essential thought process

SUGGESTED READINGS

The actual practice of writing in the content areas has been examined several ways. The following sources are useful examinations:

Applebee, A. N. (1981). *Writing in the secondary school: English and the content areas.* Urbana: National Council of Teachers of English.

Bridge, C. A., Hiebert, E. H., & Chesky, J. (1983). Classroom writing practices. In J. A. Niles & L. A. Harris (Eds.), *Searches for meaning in reading/language processing instruction* (Thirty-second Yearbook of the National Reading Conference). Rochester, NY: The National Reading Conference.

Florio, S., & Clark, C. M. (1982). The functions of writing in an elementary classroom. *Research in the Teaching of English, 16,* 115–130.

Pearce, D. L. (1984). Writing in content area classrooms. *Reading World, 23,* 234–241.

The idea of promoting writing in the content areas received new attention during the early 1970s. Insights into the early thinking about this topic are available from the following:

Donlan, D. (1974). Teaching writing in the content areas: Eleven hypotheses from a teacher survey. *Research in the Teaching of English, 8,* 250–262.

Martin, N., D'Arcy, P., Newton, B., & Parker, R. (1976). *Writing and learning across the curriculum, 11–16.* London: Ward Lock Educational.

Well-stated rationales and sets of procedures for having students maintain journals are provided in the following articles:

Hipple, M. J. (1985). Journal writing in kindergarten. *Language Arts, 62,* 255–261.

Fulwiler, T. (1980). Journals across the disciplines. *English Journal, 69,* 14–19.

Fulwiler, T. (1985). Writing and learning, grade three. *Language Arts, 62,* 55–59.

Specific steps in setting up peer response groups, peer editing groups, and writing conferences are available in several publications. Some of the most useful are as follows:

Calkins, L. M. (1983). *Lessons from a child: On the teaching and learning of writing.* Exeter, NH: Heinemann Educational Books.

Graves, D. H. (1983). *Writing: Teachers and children at work.* Exeter, NH: Heinemann Educational Books.

Murray, D. M. (1985). *A writer teaches writing.* Boston: Houghton Mifflin Company.

The following monograph chapter is a good description of aspects of writing that teachers and students might address:

Cramer, R. L. (1982). Informal approaches to evaluating children's writing. In J. J. Pikulski & T. Shanahan (Eds.), *Approaches to the informal evaluation of reading.* Newark, DE: International Reading Association.

C H A P T E R 6

Research in the Content Areas

WHAT IS RESEARCH?

Parents have learned to fear the announcement by their school-age children that, " I have a report due Wednesday. I have to do Brazil." Parents typically go through much stress and strain helping their children produce the report. Likewise, teachers often have great difficulty leading each student through the stages of research projects, and students have even greater difficulty completing such projects independently. Therefore, pupils go home with a general topic to report on, and their parents help them to limit the topic, find the resources for research, and put a report together in a reasonably organized fashion. That is, the parents who themselves produce reports provide such guidance, while other parents cannot help their children produce acceptable reports. Thus, students are often limited to their parents' level of school performance.

Classroom teachers, having few resources and little training in this area, are frequently unsure of how to teach research skills. Additionally, our society seems to have an instinctive awe of anything that smacks of research. Both teachers and students need to demystify "research," learning to define it as merely answering interesting questions. Skilled researchers become curious about some process or trend, so they set out to answer questions about their topic logically and systematically. Student researchers should be taught to generate interesting questions so that they, too, can answer questions in a logical and systematic fashion. Children who are told to "do Brazil" probably have little interest and few questions, an attitude that works against becoming an independent researcher.

CALL UP/EVALUATE
Think back to the research projects you completed in elementary and secondary school. Which projects were your favorites? Which were your least favorite? Why did you like some projects and not others?

The guidelines in this chapter on developing student researchers should lead students to conduct personalized inquiry. As you know, personalized inquiry calls for teachers to assume a facilitative role, with students at the center of the process. Students, not teachers, are responsible for asking questions, and for locating, organizing, and reporting information.

Four essential components of the research process are (1) identifying a question, (2) locating information, (3) organizing information, and (4) reporting the information. Each of these components will be dealt with separately in this chapter; however, as in composition, the components of research interact with each other. The researcher has a question and locates information, causing him or her to return to the question and refine it further. While organizing information, the researcher discovers that additional data are needed, so he or she returns to the references and locates more.

In fact, research skills can be considered a special class of composition skills. Researchers plan, draft, and revise; they have an audience, purpose, and form in mind; they follow models of finished products; they generate and organize information. The primary difference between the composition process and the research process, as we present it in this chapter, lies in the planning stage. Conducting research implies the need to discover new knowledge before sharing it. Writing activities frequently emphasize articulating what students already know; research activities emphasize learning new things so as to articulate them later.

The Benefits of Teaching Students to Do Research

We see three major benefits of developing student researchers: heightened student interest, improved evaluative thinking, and greater student independence. When students are actively engaged in collecting and sharing information about a topic, they have far more interest in the topic than if they are simply passive listeners. Students who are motivated to generate questions, suggest places to hunt for information, find that information, and share their findings typically learn more than students who merely carry out directions from the teacher. These students are building background knowledge about a topic, and generally, the more one knows about a topic, the greater interest one has in it. Teaching interested students is far easier than teaching uninterested ones.

Secondly, teachers have tended to focus so exclusively on a single textbook as the sole source of information that students have little opportunity or motivation to evaluate the materials they read. It is difficult for students to judge the content and writing style of a text when that is the only material they read. Developing student researchers requires pupils to identify a wide range of information sources—visual, oral, and written—and to learn to use them well. They must learn how to reconcile contradictory information and how to identify complementary facts. It is very difficult to teach such evaluative reading skills using only a single text.

Finally, a major goal of schooling is to help students become independent

Figure 6.1   Research projects motivate students to evaluate and synthesize information.

learners who not only know how to read and write but who actively desire to do so. When students are taught a process for generating questions that they genuinely want to answer, and are then taught a strategy for answering those questions, they begin to see reading and writing as useful and enjoyable activities, not just as required assignments. The processes that students have been taught should help them to search for answers to the other questions they will encounter throughout their lifetimes.

IDENTIFYING QUESTIONS

All students have questions. No one ever has to teach a four-year-old to ask a question. Why then do students have problems asking questions in school? Much of the difficulty in helping students develop research questions stems from their lack of interest in the topic being studied, and from their lack of knowledge about it. In order to ask a good question, we have to be aware of the gaps in our knowledge, to know what we don't know. Indeed, ''problem finding'' might be an even more complex activity than ''problem solving.'' A critical aspect of helping students to identify questions, then, is the promotion of students' interest and knowledge about a particular topic.

To begin planning research lessons, the teacher should examine the year's units of study for every subject area, and sort these units into three groups: high interest (such as dinosaurs for young children, or death for older ones); medium interest (such as explorers in the New World or propaganda techniques); and low interest (such as Brazil or forms of government). High interest topics of study are especially appropriate for research because students are inclined to be more thorough and are better able to sustain their interest through difficulties with these topics. Some medium interest topics can be developed into high interest ones. Since students can't do reports on all aspects of the curriculum, teachers should simply not assign reports on topics in which student interest is low.

Strategies to develop students' knowledge about a topic have been presented in earlier chapters. Assuming then that students have at least moderate levels of interest and background for a topic, the following four strategies are appropriate for helping students identify specific research questions.

WH Questions

Teachers should provide students with the *WH* questions: who, what, when, where, why, and how. The teacher sets the unit to be studied, oceans, for example, and then helps students frame questions by attaching *wh* words to the subject of the unit. Thus, students ask questions such as, ''Who were the first people to explore the Atlantic Ocean?'' ''What dangers do oceans present to people?'' ''When was the Pacific Ocean named?'' ''Where is the deepest part of an ocean?'' ''Why is the ocean salty?'' and ''How do oil companies drill in the ocean floor?''

APPLY

Take the general topic ''Spelling'' and generate *wh* questions about it for ten minutes. Notice how some questions come easier than others. Why does that happen? Why were you able to ask many questions with one *wh* word and fewer questions with another?

Poster Questions

For *Poster Questions,* a topic is listed on a sheet of chart paper, an overhead transparency, or the chalkboard, so that students can brainstorm questions with the teacher. The questions are posted and inspected by the students, who then go off to do their reading on the topic. The reading need not consist only of trying to find answers to the posted questions. Indeed, the purpose for reading may be to try to generate additional questions or areas of research. After about a week of independent reading, students look again at the posted questions and compare the answers they have gathered. The students then inspect the original questions, modify them, and go off again to find additional resources. Figure 6.2 shows young students comparing the information they learned in answer to poster questions.

What You Know and What You Don't Know

What You Know and What You Don't Know is another good strategy to build motivation, with the added advantage of helping students call up what they already know. As with poster questions, a topic is given. Students are then asked what they think they know about the topic. All information is put down, whether accurate or not. Students then sort the bits of related information into groups, and display it in a web as presented in Chapter 2.

Once the known information is displayed, unknown information becomes much more readily apparent. For each area of information, students must list ''What We Know'' and ''What We Don't Know.'' For instance, if the topic is

Figure 6.2   Children discuss poster questions in order to evaluate what has been learned and to generate additional areas of investigation.

the human circulatory system, students might develop a category for diseases. Anemia, leukemia, and hemophelia might be listed. Questions then can be generated about other blood- and heart-related diseases, as well as on the nature and treatment of each disease. Under "What We Don't Know" students might list "What other circulatory diseases are there?" "What causes each circulatory system disease?" and "What cures each circulatory system disease?" Groups of students then take questions, searching for information that validates what is already listed and adding new information to the list.

Question Box

Question Box involves placing a box for questions where it is readily available to students at all times. The teacher encourages students to write down (or, for younger students, to have someone else write down) questions that occur to them. Students might ask questions such as, "Why is the sky blue?" "What is France like?" "Why do the number of degrees in the angles of a triangle always equal 180?" or "Why is oxygen necessary for combustion?" Once or twice a week some questions are taken out of the box and the teacher models putting the question into a form that can be answered. For example, "What is France like?" could be recast as "How is the geography of France different from that of the U.S.?" or "What do U.S. tourists notice most frequently when they visit France?" As can be seen with this example, the teacher rewrites the pupil's personalized query into a number of focused questions that can be answered through research. When teachers demonstrate how to limit broad, unfocused questions, students become better able to formulate good questions themselves. As with the other strategies presented in this book, fading from teacher modeling to student independence is the goal of this technique.

But modeling researchable question asking is only part of the question box teaching strategy. Once questions have been focused, the teacher and students brainstorm places where students might find the needed information. Students are encouraged to list specific types of books and magazines as well as to mention resource people whom they might contact. For the question, "Why is the sky blue?," students might list the titles of science magazines, their science book, the school principal, the encyclopedia, the almanac, and the TV weather forecaster. After a list is compiled, pupils are encouraged to search the library to find more science books to add to the list. Once this large list has been compiled, students are ready to set out to find the answer. Meanwhile, a chart in the classroom with the question at the top can list the answers that students predicted before beginning the search, as well as what was found during and after the search.

CONNECT

Have you ever been involved in any research procedures similar to the ones presented here? Compare the way you generated research questions in elementary and secondary school with the procedures described here.

Maintaining the Focus of Research

A word of caution: students who are seeking information frequently lose their focus. Students can become so involved with the tangential information they encounter in their research that they are led far astray of their original question. One way to help students remain focused is to have students carry a folder with the question written on the front so that they can frequently refer to it. Students should be told that the only information to be put into that folder is information related to the particular question. It is a good idea, however, to give students another folder labeled "Miscellaneous" or "Other" into which they can put all of the other bits of interesting information that they accumulate. Who knows? The second folder may become the basis for another piece of research.

LOCATING INFORMATION

Once students have identified a specific question, they need to locate information to answer it. They must learn to efficiently locate appropriate sources and the necessary information therein. One way that teachers can help students in this task is to have students use *key words*.

First, tell students that key words are the keys that open the storehouses of information: textbooks, encyclopedias, library references, and people. Second, tell students that key words help to organize ideas. "If you are going to the store for milk, Kool-aid, orange juice, root bear, and diet cola," you might say, "what word could you use to describe all those items?" Discuss students' responses, such as *beverages* and *drinks,* in order to demonstrate how different words can be used to organize the five items. Point out that a few key words lead to many specifics. Finally, once students grasp the concept of key words, teach them how to use key words when researching single texts, multiple written sources, and oral interviews.

Single Texts

Three key word teaching strategies appropriate for single textbooks are presented here: Key Word Guess, Key Word Questions, and Key Word Scavenger Hunt. These lessons can be taught using content area textbooks.

Key Word Guess   *Key Word Guess* is begun by writing questions about the unit. Possible key words that might lead to the desired answer then are written underneath the question. The following is a Key Word Guess that fourth graders created:

Where did Native Americans live?

Indians	homes	states
teepee	countries	climate

Who were Native American leaders?

chiefs	Sitting Bull	Chief Joseph
Crazy Horse	medicine men	shaman
Indians	leaders	

What did Native Americans eat?

cooking	hunting	farming
gatherers	food	survival
Indians	basic needs	

It is clear that not all of the above key words would easily lead to the information being sought; however, that is also true of the key word lists that adult researchers generate. Adults list the most likely candidates for key words and then go to check them out. While checking, the list of key words is altered to become better focused for the question. Recently, in trying to locate articles about oral language use, we came up with the following list of key words to check in the *Education Index:* oral language, oral communication, and talking. While searching for articles under these phrases, the index directed us to yet another term, "conversation." The altered list, with "talking" dropped and "conversation" added, yielded several appropriate articles. Student researchers can likewise alter their key word lists once they are shown how.

After students list their key word guesses, they go to the index in their textbooks to see what can be found. In the example above, the class decided that *Indians* would be a good key word for all of the questions.

After a few sessions with key word guess, it is useful to change the strategy a bit in order to help the students apply what they are learning and gain independence. In the variation, students turn to major headings in their text's table of contents and make up a question for one of them. These questions are given to their classmates who then guess at key words that might help locate the needed information.

Key Word Questions   With *Key Word Questions,* the teacher groups related words, lists them on a transparency or the board, and asks students to come up with appropriate questions. As you can tell, key word questions is the obverse of key word guess. An example of grouped key words and students' guesses for appropriate questions is as follows:

Indians	pots	open fire
seeds	meat	woven baskets

How did Native Americans cook their food?
What kinds of foods did Native Americans eat?

Indians leaders	Chief Joseph	Squanto
Sequoyah	chief	ruler

Who were some Native American leaders?
Who were some peaceful Native American leaders?

It is clear that the grouped key words lead into a wide range of possible questions. In order to promote independence, have students look at the table of contents and the index in their textbooks to find a heading with related words and phrases. The students then list the words and have other students generate key word questions from their list.

Key Word Scavenger Hunt   *Key Word Scavenger Hunt* is a third strategy for teaching students how to use key words. The strategy emphasizes actual searches through materials using key words. Students are first led through a practice exercise as a whole class to learn through modeling how to find answers to various questions. Students then work in small groups to answer questions from a key word scavenger hunt list. Following are some practice items we have used:

1. A word used in New England for "factory" is "mill."
   How many kinds of mills does your textbook tell about?
2. What does "adobe" mean?
3. What is nuclear reactor? What key words could you use to find information?
4. Look at the key word "Dallas" in your text's index. Then find the listing "Dallas, early history of, 263–264." Write a question whose answer you think you might find in those pages. Do not try to answer the question.

As you can see, some of the questions can be answered by turning to the index only, whereas others require the student to look in the textbook to locate information. After practice-answering the questions above, students generally are ready to find the answers to some real questions generated within their small groups.

Multiple Written Sources

Locating information in textbooks is only part of being a researcher. Library books and magazines also provide enormous amounts of information. Indeed, a library card catalog can yield a surprising number of references, as can an index such as the *Readers' Guide to Periodical Literature*. If students turn to the heading "Indians" in the *Readers' Guide*, they will discover an enormous number of articles on the topic. To help students gain access to the information contained in these references, teachers must help students apply their understanding of key words to the specific format of each reference work. Teachers can easily connect the process of looking for key words in a textbook index to that of using key words when searching an encyclopedia, card catalog, or the *Readers' Guide*.

As for the other strategies we have described, we recommend that you fade your instruction. Demonstrate what you want students to do, give them some practice exercises, then launch them into real inquiries. Most teachers find their school librarians extremely helpful in introducing students to specific sources; the teacher needs to provide the guided practice and independent application to follow up the initial demonstration.

REVIEW

This chapter has described four teaching strategies to help students learn to identify researchable questions, and three strategies to help students locate pertinent information. Without looking back, list those strategies and describe each with a few terms. Then check your response against the text.

Interviews

So far, we have emphasized locating information in written sources. Conducting oral interviews also is a worthwhile way for student researchers to gain access to information.

Young students should begin interviews with familiar, friendly sources. Family members, school personnel, and peers are appropriate candidates for interviews at the early grades. Secondary students can begin interviewing unfamiliar people who are expert in students' research topics. Once a person has agreed to be interviewed, many teachers send the person a brief letter outlining the nature of the students' projects and a description of how the information will be used. Such a letter is especially helpful if the interview is to be tape-recorded.

Interviews work most efficiently when the researcher has specific questions written in a set order. If students are investigating schools of the past, asking the interviewee to "Tell me about your school days" may not be very productive. Instead, the students should be prepared to ask questions about teachers, fellow students, lessons, tests, discipline, and so on. These words might be jotted down at first and then developed into complete questions before interviewing a subject. Questions should be specific, but not so narrow that they can be answered with a "yes" or "no." Asking source people follow-up questions such as, "Tell me more about that" or "What else do you remember?" is a useful way of getting more complete information.

Tape-recording the interview is a good way to maintain a record of what was said, with taking notes during the interview also recommended. Figure 6.3 shows a good seating arrangement for an interview. Note that the interviewer has a clipboard to facilitate notetaking as well as a tape recorder. After leaving the interviewee, students should write down what they learned. This summary might then be shared with the interviewee in order to check for accuracy and to elicit additional pertinent information.

Before sending students out to conduct interviews, teachers frequently demonstrate the procedure by interviewing a guest in the classroom. Students

Figure 6.3   Interviewing is an important component of research.

also may want to practice interviewing one another before going outside the classroom.

ORGANIZING INFORMATION

Organizing information is perhaps the most difficult task facing student researchers. Students must learn to record only the information that answers their specific question. Students frequently pull out all the information they find because they consider everything to be of equal importance ("If it's not important, then why was it written there?"). Teachers must show students how to be selective.

Students must also be taught how to categorize information according to various aspects of their question. Young students who are seeking answers to "What do bears eat?" soon discover that information is available about the eating habits of different types of bears, different times of the year, and different ages and locations. Older students looking at how people measure time soon discover the great complexity with which scientists have addressed this issue. Organizing information is a complex skill. Producing notes, categorizing information, and citing information are three aspects of this phase of the research process, all three of which teachers must demonstrate and explain.

Producing Notes

In order to help students attend selectively to the information that answers their questions, we recommend regular comprehension lessons as described in Chapter 2. Reading for specific purposes is a dominant feature of those lessons, as well as a central feature of research. Producing notes about what one reads is a logical extension of reading for specific purposes; students producing notes record both the targeted information and their initial reactions to it.

We like to distinguish *notetaking* from *notemaking* because we see different skills being used in the two. Notetaking implies that the reader mainly lifts information from a source, using phrases from the passage itself. Making notes may also involve jotting down exact wordings, but it should also include personal examples, questions, and related information from other sources. The notemaker is not only taking from the source, but also evaluating the information. When you make notes you are far more likely to learn the material than when you merely take notes, because in making notes you are consciously connecting the new to the known. You are also monitoring more information when you make notes because you need to be aware of how much you know in order to add personal examples or raise questions about the material.

Partial Outline   A *partial outline* is a good tool for introducing students to notetaking. Teachers give students a partially completed outline or diagram of the content of a reading selection and then demonstrate how to go about completing it. After a few such lessons, teachers provide students guided practice for completing a partial outline on their own. The following is a partial outline of Chapter 1 of this book. To see how this activity works, complete this outline as you reread Chapter 1:

The Essentials of Content Area Reading and Writing

I. The challenges of content area reading and writing

   A. Functions of literacy

      1.

      2.

      3.

   B. Structure of materials

      1.

      2.

      3.

   C.

      1.

      2. Acquire information independently

II.
   A. Call up
   B.
   C.
   D.
   E.
   F.
   G.
   H.
   I. Apply
III. Approaches to content area reading and writing instruction
   A.
   B. Fading instruction
   C.

By filling out this outline as you read, your attention is drawn to the chapter's major ideas, to the relationships among the major ideas, and to the relationships between major and minor ideas. Notice that by providing you with the outline skeleton, your attention does not have to focus on the trivia of making an outline, ("Do I need an upper-case or lower-case a?"). By providing you with a fixed number of slots to be filled in, you can easily determine how many ideas to list, and what the relationship among them should be. A partial outline helps you to focus on selecting the important information from a text. The amount of information provided in the outline and the amount of instruction you need to provide will vary with the sophistication of the students and with time as you fade yourself out of the picture.

Transparency Notes   *Transparency Notes* is a good teaching strategy for helping students make notes. The teacher provides students with the main headings for an outline of a portion of their textbook, covering, say, a third of a chapter. The partial outline here would consist of only the title and the main headings, with completely blank spaces in between. Your students would have a copy of the outline at their desks, and you would have one on an overhead transparency. You then have the students read a portion of the text and make three notes about the information. While the students read, turn off the overhead projector and write your own three notes under the appropriate heading on the transparency. Next, have a volunteer read one note and explain why he or she included it. After three notes obtained from the students are recorded, turn on the overhead projector light, reveal your own three notes, and explain your reasons for making them. Compare your notes with the students', then turn off the light and repeat the procedure with the next portion of text. Continue throughout the passage, allowing students to copy your notes next to theirs.

As can be seen, transparency notes is quite similar to partial outline. Both strategies call for students to note information from a reading passage in a step-by-step fashion. However, transparency notes encourages students to evaluate information; students make, rather than take, notes. As this strategy is repeated through the school year, students generally begin to see their notes resemble yours, and you can begin to fade out your instruction.

Categorizing Information

As the notes accumulate in a research project, students need to categorize what they find. It is not efficient to write bits of information on separate file cards or sheets of paper and organize them later. It is far better to establish the categories of facts and to group facts into the categories as the research progresses. In that way, students can see which categories are lacking information, and whether new information corroborates or contradicts earlier findings. Students using this method may also see the need for establishing new categories or revising old ones. Three ways to establish research categories are Question Cards, Data Charts, and Webs.

Question Cards   A simple technique for maintaining category identities is to use *Question Cards*. Students list questions to be answered on note cards or on paper, one question per card or sheet. Whenever pertinent information is located, students write notes underneath the question. Later on, students group the information on each card or sheet according to its various aspects. This grouping becomes the outline to answer that particular question. Figure 6.4 is an example of a student's question card for a study of Connecticut, and Figure 6.5 shows how the information about that state was organized into categories.

Data Charts   McKenzie (1979) describes *Data Charts* as a tool to help students organize content information. He suggests making a grid on paper, with the research questions listed across the top and the resources to be used listed along the side. Each box of the grid then contains the source's information related to the question. Sparsely worded notes are used in order to conserve space and to encourage students to use their own words when writing the report. If a particular source provides no information about one of the questions, an *X* is placed in that square. Figure 6.6 shows a data chart for investigating the career of Ernest Hemingway.

   When introducing data charts, we have found that it is helpful to have a large sheet of paper posted in the room, or to use a transparency on an overhead projector. Students must be shown how to record information in the proper location of the chart. Students should also be sent out to locate other sources to add to the left-hand column.

   Another type of data chart lists questions across the top of a chart and as-

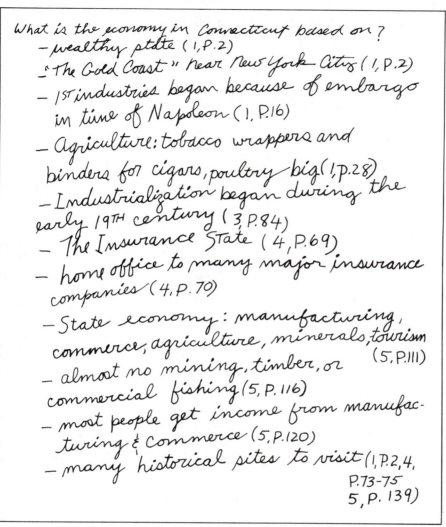

What is the economy in Connecticut based on?
- wealthy state (1, P.2)
- "The Gold Coast" near New York City (1, P.2)
- 1st industries began because of embargo in time of Napoleon (1, P.16)
- Agriculture: tobacco wrappers and binders for cigars, poultry big (1, p.28)
- Industrialization began during the early 19th century (3, P.84)
- The Insurance State (4, P.69)
- home office to many major insurance companies (4, P.70)
- State economy: manufacturing, commerce, agriculture, minerals, tourism (5, P.111)
- almost no mining, timber, or commercial fishing (5, P.116)
- most people get income from manufacturing & commerce (5, P.120)
- many historical sites to visit (1, P.2,4, P.73-75, 5, P. 139)

Figure 6.4   Unorganized question card.

pects of the questions down the side. For example, if the topic is "wild animals," the questions across the top might be "What does the animal eat?," "Where does the animal live," and "What dangers does the animal face?" Down the side, rather than listing sources, several different wild animals such as tiger, leopard, and lion are listed. Figure 6.7 is an example of this type of Data Chart.

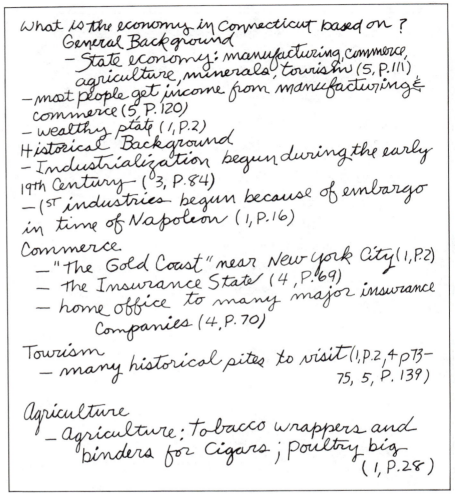

What is the economy in Connecticut based on?
General Background
  - State economy: manufacturing, commerce, agriculture, minerals, tourism (5, P.111)
- most people get income from manufacturing & commerce (5, P. 120)
- wealthy state (1, P.2)
Historical Background
- Industrialization begun during the early 19th Century (3, P.84)
- (1ST industries begun because of embargo in time of Napoleon (1, P.16)
Commerce
  - "The Gold Coast" near New York City (1, P.2)
  - the Insurance State (4, P.69)
  - home office to many major insurance companies (4, P.70)
Tourism
  - many historical sites to visit (1, P.2, 4 p 73-75, 5, P. 139)

Agriculture
  - agriculture: tobacco wrappers and binders for cigars; poultry big (1, P.28)

Figure 6.5   Organized question card.

Data charts are useful for ordering information, and they also help students evaluate what they have gathered. For example, students might be directed to the "wild animals" chart and asked to decide which animal ate the widest variety of food, lived in the most unusual habitat, or faced the greatest dangers.

Webs   A *web* is a very flexible outline that graphically depicts the relationships of the parts to the whole and to one another. Teaching students how to use a traditional outline is much easier if they have already been organizing

Sources	What was his life like?	What themes did he pursue?	What was his influence?
Smith & Jones			
Brown			
Linn			

Figure 6.6   Data chart for Ernest Hemingway report.

information through webbing. Figure 6.8 is a web of the history of Connecticut produced by a middle-school student. In the middle of a web is the topic being researched, and radiating out from the center are the subtopics stated either as questions or as words and phrases. Pieces of information about the

Animals	What does the animal eat?	Where does the animal live?	What dangers does the animal face?
Tiger			
Leopard			
Lion			

Figure 6.7   Data chart for wild animals report.

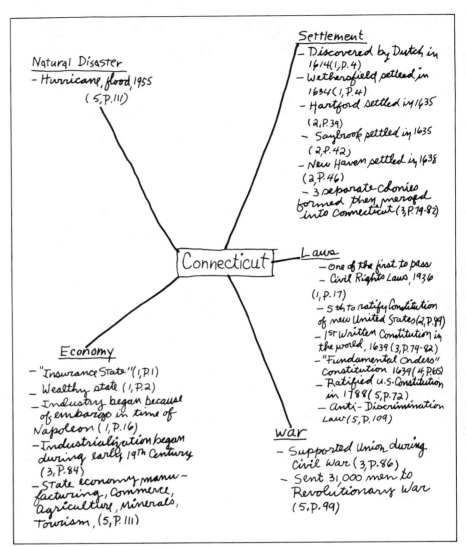

Natural Disaster
- Hurricane, flood, 1955
   (5, P. 111)

Settlement
- Discovered by Dutch in 1614 (1, P. 4)
- Wethersfield settled in 1634 (1, P. 4)
- Hartford settled in 1635 (2, P. 39)
- Saybrook settled in 1635 (2, P. 42)
- New Haven settled in 1638 (2, P. 46)
- 3 separate colonies formed then merged into Connecticut (3, P. 79-82)

Connecticut

Laws
- One of the first to pass
- Civil Rights Laws, 1936 (1, P. 17)
- 5th to ratify Constitution of new United States (2, P. 99)
- 1st written Constitution in the world, 1639 (3, P. 79-82)
- "Fundamental Orders" Constitution 1639 (4, P. 65)
- Ratified U.S. Constitution in 1788 (5, P. 72)
- Anti-Discrimination Law (5, P. 109)

Economy
- "Insurance State" (1, P. 1)
- Wealthy state (1, P. 2)
- Industry began because of embargo in time of Napoleon (1, P. 16)
- Industrialization began during early 19th Century (3, P. 84)
- State economy, manu-facturing, Commerce, Agriculture, Minerals, Tourism, (5, P. 111)

War
- Supported Union during Civil War (3, P. 86)
- Sent 31,000 men to Revolutionary War (5, P. 99)

Figure 6.8   Web for Connecticut report.

subtopics are listed around the subtopics, though not necessarily in any specific order.

A web is a good way to depict information that students produce during sessions of what you know and what you don't know, and that students eventually gather. When you introduce webs to students, you might begin by using a topic that they are about to begin in a unit of study. Put that topic in the middle and list questions around it. Next, have students tell what they know or think they know about the topic and you list that information next to the questions. Students then find more information in their textbooks, return to the web, and revise it in light of the new information. The initial web gives you a good idea of what your students already knew about the topic, with the final web a good basis for a unit review.

Citing Information

An important point to convey to students is the need to accurately record their sources. Accurate records are necessary both for others to check the information, and for the students themselves to return to, if necessary. The simplest way to record sources is to make a numbered list of all sources by title and date, including all visual, oral, and written sources. Then, when students find something they want to use in the report, they can jot down the information, placing the appropriate identification number after the information, and include a page number if using a written source.

Another Look at Planning

As can be seen, the initial steps in teaching research (identify researchable questions, locate information, and organize the information) differ only slightly from the planning steps for guided writing lessons presented in Chapter 5 (design the task, develop background and motivation, model the process, generate and organize information). The main difference is that planning a research report places great emphasis on locating and organizing new information. The final step of the research process—reporting information—encompasses the drafting and revising stages of the writing process that were detailed in Chapter 5.

REPORTING INFORMATION

Student researchers at all levels face the task of reporting to others what has been learned. Such reporting deepens the understanding both of those who did not conduct the research and of those who did.

Student researchers generally feel compelled to share all the material that they garnered during their searches. They want credit for all the information that they worked so hard to obtain, and frequently have difficulty paring down the information to that which directly answers their questions. Such unwieldy reporting results in undesirably long pieces. Inform your students that expert researchers generally know more than they include in their reports, and that students should likewise not try to include every bit of information that they gather.

Reporting sometimes is done in an informal, casual manner. Students are assembled after spending time conducting their research in order to share what they have learned in impromptu fashion. If the class spent time in the library investigating customs of dress, then a discussion about those customs might ensue; if students were sent home with the task of asking available adults how they came to their current occupation, then the findings are informally shared the next day.

As you know from Chapter 4, students should have several options for how to respond to what they read. Students might produce visuals, such as maps or homemade transparencies; they might produce or collect realia, as is done in most science fairs; or they might dramatize scenes. However, research findings frequently are reported in a more formal, strictly prescribed manner. Teachers provide a set of specifications (e.g., how long the report is to be; who the audience is; how many visuals, if any, are to be included; how citations are to be listed) and students frame their reports accordingly. Following is a discussion of two aspects of reporting information according to a somewhat formal set of specifications. Transferring information and sharing information are two important techniques for students to learn.

Transferring Information

Transferring information involves moving what has been gathered from sources into a final written or spoken form.

Written Reports Students must be taught how to transfer information from their question cards, data charts, or webs into written report form. Question cards lend themselves most easily to long reports, as students group all the pieces of information listed under each question into even smaller categories. Show students how to transfer each piece of information under one question onto a small strip of paper and then to physically arrange those strips into categories. Each question might include two, three, or more categories. Students might glue or tape the strips of information onto another sheet of paper with the question at the top to create a reorganized version of the original question sheet.

After this reorganization, show students how to turn each question into a topic sentence for a paragraph or section in a manner similar to that used with one-paragraph essays. For example, the question "What are the main industries in Connecticut?" might be recast into the topic sentence "Connecticut has five main industries." The bits of information beneath the question on the Question Card then become the supporting details for the topic sentence.

Reporting the information gathered onto a data chart is even more straightforward. For example, the data chart in Figure 6.6 can be the basis for a five-paragraph essay. The first paragraph is the introduction, which prepares people for the upcoming questions (e.g., "Three aspects of Hemingway's life seem to have been very important."). It may also tell why the topic is important (e.g., "Ernest Hemingway was one of the most influential and well-known American authors of the twentieth century."). Paragraphs 2 through 4 address the three questions, turned into topic sentences, along the top of the data chart (e.g., "Hemingway had a vigorous life style," "Hemingway focused on five primary themes in his writing," and "Hemingway influenced a generation of writers."). Paragraph 5 is a summary of important findings. Using a data chart works especially well for short reports.

Turning a web into a written report follows a similar pattern. Show students how to arrange the details for each subtopic according to the desired order of presentation. Subtopic headings become topic sentences and the bits of information become the supporting details. Be prepared to demonstrate this method of organization more than once, and to provide sufficient guidance when students practice it.

Once information has been organized, students draft and revise their written reports following the guidelines presented in Chapter 5. Reports can be improved by having students go through the revising step of the writing process. Peer response groups work especially well, since each student has been trying to write a similar type of paper, and so he or she brings to the group the same knowledge of the paper's form.

Oral Reports   Transferring information for oral reports is slightly different from the procedures for written reports. Students giving oral reports must rely on note cards, or some other type of reminder, to help keep the order of

Figure 6.9   Webs provide a basis for writing well-organized reports.

presentation straight. Key words and apt phrases should be recorded so that students can glance at them to maintain their flow of speech. For instance, a student reporting on Connecticut might have made the following list: "Industries . . . manufacturing . . . defense products . . . ship building at Groton . . . transportation equipment . . . electrical machinery." Such telegraphic writing clearly differs from the form of a written report.

A good aid for students giving oral reports is to support their talks with visuals and realia. Props allow speakers to maintain focus by discussing the aspects illustrated by each prop one at a time.

Oral reports allow immediate questioning, prompting researchers to give additional information about what they have learned. Thus, teachers should allow time for questions after an oral report.

Sharing Reports

Allotting class time for the presentation of reports has always been a problem. No teacher ever has enough time to do all that must be done. If you are going to ask students to make written or oral reports of their completed research, you might consider the following suggestions for saving time.

PREDICT
How can you save time yet still allow each class member to share the fruits of their investigations? Jot down some suggestions.

Some teachers have students sign up for only one type of presentation—oral or written. The teacher uses a signup sheet with only enough spaces under each type of presentation for half the students in the class to sign up. Other teachers prefer to rotate assignments among the students to give each student the chance to prepare equal numbers of oral and written reports during the school term.

Written Reports   In the elementary school, where teachers have students for longer than 50-minute periods, a group-oriented approach to sharing reports is frequently useful. For a class unit on domestic animals, for example, the class would generate a series of basic questions. Questions might include, "How does this animal help us?," "Where does it live?," "What does it eat?," and "What does it look like?" Each child selects a different domestic animal from a group they have previously called up, and writes a web about the animal. When it is time to produce the written report, the class decides how many paragraphs each report should have, as well as the order of each paragraph. They might also talk about what the introductory and concluding paragraphs should include. Each student then goes off to write a short report on his or her domestic animal, using illustrations if possible. These individual reports are revised through writing conferences, peer response groups, and peer editing groups, and the revised reports are bound into a classroom book on domestic animals.

Students frequently prepare constructions or artistic presentations for a report, such as scale models of the Parthenon, the Globe Theater, or the solar system. Consider leaving the objects on display around the room for a few weeks, letting written explanations serve as the means of sharing.

In secondary school, be sure to balance the reports that are due in each class. If you teach two class sections of the same course, require a batch of reports to be done at staggered times during the semester, rather than assigning everything for the final week of the term. Maintaining such a balance allows you to spend more time helping students prepare their reports, and you also have more time to react thoughtfully to the final products.

Oral Reports   One possibility to save class time during oral reports is for only some students actually to report to the whole class. The others can tape their presentations and place them with explanatory material in the classroom or school library for others to hear on their own time. One advantage of this technique is that no matter how well done the reports are, listening to thirty oral reports in a few days is bound to drag, whereas listening to ten over several days can still be interesting.

Another time-saving device is to put students into teams to prepare a panel presentation. Each panel member could be responsible for researching an aspect of the topic. Some teachers station students with reports to give at separate locations throughout the classroom, and then have various groups of listeners rotate among the presenters. This strategy forces the presenters to repeat themselves, but repetition can be beneficial and the class routine has been varied a bit.

PROMOTING STUDENT INDEPENDENCE IN RESEARCH

As was suggested in Chapter 1, you develop student independence as you first demonstrate what you expect students to do, fade out your assistance as your students practice the task with your help, and finally provide opportunities for independent application. Such fading applies to developing student researchers, also. You should model how to identify questions, locate information, organize information, and report information. Students as a whole class can observe the demonstrations, then perform the tasks in small groups with continued teacher guidance; finally, students should embark on their own investigations with minimal teacher intervention. Such fading should occur throughout the school year.

In the elementary grades, teachers might walk the whole class through the entire research process. Teachers should show students how to investigate and report a subject, with teacher and students jointly producing a finished product. Later in the year, when a different unit is being studied, teachers can remind students of the processes they used before. For the second unit to be researched, students might work in small groups rather than with the whole class. As students develop research skills, they are able to carry out the research task more and more independently.

At the secondary level, teachers should refine students' research skills. If students are already adept at locating information through an index, teachers might teach them to use a card catalog. Practically all students at the upper grade levels benefit from attention to their notemaking skills. Secondary teachers also must remind students of the skills they learned in earlier grades.

WHAT ABOUT . . .

What about Plagiarism?

In our experience, most students who copy their reports from another source do so out of ignorance and desperation. They are unaware of any other system for generating the required report. Several techniques can help prevent copying in your classroom. Taking students through the steps described in this chapter will model the research process for them. You might further want to require checkpoints to see what progress is being made. These checks should not be presented as punitive; rather, make it clear that all students need your feedback about how successfully they are dealing with the various stages of a report. Thus if a student is organizing information on a data chart, you need to check whether or not key words are being used, whether a variety of sources have been located, and whether sources are being identified with page numbers. Such checking, by the way, also helps teachers prevent student procrastination.

You might also make all initial reports oral or visual to prevent copying, with students not permitted to read reports but only to use notes. Most students are unable to memorize a long selection from the encyclopedia, so they must use their own words. When you praise their ability to speak from notes, you raise their confidence in their ability to write their own reports.

However, there are some students who are well aware that copying is wrong and who know of alternative ways to prepare reports, yet who still persist in plagiarizing information. Unfortunately, many of them are capable students who have been rewarded through the years for their plagiarism by receiving good grades from teachers. How many students have the ability to write as well as the author of a science trade book? As long as more emphasis is placed on the product of the research, rather than on learning the process well, such copying will continue to be a problem. Typically, we can assume that a good grasp of the process will result in a good product. However, we have all known students who were very good at finding information, but whose verbal skills prevented them from sharing what they found in a clear manner. By the same token, many good students admit to moving effortlessly through school, doing little work, but presenting their material so well that they get good grades.

In your classroom, you might grade students at each step of the research process. Thus, students need to produce good questions, locate valuable sources, and produce and organize effective notes before they get to exercise their drafting and revising skills. Remember that your main concern is teaching the process of finding and sharing information on a topic; the final product, the report, only reflects students' proficiencies with that process.

What about Lack of Materials?

Many states have area education agencies that provide teachers various types of in-service opportunities as well as a wealth of curricular materials. You can always contact such an agency, saying that you want a good idea of what materials and services are available in your area. You might also ask whether the agency holds in-service sessions on using a variety of materials in the classroom to get away from over-reliance on the textbook. You can also check in the textbooks themselves: texts frequently list books and films to supplement particular units.

What about Length and Depth?

One of the first questions students ask when they are assigned a report is, "How long does it have to be?" As we pointed out in Chapter 5, this question embodies concerns not only about the amount of work required but also about the depth of investigation that is expected. If a college science professor tells students to prepare a four-page report, students assume that is a more superficial and less demanding project than a 25-page paper.

Thus you can set your priorities by setting the length of the reports you require. If you judge a particular unit or topic of study to warrant careful research, then provide students sufficient instruction, time, and resources to execute it. If another part of your curriculum deserves less emphasis, then require less in the way of research.

What about Grading?

As stated above, learning the research process is more important than producing a polished report. Otherwise, teachers could be satisfied with students who submitted reports purchased from commercial services. Therefore, it is wise to award multiple grades for each research effort, possibly giving a grade for each checkpoint you set up. You should evaluate each checkpoint according to how well students are learning each process. Another grade could be given for the first draft of the report, and yet another for the final draft.

We believe it is a good idea to give students the checklist you will be using to evaluate each of their efforts. This allows students to see how you weigh the different aspects of the assignment. Allow room on the list for your comments, and for their comments back to you, for each evaluation point. This checklist should be passed back and forth between you and the student several times throughout the research process to help students give you what you expect. Be specific with your comments. If instructors write nothing or just ''Good job,'' evaluations are largely ignored, whereas more specific comments receive attention. Teachers should write general notes on the top of the paper or evaluation sheet, and specific comments within the paper at appropriate points.

APPLY
Review this chapter and construct a research report checklist that would be appropriate for the grade level you intend to teach or currently teach. Your checklist should contain at least four categories: (1) research question, (2) location of information, (3) organization of information, and (4) report. The number and type of subcategories, their grade value, if any, and the format of the list depends on the sophistication of your students.

REFERENCE

McKenzie, G. (1979). Data charts: A crutch for helping students organize reports. *Language Arts, 56,* 784–788.

SUGGESTED READINGS

Four sources provide especially useful information about helping students research topics and report what was learned. Although these sources address elementary students, the processes described apply to secondary students as well.

Beach, J. D. (1983). Teaching students to write informational reports. *The Elementary School Journal, 84,* 213–220.
Cassidy, J. (1981). Inquiry reading for the gifted. *The Reading Teacher, 35,* 17–21.
Hennings, D. G. (1982). A writing approach to reading comprehension: Schema theory in action. *Language Arts, 59,* 8–17.
Stauffer, R. G., & Harrell, M. M. (1975). Individualizing reading-thinking activities. *The Reading Teacher, 28,* 765–769.

The processes described in the references below also apply to elementary students, but they specifically address secondary school students.

Doubleday, N. F. (1971). *Writing the research paper* (rev. ed.). Lexington, MA: D. C. Heath.
Schumm, J. S., & Radenich, M. C. (1984). Readers'/writers' workshop: An antidote for term paper terror. *Journal of Reading, 28,* 13–19.

Identifying researchable questions is a valuable skill that deserves considerable emphasis. Helping students learn how to isolate a problem is an intricate process, as the following reference makes clear.

Getzels, J. W., & Csikszentmihalyi, M. (1975). From problem solving to problem finding. In I. A. Taylor & J. W. Getzels (Eds.), *Perspectives in creativity*. Chicago: Aldine.

Notetaking and notemaking are traditional learning strategies that teachers have emphasized through the years. The first reference included here reviews research about the specific effects of notes on learning; the second reference presents a procedure that is more intricate than the ones we presented in this chapter.

Carrier, C. A., & Titus, A. (1979). The effects of notetaking: A review of studies. *Contemporary Educational Psychology, 4,* 299–314.
Palmatier, R. (1973). A notetaking system for learning. *Journal of Reading, 17,* 36–39.

CHAPTER 7

Classroom Complexities

For many of you, the ideas and teaching strategies introduced in this book are new. When first faced with new ideas, we all tend to be pulled in opposite directions. The new often sounds exciting and profitable, and part of us wants to plunge ahead. The other part of us, however, is more cautious. That side of our nature comes up with a lot of objections: But what if I can't? But what if they won't? But I don't have time! This resistance is an important check and balance against a natural fascination with new things. All of us should be cautious, consider risks, and think about the problems involved in new adventures. But our growth as teachers and people will be limited if our cautious nature completely takes over.

Teachers frequently express concern about the complexities of life in the classroom. Elementary school teachers work with about twenty-five students during the entire school day; secondary-school teachers face about 150. These students vary substantially in ability and attitude toward school. Teachers have several lessons to prepare and present each day, in addition to their supervisory duties such as checking daily class attendance. Given the demands of managing a classroom, teachers frequently become concerned about conducting effective content area reading and writing lessons. This chapter presents answers to some normal concerns (prefaced with the introduction *But . . .*) that are commonly expressed by teachers when they consider content area reading and writing instruction in the complex environment of classrooms.

BUT MY TESTBOOK IS TOO HARD

Even when teachers have a variety of other resources available, they frequently have class sets of only one book. This text is often difficult, perhaps impossible, for many students to read. When faced with this problem, teachers may feel that their text is too hard.

If you confront this problem, begin by considering how you decided that the book was too hard. Did you make that decision based on the book's level of readability? Most textbooks have a teacher's edition with a number that is supposed to represent the book's level of readability. If, for example, a text has a readability level of 5.6, that means it is predicted to be appropriate for students in the fifth grade, sixth month of school. If the readability level ranges from 8.0 to 9.0, that means the various sections of the book range from eighth to ninth grade level in difficulty—at least in theory. There are many problems with readability estimates and with reliably estimating the difficulty of a text.

All commonly used readability formulas are based on two factors, sentence difficulty and word difficulty. *Sentence difficulty* typically is determined by the average number of words in a sentence. Long sentences usually are considered more difficult to follow than short sentences. *Word difficulty* is harder to define. Various formulas measure the incidence of long words, assuming that long words are more difficult to read. If someone were applying a readability formula to this textbook, for example, they would select several passages, determine the average sentence length and number of difficult words, consult a formula, and produce a number to be called the readability level of this book.

There are several problems with this apparently scientific approach. First, the formulas take into account only two of the characteristics that make texts difficult. The number, quality, and appropriateness of the visuals can make a text more or less readable, as can the organization of the passages and the connections that are made between students' experiences and new information. Clear content-related headings and good transitions are also important. Introductory and review activities that help students to determine key information and to monitor how well they are learning are important text characteristics commonly ignored by readability formulas.

In addition to these text variables, there is the more important reader variable. No readability formula can take into account what level of prior knowledge, interest, or motivation readers bring with them to the text. Imagine that a book on United States history has a readability level of 8.0 and is used by average eight-graders in Williamsburg, Virginia and Sydney, Australia. The superior knowledge, interest, and motivation of the Williamsburg eighth-graders would make them much more able to benefit from the text than the Australians, most of whom probably would lack prior knowledge, interest, and motivation to study U.S. history.

Yet another variable that formulas don't consider is you, the teacher. Remember that you have control over which sections to use and which to skip, what kind of preparation you will do before reading, how long a segment you will assign, and what kind of follow-up you will do after reading. Your instruction can do much to make a text more or less readable.

Readability formulas have one final problem when they are applied to school textbooks. Because writers of textbooks know that they must achieve a certain readability for a book that is designated for a certain grade, writers compose with the variables of sentence length and difficult words constantly in mind.

The finished writing is checked against a readability formula and if the score is too high, long sentences are made into short ones and long words are replaced by short words. As an illustration, note the difference between the following two examples:

> Furthermore, the finished writing is checked against a readability formula and if the score is too high, long sentences are made into short ones and long words are replaced by short words.

> Then the writing is checked with a readability formula. Sometimes the score is too high. Long sentences are made into short ones. Short words are used for long words.

Both the first long sentence and the rewritten four sentences contain essentially the same information. If the readability formula were applied, the four sentences would be rated as much easier to read. But were they? Most people would find them harder to read. In the four short sentences, the reader has to infer that the score being too high results in the long sentences and words being adjusted. In the long sentence, this inference is made by the word *if*. While most readers can make that inference, doing so takes more attention. Numerous short sentences and vague little words (*that, these, things*) may actually make comprehension more difficult. Defenders of readability formulas would respond to this criticism by stating rightly that readability formulas were meant to measure the difficulty of "naturally occurring text" and were never intended to be used as a guide to rewrite material. Unfortunately, because most states demand that all textbooks meet the readability requirements for a given grade level, that is the way readability formulas are currently being used.

You should therefore avoid basing your assessment of text difficulty on the stated readability level. Carefully inspect the text and answer the following questions:

1. Are difficult words clarified in the text by visuals, examples, and other devices that help students make connections?
2. Are paragraphs clearly written so that main ideas are apparent?
3. Do headings cue readers on what the section is about?
4. Are there good transitions between paragraphs and sections?
5. Are visuals abundant, clear, and closely related to major topics?
6. Do introductory and review activities help students to focus on what is important?
7. Can I, the teacher, readily develop my students' prior knowledge, interest, and motivation so that they can connect what they already know with the new information presented in this text?

In addition to looking carefully at your text, you may want to try out the text with some students. Plan a good comprehension lesson, teach it well, and see how your students do. If after a good comprehension the class is still unable to read the textbook, your book is in fact too hard!

BUT I MUST USE THE BOOK SOMETIMES

No matter what the actual readability of a text, teachers are often forced to use it. There may be little money to buy supplemental materials, the library may be in poor shape, and no films may be available. Using a difficult textbook may be preferable to simply lecturing because lectures bypass reading and lead students to become dependent on the teacher for information. What can be done when you must use the book?

1. Hold students responsible for only part of a text. Textbook difficulty varies tremendously among and within chapters. In Chapter 2, we suggested that you use importance as a criterion for which parts of the textbook to teach. If your book is too hard, you will also want to consider the criteria of interest and vocabulary. Go through your textbook and identify the chapters that cover topics of particular interest to you and your students. These chapters will be easier for your students to read because high interest is closely related to high prior knowledge, as well as generating extra motivation. Next, look at the text for vocabulary. Chapters that introduce numerous words for which students have no meaning will be more difficult than chapters that introduce words for which students have already experienced the meaning. In sum, have students read portions of the book that seem most appropriate based on your decisions about importance, interest, and vocabulary load.

2. Help students with good preparation and clear purposes. Remember how much preparation you got for most of your subject-area assignments? "Read the chapter for tomorrow, and we'll discuss it" is a common way of making a reading assignment. There are many students who could not read any chapter after receiving such a minimal amount of preparation and purpose. But remember what you learned in Chapter 2. You can help students call up prior knowledge before they read, and have them predict what they will find in a passage. You can make clear to students what you expect them to have learned when they finish reading, thereby helping students monitor their progress. Reading comprehension is far easier when students are prepared and have a clear purpose in mind. This can be easily demonstrated: Imagine that you are to go to a party where there will be several hundred people. When you return from the party, your friend begins to ask who was there. You will remember some, but not all, of the people that deserve mention. Compare this with having your friend ask you before the party to notice whether Carol Smith, Janet Cates, and a specific list of several other people attend. You go to the party prepared to look for them and are more easily able to report back later. Students may be able to read more of the book when you help them call up what they already know, predict what they will find, and use preset purposes to help them monitor their reading.

3. Use difficult but important material in a listening comprehension lesson. As you remember from Chapter 2, a listening comprehension lesson has all the components of a reading comprehension lesson, except that students listen rather than read. To be sure that they listen well and purposefully, prepare them for listening as you would for reading. Build and call up prior knowledge. Set clear purposes. Limit the amount they will listen to. Conduct a group follow-up to make sure the purposes have been met.

Some teachers like to tape a section as they read it to students. Then, if there is any disagreement about what the students heard, the teacher can replay that part of the tape, a practice analogous to rereading part of the text. Some teachers also assign students to read the text aloud, but such an assignment is valuable only when students have the opportunity to polish their oral reading before actually performing for the class.

4. Use the visuals if nothing else. Even those chapters that are too hard for your students may have useful visuals. Pictures, charts, maps, graphs, diagrams, and other visual aids provide some alternative to words. We know a teacher who begins every unit by first leading students through the visuals in the text. The students soon learn to look forward to this introduction to a unit. This teacher gives students five minutes in which to learn everything they can from visuals alone; students are not allowed to read any text except captions or keys included with visuals. As they are timed for exactly five minutes, students go quickly through the chapter, making as big a list as possible of what

Figure 7.1   A student learns information from visuals.

they can learn from visuals alone. When the five minutes are up, all books are closed and the teacher compiles the lists on the board. He or she then focuses on particular information by asking the students who included it to point out the appropriate visual. All students turn to the appropriate page, and the student who figured out something particularly clever explains how he or she learned it from the visual. By the end of this lesson, the class has built a lot of prior knowledge and learned a lot about how to interpret visuals. Figure 7.1 shows a student learning from the visuals in a text.

BUT MY STUDENTS DON'T ALL READ AND WRITE AT GRADE LEVEL

Very few classes contain only students who read and write at grade level because *grade level* is only an average. A "ninth-grade task" is one that "average ninth-graders" can effectively complete. In all areas of life, there is an average. Size ten clothes fit the average ten-year-old. But many ten-year-olds, because of the genes they inherited from their parents and because of the good or poor nutrition they have had since conception, wear clothes one or more sizes larger or smaller. If you are the parent of a ten-year-old boy who wears size twelve, you complain "proudly" about not being able to keep him in clothes. If you are the parent of a ten-year-old who wears size eight, you worry a bit because undersized boys tend to have a harder time in our society. It is perfectly normal to wish everyone were average or above. But we must accept the fact that *average*, by definition, implies that some are above and some are below a middle point.

What constitutes average ability is constantly changing. A child who wears a below-average size eight today would have, at the same size, been average a generation ago. As the average size ten child grew taller, size ten clothes were made bigger. If all the children in the schools were to start reading a year better than they presently do, expectations would be adjusted and the grade-level book would still be just right for some, very easy for others, and very hard for others. Indeed, this shifting standard of literacy raises society's expectations, so that public education continually looks as if it were not producing literate citizens. "Illiterates" today might have been considered well educated years ago when reciting Biblical passages from memory was the accepted criterion of literacy.

Parents of a ten-year-old boy who wears size eight may worry about him, make sure he gets the best nutrition, and take him to the doctor to be sure that he is continuing to grow, but they buy him size eight clothes and don't constantly berate him because he can't wear size ten. Teachers of children with below-average ability may worry about them, make sure they get instruction from which they can grow, and monitor their progress more carefully than they monitor the progress of others. But pretending that students with below-average ability could do average work if they would just try, and assigning the work as if they could do it, would be like demanding that, regardless of size, all ten-year-olds must wear size ten clothes. This would be humiliating and would not help them to grow!

To cope with students who don't read at grade level, you need to adapt your instruction. Throughout this book, we have suggested ways of adapting instruction so that everyone can learn something. For instance, in Chapter 2, you learned how to plan and carry out a comprehension lesson. When whole-class comprehension lessons are taught, students who simply cannot read the book still learn the major content by participating in the prereading activities and by paying attention to the follow-up activities. If you have wide variations of ability in your class, you will want to make sure that across any unit, you teach lessons with a variety of purposes. When your purposes are easier, your slower students will benefit more from the lesson. When your purposes require more, your high-achieving students will benefit correspondingly. You can't meet the varied needs of each student every minute of the day. But you can meet the needs of every student during some part of the day.

Because writing activities have no established level as reading materials do, all students work at their own level as they write. Chapter 5 provides a variety of ideas for directing students' composition. As with comprehension lessons, your composition lessons should have a balance of fairly easy, moderate, and more difficult tasks.

APPLY

Of the following three writing assignments designed for middle-school students, which do you consider fairly easy, which moderate, and which fairly difficult?

Pretend you are writing a gourmet cookbook and compare the benefits of cooking, seasoning, and chopping foods as an aid to digestion.

Explain in a few sentences to your younger brother why he should chew his food completely before swallowing.

Describe in a letter to a Chinese homemaker the various ways that American cooks heat, season, and chop foods.

Make up another three assignments, one for each level of difficulty, for a topic that you select.

All of the chapters in this text provide guidelines for helping students develop independent reading and writing proficiencies. Students with such independence are able to carry out reading and writing projects that fit their interests and capabilities. Indeed, the chapters on content area literature and on developing student writers and researchers are especially pertinent for adapting instruction to fit the range of students one inevitably encounters in a classroom.

Another way to adapt instruction is to provide students with choices. You may not give a four-year-old a choice of whether or not to take a bath, but you may give a choice of when to take that bath. ''Do you want to take your bath now or in twenty minutes?'' is a ploy used in many households. Young children typically respond, ''Twenty minutes!'' and in twenty minutes they take their baths without complaint. Students like to schedule their own time. You may require some tasks, but allow your students to decide the order in which to complete them. Or, you might allow students to choose which assignments from a given list they wish to complete. Given two possible writing assignments, students could pick the one they are most interested in completing. Given ten vocabulary words, students could pick two to learn well enough to teach them to a small group. All of us want to control our lives. The statement attributed to Winston Churchill aptly sums up how many students feel: ''I have always enjoyed learning, but I have not always enjoyed being taught.'' Letting students make choices within parameters set by the teacher is a nice balance of authority.

APPLY

Obtain a copy of the journal article entitled ''The Half-Open Classroom'' by R. A. Earle and R. Morley (*Journal of Reading*, 1974, vol. 18, pp. 131–135). Compare this chapter's discussion of adapting instruction with that presented in the article.

BUT THEY WON'T WORK IN GROUPS

Students generally will work productively in groups when the assignments are clear and feasible. However, students may not have had much experience working in groups, and you may have to teach them how. If your students have difficulty working together, you need to begin by building a lot of structure into groups. As time goes on and they become more comfortable, you can let them take on more responsibility. Following are some general rules for initiating successful group work:

1. Keep your group size at three to five members. More than five students in a group seem unable to work together well. Some will just sit and let the others work. Some teachers believe that four is not a good group size because the group can become deadlocked when decisions must be made—two for, two against. This is a factor to consider if your group work involves much decision-making.

2. Assign members to fixed groups with a balance of individuals. Make sure that each group has leaders and followers, slow and fast learners, students who are paragons of virtue and some who are less than perfect. Avoid assigning students whom you know don't get along to the same group. If your students are at that terrible age when boys and girls secretly like each other but can't admit it, don't assign boys and girls to the same group. This applies only to students going through that stage; otherwise, it is a good idea to mix boys and girls in the groups. Most teachers like to keep groups together for several weeks or months so that a group develops a sense of cohesion and pride, and is used to working together.

3. *Have assigned places where each group always meets*. If necessary, have students practice getting to those places and getting ready to work. You may want to time the class to see how long it takes for all members to get quietly to their places and be ready to work.

4. *Assign a leader and a recorder for each group*. You may want the same people to assume these roles for several meetings until the groups learn how to work, but then it is a good idea to let everyone have a turn at being leader. The leader's responsibility is to make sure the task gets done—not to do it himself or herself. The leader should make sure that everyone has a chance to talk and should learn to say such things as, "I think we are getting off the track, and we only have two more minutes," and "Why don't we combine those two ideas?" Many teachers have students role-play a discussion while others watch so that the teacher can point out actions that help or hinder group functioning. Other teachers circulate during group work time making notes of the actions that helped the group to be productive. Sharing this information with the class helps students learn what is expected of them when they work in groups.

The group recorder makes notes or fills out whatever must be turned in or shared with the whole class. The recorder role should also shift from member to member, although you might want to avoid embarrassing students whose spelling and writing ability are very limited. One teacher we know writes something like "Groups—Shortest Person" on the board before students come into class. When students see this on the board, they immediately form groups, choosing the shortest person in each group as leader. They always enjoy deciding who will be leader by comparing their heights or other characteristics. In addition to shortest and tallest, leaders can be chosen by designating the oldest, youngest, most (least) letters in first and last name, where a name comes in alphabet, etc. This teacher then hands a sheet of paper and pencil to whomever she wants to be recorder in each group.

5. *Have a specific task for the group to accomplish*. Of all the guidelines for groups, this is the most crucial. You can't tell people to "Discuss." They don't know what to say, and they feel foolish.

___

CALL UP
Think back to your experiences with groups when you were told to get together and "discuss" something. What did you do? What was accomplished? Was there a lot of discussion that had nothing to do with the topic?

___

Oddly enough, to start a good discussion, you must avoid using the word *discuss*. Rather, you must set a specific task for the group to accomplish. These tasks may consist of the purposes for comprehending detailed in Chapter 2, or the purposes, audiences, and forms for writing you learned about in Chapter 5. In fact, you can have the group perform those comprehension tasks rather than the individual. These are some sample group tasks:

1. Make up five questions to ask the other groups regarding the major information we have learned about the USSR.
2. From our brainstormed list of twentieth century leaders, pick the five that your group believes most influenced our lives.
3. List all the insects your group can think of.
4. Write five questions a reporter should ask William Shakespeare if he were suddenly here today.

As you can see, in order to perform its task, the group will have to discuss the topic.

6. *Give the groups a limited time and stick to it*. Many teachers use a timer or appoint one student to be the official clock watcher. Once time is up, give students one minute to prepare to report back to the whole class. How long the limited time should be varies with the age of the students and with the task, but most teachers tend to give too much time. Ten minutes is generally a good length unless you have an unusually complex task for your groups. At least in the beginning, limit groups to ten minutes or less. While this may not seem long enough, your groups will get in the habit of getting right down to business and not wasting time if they are always a little pushed for time. Most teachers who say they have never been able to get groups to work in their classes were trying to keep the students in groups too long.

7. *Follow up the group work with some sharing from the groups*. Do not spend too much time on sharing and do not let the groups share everything they have done. For the tasks listed previously, you might follow each one up as follows:

1. Have each group ask another group one of their five questions.
2. Make a tally from the groups of the most commonly picked leaders and then open a discussion of the whole class about why these were picked.
3. Let each group list one insect on their list until all insects on every list are compiled on a list you make on the board.
4. Have each group share their best question for Shakespeare, and then see what volunteers from other groups think Shakespeare would have answered.

Teaching is a hard job. It is an impossible job if only the official, paid teacher is allowed to teach. When you arrange for your students to work in groups, they have the opportunity to teach each other. If you feel that you are the only person in your classroom working hard, follow these guidelines and try some group work. Figure 7.2 shows students of different ages working in groups.

Figure 7.2   Students of all ages can work together.

BUT THEY WON'T DO IT IF IT DOESN'T COUNT FOR A GRADE

Make assignments count for a grade if students require such motivation. Grading is an extremely difficult part of teaching because of the differences in student ability. If students came to us with exactly the same amount of prior knowledge and learning ability, we could expect them to all gain exactly the same amount from our good instruction. But students do start at different places, with different amounts of ability. How do we grade fairly? Should the student who knows almost nothing about social studies and whose learning ability is limited fail social studies if a good effort is made? Should the student who knows a lot about social studies and is very bright and advantaged get an A even if that student need put forth only minimal effort to do so? These are not easy questions to answer, but teachers must come up with a grading system, one that will encourage rather than discourage students from learning. Following are some guidelines to consider in designing a grading system that encourages all students to work and learn.

1. Make sure that your essential learning activities count toward the grade. Teachers typically assign grades derived from three types of school work: daily work, projects, and tests. One way to motivate students to effort in the classroom is to regularly monitor daily work. If students work in groups, give each group member a point when the group completes the assignment. If a writing assignment is made, give those who complete it on time a point before assessing the content and mechanics of each piece. Generally give points for tasks completed on time and with good effort. By combining good instruction that focuses on concepts of varying degrees of difficulty with rewards for completing assignments acceptably, you go a long way toward motivating your students to work with you.

Students who regularly succeed with their school work demonstrate the best progress. Thus, students must be successful at their tasks if they are to continue to work and learn. To guarantee success to students of all different levels of achievement, define success as good effort.

2. Have some projects that allow hard workers and talented students to excel. As you know from Chapter 4, involving students in projects allows students to pursue individual interests as well as to develop their talents. Much is said these days about helping students develop the right half of the brain which is the side believed to be responsible for artistic or creative endeavors. Students who seem to be better "right half" than "left half" thinkers are at a disadvantage in most of our logical, sequentially oriented classrooms. Assigning projects allows students to go beyond linear thinking to creativity.

Of course, any student who does a satisfactory project should get the number of points designated for "satisfactory." But those who go beyond the minimum requirement should get more points. Giving everyone equal credit for a good effort for daily work rewards students for a normal, good effort. Grading projects according to their quality allows those who can and will work hard to feel their efforts are appreciated.

3. Make your tests as fair as possible to students of all abilities. Tests are the hardest element of a grading system. Some teachers, particularly at lower grade levels, don't give tests. But many teachers feel the need for some "objective" measure of learning, and many school systems demand that teachers have test grades for students. How do you produce tests that don't penalize students who began your unit with little prior knowledge and who have limited learning skills?

As a general guideline, 80 to 90 percent of material tested should have been thoroughly taught and reviewed during class. Include on your tests information taught in guided comprehension and writing lessons as well as information taught through lecture and demonstration. Those students who worked with you on a daily basis—even if their ability is limited—should be able to answer 80 to 90 percent of such a test correctly. The other 10 to 20 percent of the test may include material that was assigned but not thoroughly taught. This is, of course, a compromise position. Some teachers believe it is unfair to students with limited ability to test anything not thoroughly taught in classes. Unfortunately, if you try to test only what was thoroughly taught and reviewed, and you taught and reviewed it well, everyone in class should get an A. Most schools won't permit this, and your more able students won't be motivated to learn from assignments. Other teachers believe that everyone should learn everything—both what was taught and what was assigned. Following this system, many students who worked with you on a daily basis but who cannot learn from assignments done independently will fail the test. And if they always fail tests, they will not continue to work with you on a daily basis. Since success on a daily basis is such an important determinant of content learning, a grading system that does not assure success is bound to create students who learn little.

4. Make sure your tests are testing content, not reading and writing abilities. While we want students to develop reading and writing abilities as they are learning content, we do not want the lack of their abilities to mask what they have learned. Imagine a student who is a very poor reader and a very poor writer but who has worked hard in class, listened well, contributed to group discussions, and done everything else you could possibly want a good student to do. Now, imagine that student taking your test, 80 to 90 percent of which is material that was taught and reviewed in class. The student knows the information but, because of limited reading and writing abilities, cannot answer the questions and fails the test. As time goes on, these good students cease being good students. Why bother to listen and try if you learn the important information and fail the test anyway? For such students, consider the following possibilities:

1. Read the test to everyone. This may seem a little foolish to older students but you can generally get by with it if you ask, "How many of you have ever gotten a question wrong on a test just because you read it wrong?"

Most students will nod and groan as they remember this experience. Next explain, ''When we take a test, we are sometimes anxious and when we get anxious, we can read things wrong. I am going to read the test to you to minimize that possibility.''

2. Let students choose whether they would rather read the test to themselves or have it read to them. Say, ''When I give a test, I really want to know how much you have learned. I don't want you to get something wrong because you misread it. Some people prefer to read the test to themselves. Others like to have the test read to them. If you want to read the test to yourself, go to this side of the room. If you want the test read aloud, go

General Strategies

1. Survey the test. Estimate its difficulty and plan your time for each section.
2. Underline the important words in each question. Be especially alert for closed terms such as ''always,'' ''never,'' ''most.''
3. Be sure to answer every required question (unless there is a penalty for guessing).
4. Don't spend too much time on any one question.

Strategies for Objective Tests

1. Answer the easy questions first. Mark the ones you skip and go back to them when you're ready. Remember, information contained in later items can help you answer previous items.
2. Look for the most correct answer when two items seem to be similar.
3. Narrow multiple-choice items to two and then make your choice when you're not sure of an answer.
4. Rephrasing questions and answering questions in your head before inspecting the choices frequently helps.
5. Change your answers only if you misunderstood the question the first time or if you are absolutely sure that your first response was wrong.
6. False items on true-false tests usually contain one essential word that converts the item into an overstatement, understatement, or misstatement.

Strategies for Essay Tests

1. Briefly outline all answers before writing. Jot down key terms and then add to those terms while working on your answers.
2. Only include information that you believe is correct.
3. Plan your time for each question and stick to that schedule.
4. Include topic sentences and supporting details in each paragraph.
5. Proofread your writing.

Figure 7.3   Test-taking strategies.

to the other side.'' Then you, an aide, or a student volunteer can read the test in a low voice to those who so choose.

3. Provide alternatives to essay answers. Essays are very difficult to write. When you want students to show what they have learned about a major topic, consider requiring an outline, web, or word sort rather than an essay.

4. When students do write, correct their answers for content only. Mechanics such as punctuation, capitalization, usage, and handwriting should not be allowed to detract from what a student has learned.

5. Teach test-taking skills. Figure 7.3 contains a list of test-taking strategies that are appropriate for middle-grade and older students. The strategies are best presented following an actual test. Return the papers to your students, and direct their attention to specific test items as you explain each strategy. Demonstrate how you would perform each strategy. Point out the questions you think most difficult and explain that you would mark them and return to them later. As with all teaching, fade out your instruction by reminding students of the strategies before the next several tests and then gradually omitting mention of the strategies as your students become proficient with them.

EVALUATE

How do you feel about our five guidelines for making tests fit students' reading and writing abilities? What parts are you comfortable or uncomfortable with? How would you modify our suggestions to fit your teaching situation?

BUT SOME STUDENTS JUST DON'T CARE

Motivating students is one of the most difficult tasks teachers have. While all humans seem to be born curious and anxious to learn, this curiosity often doesn't last, and some students seem to not care about what we are trying to teach them. Students do care more when their prior knowledge is called up and developed so that they can connect what they already know to what they are reading. Students care more when there are a variety of whole class, small group, and individual learning opportunities. They care more when they know that they can make a satisfactory grade if they put forth their best daily effort. Consider as well the following suggestions:

1. Remember that motivation generally follows success. Think of something you are not successful at. How motivated are you to engage in this activity? If you are not a very good cook or runner or singer, you probably don't engage in these activities very often, and when forced to participate, you are probably not the most enthusiastic participant. In fact, you may even display a "Who cares?" attitude. Now imagine that someone must teach you to do something that you are not good at, such as cooking. The cooking teacher is probably a good and enthusiastic cook. If the good cook is also a good teacher, he or she will turn you into a decent cook and even have you liking cooking better. Some "can't fail" recipes will be tried first, for which you will be given much guidance and encouragement. When you burn something or forget the sugar, your teacher will proclaim, "No one's perfect," and tell a story about a real disaster made by an expert cook when he or she was just learning.

Or, the good cook will be a poor teacher who believes that his or her role is only to provide information and skills; motivation must come from the students. "If they aren't motivated, I can't teach them," this cook might say. This person would soon become discouraged by your lack of enthusiasm, and if you failed to learn to cook, this teacher would blame you and your lack of motivation. Thus if your own students appear unmotivated, we prescribe a steady diet of success, teacher enthusiasm, and an attitude of "no one's perfect." Once students experience some success, they generally decide that schooling isn't so bad. Once they start to like school, they will care more and learn more.

CALL UP
Can you remember a time when you were forced into a group activity, such as a singalong, a game of softball, or a board game, when you really didn't want to join in? Did you go home afterwards amazed that you had a good time?

---

2. Every-pupil-response activities get everyone involved. Sometimes we aren't motivated because we refuse to get involved. If we are forced to get involved, we may find ourselves getting caught up in the activity.

Every-pupil-response activities involve everyone. Imagine that you are teaching a group of first-graders a lesson on living and nonliving things. You have taught the differences; now you want to show some pictures so they can decide whether each picture represents a living or nonliving thing. You could simply call on volunteers. But then only one child at a time would be responding, with many children uninvolved and not attending. To make this an activity in which all are involved, have each draw a picture of himself or herself on one side of a piece of drawing paper and a picture of a book on the other side. Then as you display each of your pictures, say "Ready, set, show," and have the children show the picture of themselves if they believe the object is living (like them), the picture of their book if they believe the object is nonliving (like the book). Teachers of young children often use yes/no cards for such activities. Another variation is the smile/frown activity. The teacher says, "I am going to try to name living things. If I do name a living thing, smile at me. But if I make a mistake and name a nonliving thing, frown at me!"

For older students, writing is the obvious every-pupil-response activity. Imagine that you want to review the major aspects of communicable diseases. You could ask, "Who remembers something we learned about communicable diseases?" You would probably get some hands, but most teachers complain that the same hands are always raised. Do the ones whose hands aren't raised not know or simply not care to participate? *Three To a Customer* is a review activity that gets everyone involved. The teacher asks everyone to take out a sheet of scrap paper and write down three things they remember about communicable diseases. After giving students about two minutes to do so, go around the room having each student tell one of the things written down. If, all of a student's items have been mentioned, that student simply says, "Pass." When there are several passes in a row, ask if anyone has something written down that hasn't been mentioned yet. Students like having something no one else thought of. You might then collect the papers and assign points for good effort.

Many other formats for such written every-pupil-response activities are possible. To call up prior knowledge about Shakespeare, you might give students three minutes to write down as many of his plays or characters as they can. Before introducing some new geometric shapes, you might write the names of the shapes on the board and let the students see how many of the shapes they can draw. Be a mind reader, as described in Chapter 3, requires every student to think and respond.

Be sure to acknowledge the right answers in these activities, rather than focusing on the wrong answers. Say, "Good, most of you are frowning because a table is not a living thing" and let students share the answers they wrote down that they think are right. If a student does volunteer a wrong answer, indicate that the answer was not right but was a "good try." ("*Our Town* is a play, but Shakespeare didn't write it." "That's close, but a trapezoid has to have two parallel sides and two nonparallel sides.") Every-pupil-response activities help students form the habit of thinking and participating. And once they begin participating, they might become more interested in class.

3. Prediction improves participation and motivation. To test this assertion, take a sheet of scratch paper and number it from one to five. Write *yes* or *no* to indicate whether each of these statements is true or false.

1. Babe Ruth was an orphan.
2. Babe Ruth was a good kid.
3. Babe Ruth was left-handed.
4. Babe Ruth was over six feet tall.
5. Babe Ruth was a New York Yankee.

Many of you are sure about some of the statements and unsure about others. If you actually committed yourself to some guesses about Babe Ruth, you would be anxious to find out how you did. This desire to find out how you did is one of the main reasons why prediction is motivational. When you make a prediction, you have invested something of yourself in the activity. You have something at stake in the reading assignment—if only to see how you did.

The other motivational factor in prediction is that you find out what you don't know. It is a strange but true phenomenon that once we learn something, we think we always knew it. That may be the reason that so many youngsters go home and answer, "Nothing" to the "What did you learn in school today?" question. When you are forced to predict prior to reading, you know what you know and, as importantly, what you don't know.

As to your Babe Ruth guesses, he was not an orphan although he did grow up in an orphanage. He was a bad kid whose mother couldn't control him, so he lived in the orphanage in the same neighborhood as his mother. He was left-handed, short, and a New York Yankee. If you found yourself enjoying our prediction activity in spite of yourself, you have realized the power of prediction.

There are many ways to get students to predict. Chapter 2 described prediction comprehension lessons including forecasting, expectation outline, and possible sentences. Chapter 3's context power helps students determine which words they know meanings for and which they don't. Another simple activity is called *Don't Turn the Page*. Imagine that you are leading the students through some content area material and their attention is wavering. We have just read about Napoleon's conquests. Before going on to the next page, ask students to take a sheet of scratch paper and tell them, "Don't turn the page." Then ask one question that can be answered "Yes" and "No." "If you think Napoleon's army is going to be successful in the next battle, write 'yes' on your scrap paper. If you don't think so, write 'no.' When you have written yes or no, turn the page and read to find out." Don't turn the page is a quick strategy to use whenever you want to reengage students' interest and motivation.

BUT MY STUDENTS JUST WON'T THINK

Students think all the time. Much of that thinking, however, might not be focused on what you want them to think about! In Chapter 1, we defined the essential thinking processes as call up, predict, organize, connect, image, monitor, review, evaluate, and apply. Throughout this book, we have indicated how helping students read and write better is intimately tied to helping them think about the content being presented. Two more ways to help students think are as follows.

PREDICT

How many seconds are students generally given to think between the time a teacher asks a question and the time a student is called on to respond?

   a. one second   b. three seconds   c. five seconds   d. ten seconds

   What did you predict? Research reveals that the average amount of time teachers wait before calling on someone to respond to a question is less than one second. How can a student employ worthwhile thinking processes in such a short time?

   1. Allow students wait time. A strategy you can use to allow wait time is called *You Think, I Count*. Before you ask a question that requires students to think, tell the students that they will not know the answer right away and will have to think about it. Tell students that they should think about their answer as you count five seconds to yourself. Do not allow students to raise their hands or do anything until you have counted out five seconds. Some teachers of young students like to have everyone close his or her eyes while thinking so that distractions are minimized. Once the time has elapsed, let students respond to the question.

   2. Avoid "popcorn" recitation questions. Often after students have read, teachers ask a series of quick questions about the facts to make sure the students have understood the reading. These rapid-fire, low-level questions are termed *popcorn* questions because of the rapidity with which one follows another. These questions, like popcorn, also tend to be lightweight and to go out to students randomly. The comprehension lesson plan outlined in Chapter 2 will help you to structure and guide reading activities that circumvent popcorn questions. The writing activities in Chapter 5 also suggest ways to have students share information without resorting to many quick oral questions.

   If you do want to ask students some checkup questions after reading, have them number a sheet of paper and write the answers to the questions you give. The time that writing takes will slow down the process, and since everyone is answering, all students can be involved in reviewing pertinent facts. Once the answers are written, you can have volunteers share the answers so that all class members can check the accuracy of their recollections.

BUT I DON'T HAVE ENOUGH TIME

No teacher has enough time to do everything he or she wants to do. Therefore, you must set priorities. You set priorities by deciding what information is most important and making sure that you use your in-class time to help students obtain that information. You set priorities by assigning less important material and by skipping relatively unimportant material altogether.

But you have still more decisions to make. How much time each week can you spend in guided lessons that teach content through reading and writing? How much time can you spend increasing student vocabulary? Finally, you must decide which teaching strategies appeal most to you. Teachers, being human, have individual preferences and styles in their teaching as in all other facets of their lives. Some of our teaching strategies for improving reading and writing will seem very "do-able" to you and others will fall into the "I just can't see myself doing that" category. Once you know what content you will stress and how much time you can give to the various literacy goals, choose strategies which particularly appeal to you to reach these goals.

One warning is in order for anyone trying a new teaching strategy: Don't expect great success the first time. It takes a while to get things into a workable routine. That's one reason why the first year of teaching is so hectic. Why, when doing something you have never done before with students who have never done it before, would you expect everything to go smoothly? We recommend the rule of "Three strikes and you're out." Try each strategy three times with the same group of students. During the three trials observe your students' behavior and learning and your own comfort. Then decide if the strategy is one you want to continue. Be aware that some teaching strategies require a higher energy level and more teacher involvement than others. As you decide which strategies to use and how often, consider your own physical and psychological needs. No one can perform on center stage for six hours every day. Try to stagger the teaching strategies that demand high teacher intensity with those that are less demanding. Balance demanding new strategies with more comfortable familiar ones.

Teaching is a lot like cooking. We often get in a rut of fixing the same recipes week after week. Sometimes we continue to fix recipes even when we are tired of eating them. We have other recipes; we may even have a little box of ones to try someday. But new recipes require more preparation as we make the shopping list, more thought as we prepare them, and more risk. We worry, "What if it flops?" "What if everyone hates it?" Trying one new recipe a week is a compromise that doesn't demand too much of the cook but that holds the promise of better meals to come.

REVIEW

This chapter presented some common concerns many teachers have expressed as they began to implement content area reading and writing strategies in their classrooms. Here is a list of the "buts" to which we tried to provide answers. For each one, try to remember the solutions we suggested and try to think of one more possible solution we didn't suggest.

1. But my textbook is too hard.
2. But I must use the book sometimes.
3. But my students don't all read and write at grade level.

4. But they won't work in groups.

5. But they won't do it if it doesn't count for a grade.

6. But some students just don't care.

7. But my students just won't think.

8. But I don't have enough time.

SUGGESTED READINGS

Strategies for organizing and managing classrooms so that effective instruction can take place can be found in the following books:

Charles, C. M. (1984). *Building classroom discipline.* (2nd ed.) New York: Longman.

Duke, D. (1982). *Helping teachers manage classrooms.* Alexandria, VA: Association for Supervision and Curriculum Development.

Kounin, J. (1970). *Discipline and group management in classrooms.* New York: Holt, Rinehart and Winston.

Good, T. & Brophy, J. (1984). *Looking in classrooms.* (3rd ed.) New York: Harper & Row.

Readability formulas have a long history. For more about their use and abuse, read the following articles:

Klare, G. R. (1984). Readability in P. D. Pearson (Ed.) *Handbook of reading research.* New York: Longman, 681–744.

Campbell, A. (1979). How readability formulae fall short in matching student to text in the content areas. *Journal of Reading, 22,* 683–689.

Information on developing students' test-taking skills can be found in the following article:

Stewart, O., & Green, D. J. (1983). Test-taking skills for standardized tests of reading. *The reading teacher, 36,* 634–638.

In the following two articles, the research on think-time and its effect on reading comprehension is reviewed. The articles also describe practical strategies for teachers who want to provide think-time.

Gambrell, L. (1983). The occurrence of think-time during reading comprehension instruction. *Journal of Educational Research, 77,* 77–80.

Gambrell, L. B. (1980). Think-time: Implications for reading instruction. *The Reading Teacher, 34,* 143–146.

The following article identifies outstanding teachers and describes the characteristics that set them apart from other teachers:

Tschudin, R. (1978). A+ teachers set goals that develop student confidence. *Instructor,* 66–74.

. . . IN THE CONTENT AREAS: K–12

Part II of this book illustrates how the principles and methods of instruction described in Part I can actually be implemented in the classroom. The information is presented in the form of a chronological narrative through fictional teachers' journals. This part of the book demonstrates how teachers might integrate the many aspects of reading and writing in the content areas throughout an entire school year. Part I compartmentalized information according to topics, but life in classrooms is not so orderly. Teachers must balance instruction in comprehension, vocabulary, literature, composition, and research within each day and across 180 days of school. Part II provides perspective on how teachers make this balance work.

In the next chapters you will meet four fictional teachers. Dee Klare teaches first grade. She is entrusted with the crucial task of getting youngsters off to a good start. Dee's beginning students have only rudimentary reading and writing skills, and she must launch them on the way to independence. Along the way, she must develop students' understanding of subject matter such as transportation, measurement of time, the five senses, and human wants versus needs. Connie Tent is a fifth-grade teacher. Her students are more sophisticated than Dee's, but they still have much to learn. Connie directs her students to information in the content areas, and likewise furthers the development of her students' independence. Hugh Mann teaches the humanities in secondary school; he is assigned three sections of American history and two sections of sophomore English. Hugh is a second-year teacher who takes a little longer than Dee or Connie to teach as well as he would like. Finally, Annie Mull teaches high school biology and consumer math. She must both deliver information and teach students to acquire information independently. In addition, she balances a process approach with a textbook approach to biology, and must teach students to solve word problems in math.

You may want to read only one of the fictional accounts that follow if you are primarily interested in only one grade level. However, reading all the chapters will provide you with insight into how teachers develop students' thinking processes and literacy skills across the grades. Knowing what students have encountered earlier in school and what they will encounter in the future provides perspective on what they need at the present. Furthermore, instructional strategies for one grade level frequently are applicable at other grade levels.

As you read what follows, we hope you will learn how teachers engage students in meaningful instruction. We hope you will see how instruction builds and changes in one grade level and across grade levels. Perhaps most important, we hope you will evaluate the information presented here and apply what seems most sensible when you teach in your own classroom.

CHAPTER 8

First Grade

August:

Every August I experience the same excitement that I did 23 years ago, when I first began school at the age of five. Edgar, my husband, laughs at me, saying, "Dee, you're as bad as the kids about wanting to get back to school!" I guess I am, but that is a much nicer feeling than the reluctance I see from some other teachers in our school district. I have heard about "teacher burnout," but my own theory is that burnout generally occurs when you are frustrated with your job and no longer feel you are accomplishing anything. Fortunately, I do feel successful, and I am grateful that I can work at something I truly love! Nevertheless, when I come back to school each August to ready my room for September, I have a mixture of feelings: apprehension about who I will be "living with" for the next nine months and excitement about teaching yet another group of youngsters to read and write. There is nothing more satisfying or thrilling than teaching first-graders!

This year I guess I am even more charged up than usual since I just completed my Master's degree a couple of weeks ago, and I signed up to be one of our school's representatives for the school district's writing project! My thesis addressed the effects of using content area subjects to help improve children's reading skills. As a result of my findings, I am convinced that I need to integrate more reading and writing skills with the content of social studies and science in my classroom.

I've been sitting here for the past week, trying out one schedule after another, and it's not as easy as I had anticipated. I think I need to start this year as usual, with set times for science or social studies instruction every day, using textbooks as part of the reading material. If all goes well, I may come up with another plan for later in the year. I have sat here for a week surrounded by pieces of paper with lists of important elements to include in my classroom this year, and the problem has been trying to come up with a workable plan which will include them all.

First of all, there are nine essential thinking processes that I must systematically and frequently include in my lessons: call up, predict, organize, connect, image, monitor, review, evaluate, and apply. By incorporating each of the nine thinking processes on a regular basis, I will not only be teaching the content areas, but I will also be developing skills that students can use in life as well as school.

Most importantly, I am going to emphasize student independence in learn-   **Independence** ing. It really frosts my cookies to have someone I meet for the first time comment that they couldn't tolerate my profession because they wouldn't want to wipe noses and tie shoes all day. (Velcro has put an end to that at any rate!) What an idea people must have of first-grade students! Admittedly, these students cannot do what fifth-graders can, but we teachers can certainly expect that they be responsible for their learning to an ever-increasing degree. In fact, teachers who do not foster independence in learning are condemning their students to a "learning welfare" system that children will find hard to break out of later on. My battle cry for the year will be, "Get those kids off welfare!"

But, I ask myself, how can I meet these glorious goals of mine this year? I suppose the answer will unfold as the year progresses. What follows is my daily schedule, but I reserve the right to alter it should I find it necessary or appealing to do so!

Schedule

8:15–8:35	Attendance, sharing, plan the day
8:35–10:00	Four reading groups
	Learning centers
	Writing
	Independent seatwork—guided practice
10:00–10:15	Morning recess
10:15–10:30	Read to class or do storytelling
10:30–11:15	Three math groups
	Learning centers
	Writing
	Independent seatwork—guided practice
11:15–11:45	Lunch
11:45–12:00	Read to students
	SSR
12:00–12:30	Science lessons—Monday, Wednesday
	Social studies lessons—Tuesday, Thursday
	Writing groups and conferences—Friday
12:30–1:00	Art—Monday
	P.E.—Tuesday, Thursday
	Writing groups and conferences—Wednesday
	Music—Friday
1:00–1:30	Language arts
1:30–2:15	Learning centers
	Independent work time
2:15–2:40	Read to students
	Review the day
	Prepare to leave
2:45	Dismissal

I have designed many independent learning activities for the learning cen- **Learning Centers**
ters, where I will use tapes, picture directions, and color codes to help students know what to do. Students can turn on the tape recorder where I have
recorded directions for certain activities, which frees me from having to explain everything in person. I also make use of rebus pictures, using pictures
of scissors where they are to cut, and so forth. Each center is color-coded so
that students can tell where to go for the different assignments given in their
daily work folder. The math, science, and social studies centers contain materials that will help students learn more about the units of study we'll do this
year. The seven centers I have placed around the perimeter of the room are
a library corner, a language arts center, a math center, a tape and TV center,
an art center, a social studies center, and a science center. Occasionally I will
create an extra center, such as one with cooking utensils for when we have
classroom cooking, or a center with the computer when it is our turn to have
it for a while.

In the morning, students will rotate among teacher-directed group work,
learning centers, writing activities, and practice activities. In the afternoon,
since I won't have reading or math groups then, I can circulate among those
in the centers and those doing seatwork in order to do some over-the-shoul-
der teaching as children need questions answered. Each child's practice activities will include assignments to let everyone practice the skills already
taught in reading group, as well as the concepts introduced in science and
social studies units.

Additionally, I plan to read to the children at least once every day, and I **Literature**
will give them a daily opportunity to read materials of their own choice. The
reading and listening materials will be drawn from the finest of children's story
books as well as from informational books. Such models of clear and interesting writing will demonstrate to my students how to organize their own
writing. Storytelling is another regular feature that I will use frequently to model
oral composition techniques.

I'm so pleased that I got the tables that I asked for, rather than individual
desks. All of my students' work materials will be kept in individual, brightly
colored cardboard boxes stored around the edge of the room, but the tables
will allow a lot more flexibility in grouping students for different activities.

This journal will focus on how I plan to incorporate reading and writing in
the content areas. It certainly cannot represent everything that goes on each
day in a classroom. Well, only a couple of more items to put up on the bulletin
board in the back of the room and then I can call it quits until the children
arrive. Oh! I am getting so excited!

September:

And so September is over. Getting the children used to the routines took
up an enormous amount of time; schooling is not innately understood. A

good part of the month was spent just in helping them learn the appropriate behaviors to use in learning centers and at their seats.

So I could get to know all of them better, our first social studies unit was entitled "All about Me." I participated, too, partly so they would learn who I am, partly so I could model what each step of the project required. Before going into the specifics of the unit, however, I want to record some of what I learned about them from the unit as well as from their school records.

Every year I think I have gotten the most unusual group ever, and this year is no exception. (Can this condition continue forever?) I have *two* sets of twins. Michael and Michelle are both supportive and independent, rather unusual for twins, so I suspect they will have no difficulty being in the same classroom. But I fear that Steven and Stephanie are another story. Stephanie functions at a much lower level than Steven does, and he constantly picks on her for missing questions, turning in sloppy or late work, and not reading as well as he does. I suggested to their parents that they need to be separated, for both their sakes, and the parents would not hear of it! They think that Stephanie needs Steven to challenge her. None of my arguments could convince them otherwise, though they did agree to help try to tone down Steven. Other students who will be a challenge are Kazu and Mariane. Kazu has just come to the United States from Korea and speaks no English. Mariane is somewhat better off since her family came to this country from Brazil last year, though at home they mainly spoke Portuguese until she started kindergarten. I speak some Spanish, and since Portuguese and Spanish are very similar, we manage to communicate. For Kazu, however, I checked a Korean dictionary out of the public library. I've also met with his parents, who speak some English, to learn from them some common phrases I will need such as, "Do you understand?" "How do you say __ in Korean?," and courtesy phrases such as "Please" and "Thank you." Carlos is another student who is not proficient in using English, though he understands much of what is said to him.

Dave and Jim, neighbors and friends from birth, are two students who did not have an easy kindergarten year. They seem not too interested in school except for P. E., recess, and lunch. At the other extreme are those who came to first grade already reading or ready to read. John, David, Pat, and Sharon seem to enjoy everything we do, probably because they understand what is going on and why. I am glad that our school system doesn't provide gifted education for kindergarten and first-grade students since I believe, based on my reading, that there are no special methods or materials for exceptionally bright students. Good classroom instruction should challenge all students to higher levels of functioning and thinking. That is certainly my goal. My other ten students seem "average." They make up the majority of my middle two reading groups, and seem to be moving along well. It's not easy trying to plan lessons for so many levels of students. Even the "average" ones are so diverse that they certainly cannot all be treated alike.

Social Studies Unit

The "All about Me" unit took all of September since we only worked on it on Tuesdays and Thursdays. The unit is the first from our social studies curriculum, building from the individual to families to neighborhoods to the community at large. The focus in the unit is on the uniqueness of each person as well as the many things all of us have in common. Children learned about these two concepts in myriad ways. Many literature books, both old favorites and newer ones, address both concepts. For the whole month we have been reading books like *There's a Nightmare in My Closet, Leo the Late Bloomer, Frederick, I Have a Sister—My Sister is Deaf,* and *The Triplets.* In addition, I brought in concept books such as *A Snake Is Totally Tail, Is It Hard? Is It Easy?,* and *People.* I used those books both for this unit and for our science unit on the five senses—a nice compatible set of units to work on simultaneously. These books point out the similarities among people as well as provide information about those who, due to certain handicaps, must deal with life differently. The children had all expressed curiosity about Sharon's thick glasses, asking how she could see through them since they were unable to. Jakeitha's wheelchair also was a subject of study as students learned how many things she could do as well as they could without the use of her legs.

Literature

The "All about Me" unit was introduced by talking about *alike* and *different.* To start things off, students were asked to call up the names of types of transportation. Though the content seemed way off the topic, I wanted to use items that could be easily classified by children in a variety of ways. The various types, *boats, cars, trucks, trains, planes,* and so on, were listed on a chart. We talked about how all of the things on the chart were alike, with me listing, as students dictated, how the things were alike. Then students were assigned to groups and told to look for pictures or models of the different forms of transportation listed, or of new ones that they discovered. In this scavenger hunt activity, I planned the groups so that each one consisted both of very capable students and of those who needed more guidance. Students were able to use independent seatwork time for this activity on both Tuesday and Wednesday, as well as checking at home for pictures and models on Tuesday and Wednesday nights.

Thinking Processes

Vocabulary

On Thursday, each group brought its pictures and models to school. I used the big bulletin board on the side of the classroom to pin up all the transportation pictures, with the models on a table underneath. I had cut apart all the names of the types of transportation from the chart, and we placed them by the appropriate pictures or models. Then I asked if they could organize or regroup them in any other way. Total silence met this question. But I waited it out. After 10 seconds, Pat said, "Do you mean by how many wheels they have?" We had quite a discussion about wheels and had to turn to several reference sources to settle the debates which arose. I find this a good way to model using references to answer questions that we have. That broke the dam and the students realized that there were many possible ways to group the transportation pictures they had found. Next they grouped all the red pictures and models together, all the green ones, and so on, regardless of the number of wheels. Then they grouped all the forms of transportation by how many peo-ple they could carry—one, a few, or many. A fourth grouping consisted of sort-ing types by where they traveled—air, land, or water.

Social Studies Unit

So that they would apply their new understanding of grouping to our unit of study, I gave a list of each person's name in our class, including mine, to each group and asked them to think of at least two ways of organizing that could show how people are alike and at least two ways to show how they are different. On the following Tuesday they sorted us all into diverse groups by gender, hair color, and so on. They also put Jakeitha, Sharon, Michael, Michelle, and me into a group they labeled "Black people." This activity helped them to organize their world, one of the essential thinking processes.

Content Language Experience

Along with organizing, we worked on writing activities. They each com-piled a book of facts about themselves, as part of my content language ex-perience lessons. They had to draw pictures of their family, home, pets, friends, favorite things to do, and so on. Under each picture, they had to write a sentence telling about the picture. For most of the children, I wrote each dictated sentence, allowing them to copy it beneath their picture. A few, like Pat and David, wrote sentences on their own. For those unable to read or just learning how, I used sentence stems that they could easily remember, like

Stuctured Language Experience

"*This is my* (type of pet)" and "*I like to eat* (type of food)." After each person had completed his or her book, they all had to number each page and write in the numeral on the labeled table of contents page I had given them. They worked on this activity on the Wednesday and Thursday afternoons that I had set aside for writing conferences and groups. Within their small groups, they helped one another to copy over their sentences correctly and to make sure that page numbers were in order and matched the table of contents page.

Interviewing

I also gave the children five questions to go home and ask their parents about, one at a time, over a three-week period. I have found that if you give children several questions at once, they frequently forget both the questions and the answers. However, if I only give one question on each day that we have social studies, students can generally remember to ask the questions. These five questions became the basis for the single paragraphs about each student, which they dictated and which were then placed on the bulletin board along with their pictures. The five questions were as follows: When were you born? What was your parents' favorite thing about you when you were a baby? What did you like to do best when you were little? What was the funniest thing you did when you were little? and, What is the best thing about you now? Each question was turned into a statement using sentence stems

Content Language Experience

again, such as "*I was born . . .*" and "*When I was a baby . . . .*" The compiled statements were then written right after one another to make the paragraph. Only a few of the children could read their completed paragraphs, but they surely tried! And they loved having the paragraphs read to them. I used these paragraphs frequently during reading group time throughout the month since the paragraphs were planned to use much of the same vocabulary I was trying to teach from the basal and since they were intrinsically interesting. Children were using many of the essential thinking processes—calling up, organizing, connecting, imaging, and reviewing—as they dealt with information in this social studies unit, "All about Me."

The science unit on the five senses was also interesting and fun. So many activities can help develop the nine thinking processes! We made charts as the children called up things they could hear. I wrote their responses on chart paper, allowing enough room for them to add illustrations. Another chart was used when I told them that I would be writing down words and they had to find the organization I was using and predict which label would be placed on it. For this activity, I wrote a word, and asked them to predict another word to fit the category I was thinking of. If they guessed correctly, I wrote that word; if not, I said, "That is not an example." No one was to say the name of the category yet; I wanted to get many examples of each category so that nearly all the children would be in a frenzy claiming to know the category. The first word I wrote was "ice cream." The first discarded guess was "candy." The second guess, "ice cube," was added to the list. After several more guesses, both examples and nonexamples, we came up with a list that they all agreed could be labeled, "Things That Can Feel Cold," including: ice cream, ice cube, snow, my dog's nose, rocks, and a glass of milk.

They also made books for this unit: a feeling book of textures, a seeing book of colors, and a hearing book of sounds. For each of these they had to call up possibilities and organize them (for example, putting all loud sounds together). They were constantly connecting what they already knew to new information they were gathering. They then applied that knowledge by creating books. As before, they took some of the group writing time to work on their books and to help one another evaluate how well they had accomplished the assignment. At the end of the month, I used the various books they had made for the science unit as reading material during reading group time. Since sentence stems were again used ("*This is* [a color]"; "*This feels* [a texture]"), even the slowest readers did not have much difficulty reading their own or one another's books: illustrations were there to jog the memory

Science Unit

Thinking Processes

Structured Language Experience

and each book used only one sentence stem over and over. I'm keeping a page from Stephanie's book of sounds, which she proudly took home to read.

Admittedly, many children were not actually reading the words but had memorized the sentence stems and what the pictures were supposed to represent. Nevertheless, for some students like Jim and Dave, this was an opportunity to feel like a reader, an experience they had not had before. The value of this "pretend reading" has been shown to be an important component in the development of children who learn to read early, so I'm just letting some of the other kids catch up.

October:

Word Wall

Many of the children who come to school are able to count to ten or more in a rote fashion. But asking them to connect that knowledge to sentences with numbers in them is quite a leap for many students. Thus, I have made a word wall above the chalkboard just for math. Two other walls contain the list of commonly used and high-interest words that we use for writing. On the number word wall, I have the numerals 1 through 10 right beside the words and pictures of the corresponding number of objects. I have also placed $+$, $-$, $<$, $>$, and $=$ up there with the corresponding definitions of each symbol.

Be A Mind Reader

They love playing "Be a Mind Reader," in which I try to get them to guess the math word or symbol I am thinking of. Following is an excerpted version of one such exercise:

ME: It's on the word wall. Write your guess on the first line.

Ray wrote "$<$."

ME: It's a numeral.

Ray wrote "6."

ME: It's more than 1.

Ray wrote "6" again.

ME: It's less than 6.

Ray wrote "5."

ME: You get this when you add 2 and 3.

Ray excitedly wrote "5" again, waving his hand frantically in the air. He was among a group of three who had correctly read my mind before the final clue! He was proud.

Word Problems

Since each of the three math groups is doing at least some addition by this point, I decided to try yet another way to get them to understand symbols and number words better, as well as to use more writing. I had them convert the number sentences in their math series into small word problems. The first ones were very simple. Again using sentence stems, I gave them a formula for writing number sentences as word problems. For adding, I gave them the following sentences to fill in with numerals of their choice:

Structured Language Experience

I have ＿＿ books. I got ＿＿ more.
Now I have ＿＿ books.

For subtraction, they have this one:

I had ＿＿ toys. I gave ＿＿ away.
Now I have ＿＿ toys.

Dave and Jim wanted me to exchange the nouns in the two problems; they would rather give away books than toys!

John, Pat, David, and others were able to substitute their own nouns in the sentence stems as well as inserting the numbers. They enjoy coming up with unusual items to add and subtract, challenging one another to further heights of ridiculousness, especially in this month of ghoulish happenings! Here is one of David's that made the rounds to great appreciation, invented spellings and all:

I have three vanshing vampiers. I got three more.
Now I have six vanshing vampiers. But how can I have six if they keep vanshing?

The children are in three different math groups, so the reading level of most of their word problems pretty well matches their three reading group levels—though not completely. Kazu and Mariane, who are in lower reading groups due to their lack of English, have remarkable math skills and are way beyond the rest of the class in understanding concepts and performing computations. They need help with learning the English labels for the concepts they know. Therefore, they are in my top math group and doing well there. Twice a week, all the children bring to their math group a word problem that they have created. These are exchanged and as a part of their independent seat work, the children must write each word problem as a number sentence and draw an illustration to demonstrate the word problem using sets. They may go to the person who did the original word problem in order to discover what certain words mean. This is especially important for the children who cannot yet read more than a few words. They are allowed to use pictures in place of the words in their problems. Kazu, who understood David's word problem, was fascinated with the notion of vampires, even though David himself has only a fuzzy idea of what vampires are. This top math group has moved into creating three word problems a week. At this point, they leave out the answer, so that the one who has to solve the problem must figure it out. They love doing this. I often find them in the math center setting up problems for one another, using numbers way beyond what they are required to know. My middle math group has just begun to leave out the answers of their two word problems; most are enjoying the challenge not only of setting up the problem as a number sentence, but also of solving for the problem. I feel really good about how much children are monitoring, evaluating, and applying when they do these exercises.

Word Problems

Social Studies Unit

In order to help the children understand their role in their families, our social studies unit pursued several different activities this month. First we had to discuss the definition of a family. Since there are so many families today which do not fit the traditional two-parent structure, we defined "family" as a group of related or unrelated people who live together because they care about one another and who try to help one another in a variety of ways. Families could consist of any number of adults and children. Each child then drew a picture of his or her family and wrote a few sentences telling how they showed their care for one another.

Again children were sent home with questions to ask about their particular family. The questions were as follows: How many people live with us and who are they? What jobs do the adults in the family do? What jobs do I do at home? Have I always lived in this town? If not, where else have I lived? What is the most interesting thing about our family? The questions were writ-

Organizing Information

ten along the top of a sheet of butcher paper with children's names written down the side, creating a big data chart.

Using the data chart entries, children dictated or wrote paragraphs about themselves and their families. No names were written on the paragraphs, and I read them aloud to the whole class during social studies time as we sat in front of the data chart, trying to predict with each new sentence who the person could be. They loved the puzzle aspect of this listening comprehension lesson, which allowed them to review the questions asked and connect the answers with a name. Here is the paragraph dictated by Dave:

> Me and my dad, we live together. Dad, he drives a bus for the city. I have lots of stuff to do at home like take out the garbage and wash the dishes sometimes and dust the tables and stuff and help my dad wash clothes at the laundromat. I have always lived in this apartment even before my mom died. The most interesting thing about me and my dad is that we are going to win the lottery and go to Hawaii on a vacation for two weeks!

Independence

A lot of the primary grade teachers I have worked with through the years are afraid to let children write for fear they will practice spelling words incorrectly and will not form the letters correctly. All of my reading about the relationship between reading and writing indicates that far more harm is done by not allowing children the opportunity to write regularly. Children who use invented spellings become proficient written language users, learning to write in a similar way to that in which they learned to speak. I will continue to include many opportunities for children to experiment with written language, knowing that we can deal with spelling later.

Science Unit

This month's science unit dealt with the calendar. How many hours in a day, days in a week, weeks in a month, days in a month, months in a year, and days in a year? Talk about some tough concepts! We do our daily calendar during the opening exercises each day. You know, the "Today is Monday. It is sunny" type of activity. A child, with help where needed, names the month, the day, and the year. Whenever a new month begins, together we count how many days there are in it, and count other items like how many Mondays there are or how many birthdays there are in the month. Nevertheless, the concept of "what is a week" is still tough to communicate. To them, a week is five days; weekends don't count since there is no school! I've saved all the calendars for the current year from Edgar's bakery business, plus the ones the banks give away, and others I came across—it doesn't matter one whit that most of the months have been gone for some time now. The children dismantled the calendars and then organized the pages by putting all the Januarys together, and so on. After the pages were all grouped by the twelve months, I assigned two children per month and told them to figure out how all the Januarys, Februarys, et cetera, were the same. They discovered to their delight that regardless of the picture on the calendar, all the Januarys had 31 days listed, the first day of every January began on the same day of the week, and the last day of January ended on the same day of the week in every calendar.

Vocabulary

The months were then grouped by cold ones and hot ones, fitting some, like October and April, in between. We also spent some time talking about events during the past year, birthdays, Christmas and Hanukkah, Thanksgiving, Fourth of July, and so on. What kind of weather were we having then? Did the event happen long ago or not so long ago? The relativity of some of these terms only added to their confusion. When they said Christmas happened during a cold time, we went to the cold months group and found December. They always had trouble with the idea that all months don't have the same number of days. They'll begin to understand that concept a little better when they learn to divide 365 by 12! Their other concern was why all months don't start on Sunday (or Monday, if they still think of five-day weeks), but they are slowly beginning to understand. We made a continuous calendar for the bulletin board that shows the first day of each new month right beside the last day of the old one. So they are beginning to realize that each month is connected to the one before it.

Organizing Information

To help them understand days in the week better, I had them all keep journals for the month. During the school week, they wrote in their journals here, but each child took two pages home to write in over the weekend. I had dittoed off the journal pages, so that each one had the date already on it; all they had to do was fill in the day of the week and then write at least one sentence about something that happened to them, or that they saw, or about the weather. Naturally, Dave, Jim, and Ray consistently forgot their journals over the weekend and also forgot to bring back the sheets of paper on Mondays! I gave them extra sheets I had made, so that they could make up something for Saturday and Sunday during their Monday work time. At the end of

Content Journals

the month, we stapled all the sheets together with a cover for each identifying it as the October journal. I know that many parents will prize these short anecdotes in years to come. And I do believe they are gaining some sense of what a week is compared to a month. Journal writing has been highly touted in this writing workshop I've been attending and does seem to work for kids.

November:

Independence

Despite the onslaught of the holiday season, which really begins right after Halloween, it has been a great month. The children are fairly well set in our routines now, so that they know what they are to do and when, and more important, why. I make it a point to explain how the worksheets and learning center materials will help them to learn. I have found it is worth it to take that little bit of extra time to help children understand why they are doing something.

SSR

On my schedule of sustained silent reading (SSR) and read-aloud time, I am now taking 10 minutes for reading aloud, with the children up to 5 minutes of reading or examining books quietly on their own. I have found that since few of them are actually reading during this time, many students need two books to "read" during SSR. They spend their time looking at the pictures and even matching some words they know with ones found in the books. "Sustained silent reading" is probably a misnomer with first graders, since there is a low roar of "mumble reading" going on. Very young children find it nearly impossible to read silently, as do immature older readers and readers of materials too difficult for them. That's all right, at least everyone is engaged with books, even Jim and Dave!

Social Studies Unit

Holidays are big events to children, associated as they are with changes in routines, presents, special happenings, and clothing. Therefore, as an ongoing mini-unit in social studies this year, we are studying the various holidays associated with each month. Some months are chock full of holidays, while others are sparse. I have had to do some digging to come up with interesting holidays to study. However, October, November, and December are all full months. As part of our study of Thanksgiving, I brought in cookbooks like

Literature

The Taming of the C.A.N.D.Y Monster, *Kids Are Natural Cooks*, and *Kids in the Kitchen*. From these I adapted recipes to an easier form for children to follow, putting each recipe on a big sheet of chart paper back in the cooking center, so that we could do some classroom cooking for the dinner we shared with the kindergarten class. Even Kazu and Mariane were thrilled, although Thanksgiving wasn't a holiday they had heard of before. Six groups each prepared a different food for the feast: cranberry relish, pumpkin muffins, turkey soup, popcorn, salad, and a fruit juice punch.

Research

Using the cookbooks provided a real reading experience. To help them connect even more, we looked up information about all the foods in a variety of reference books, so that while we ate, each group told where its food came from and how it was prepared. I met with each group during social studies time to read them a little more about their foods, and they compiled a data chart of the information. The popcorn group told us about the Indians introducing the Pilgrims to popcorn and how kernels of corn were thrown around the edge of the fire rather than being cooked in a pot as we do now. They even told how people have gotten salt by collecting it from the sea or from natural salt deposits. **Reports**

It made sense, therefore, to tie in the measurement unit from the math series with all the cooking activities. What better way to learn what a cup is than by having to measure out a cup of something for a recipe? That's really developing meaning vocabulary with "the real thing." I had the kids do a "water run-through" of their recipe before they tried it with the real ingredients. If a cup of flour was called for, they had to measure out and add 1 cup of water to the bowl. Cleanup was pretty easy, and the children got some idea of how much they could expect to have in their bowls when working with the real thing. Each cooking group had children from each of the three math groups so that I knew I had some very capable people in each group on whom I could count. Each group practiced its recipe three times with water run-throughs, so the days of the actual cooking went smoothly. My friends are always amazed at what children can create with an electric skillet and a crock-pot! As for the thinking processes, the children certainly had ample opportunity to review the information they were learning, and to evaluate and apply their knowledge. **Direct Experience**

Before beginning the social studies unit on neighborhoods, I had the children call up their experiences with people, buildings, and activities in their neighborhoods. I then had them predict what they thought we would be learning about in our unit. We made a big chart with their predictions of the most important people, buildings, and activities they thought would be included. They also predicted concepts we might learn, such as, "People help one another," which were likewise put on another chart. As the month went on, they found that they needed to add additional words and concepts to the charts. **Social Studies Unit** / **Organizing Information**

The sources of information we used included interviews with community helpers, films, speakers, and field trips, all liberally supplemented with books that I read to them which they located on their own. For "homework," they were encouraged to check out a book from our classroom collection—pulled together just for this unit—and take it home for someone to read to them. We put together feature matrices of the people, buildings, and neighborhood activities about which they were learning. Based on those feature matrices, they dictated content language experience passages, which formed the basis for the review materials at the end of the unit. Some children are already quite good at monitoring what more needs to be located. Pat looked at the feature matrix of neighborhood buildings and noticed that we had left out houses! Here is the feature matrix done on people in the neighborhood, and the content language experience passage dictated from it: **Locating Information** / **Organizing Information** / **Content Language Experience**

People in Our Neighborhood

	Wears uniform	Works with people	Works for people	Have to have
Police officer	X	X		X
Fire fighter	X	X		X
Grocer			X	X
Mail carrier	X		X	
Medical helpers	X	X		X
Utility workers			X	X
Gas attendant			X	

People in Our Neighborhood

There are many people who help us in our neighborhood. Some do jobs we couldn't do by ourselves. We need police officers and fire fighters and medical helpers because they do jobs that we don't know how to do. We need grocers and utility workers because they bring us stuff we couldn't get if they didn't help us. We could get our own mail or pump gas into the car if we had to.

Some helpers wear uniforms like police officers, fire fighters, mail carriers, and medical helpers. That way you can tell real easy who they are when you need help. Some people just wear their own clothes to their jobs.

Police officers, fire fighters, and medical helpers help save people. But some helpers just do jobs for us, like grocers, mail carriers, utility workers, and gas attendants.

We need all of our community helpers because each one does a special job. That makes everybody's life easier because we don't all have to do everything.

Content Journals

The neighborhood unit has been quite a busy one, but I think the children now have a much clearer idea about who provides services and goods for them. And, of course, by writing or dictating so frequently about the different aspects of the unit, their composition abilities have been improving. In their journals this month, I had them each choose several community helpers, services, and buildings to draw pictures of and write about. I could even make out some of the words in Ray's invented spellings this time!

FIR FITRZ R GD B KAZ THAY HEP PEPL HO IS BRN UP I LIK TO LV WITH THM AND GO DON TAT BG PO

(Fire fighters are good because they help people who is burned up. I like to live with them and go down that big pole.)

December:

I, for one, am glad to have this break time. Not only do I plan to use my time on holiday and family obligations (my poor little girl, Vera, has hardly seen me this month), but I also find this an excellent time to regroup and plan for the next part of the year. I know that not even half the school year is over, but in first grade it seems that more than half the year has been covered by the time January rolls around. The children have come so far since September, reading and writing so many different things now.

The children have been doing some very elementary kinds of word processing on the microcomputer. Every six weeks, we have the school computer and printer in our room for a week. Knowing that this is not enough for my purposes, I brought my own small one to school for a couple of days a week as well. Up until now the children have mostly just worked on keyboarding skills with cardboard templates and the computer keyboard, and have played with some of the software designed to teach beginning programming skills. This time, however, I introduced using the computer for revising writing. What a hit! Even Jim and Dave wrote more than they usually do and begged to write more! Children love to see their revised copy emerge tidily from the printer with very little effort. I'll bet I have trouble getting them to go back to revising on paper after this. **Revising**

The continuing unit on holidays was very big with the children, of course, especially as they learned about how Christmas is celebrated around the world. They found it fascinating, if a bit disconcerting, that La Befana the witch (Italy) and little elves (Norway) deliver holiday presents in other countries. We also looked at Hanukkah and celebrations associated with the winter solstice. One strategy I have used somewhat successfully with this unit is take two. For each of the countries for which we studied the Christmas customs, I pulled four true statements from the passage I was going to read to the children. Here are the ones I selected from the passage on Italy: **Social Studies Unit** **Take Two**

1. Italian children have gifts brought by the witch, La Befana.
2. Italian people eat eels for their Christmas feast.
3. La Befana was a witch who was too busy cleaning her house to go see the baby Jesus with the Three Wise Men.
4. Italian children open their gifts on January 6, the Feast of the Epiphany.

Two were main ideas from the passage and two were details. I read the four statements to the children in advance, pointing to the words of each numbered statement on the chart I had prepared earlier. I told them that all the statements were true, and that they were to listen as I read to determine which two were most important. After I read the passage, I asked each student to write down the numerals of the two true statements that contained the most important information. They love the secrecy of revealing their answers this way. All guesses were collected, and a group composed of Ray, Mariane, Sharon, and Dave compiled a tally for each of the four statements.

Not surprisingly, the first time I tried take two, each of the four true statements got nearly equal votes. It was very clear to me that children who are only used to telling true and false are not able to detect what is the most important information. Luckily, the two main idea statements did receive a couple more votes than did the detail statements, so I built on that and helped students who had chosen the two main idea statements to explain why those two were most important. They are not very good at articulating reasons yet, so I can understand why some of my colleagues don't want to try higher-order thinking activities with young children. I still believe it's worthwhile, however. I tried to help children see that details occur just once in the text, whereas most important ideas are mentioned more than once. Also, details help give more information about important ideas. I used a web to show how we might organize information in the section read to them. Slowly, as the month went on, and as we worked through the countries' holiday celebrations, most of the children began to see what was meant by "most important" information. They were getting so good by the seventh country, that I introduced a twist on take two. After reading the four true statements to them, they predicted which two would be the most important. They listened to confirm or alter their guesses. I took a show of hands for the first guess, and wrote the numeral beside each statement. The second guess was done in writing as before.

Science Unit

Organizing Information

Vocabulary

The science unit we worked on was solids, liquids, and gases. I began the unit by starting a big content web on the back bulletin board. In the center of the web were the words, "Forms of Things." Radiating out from the center were the terms "solids," "liquids," and "gases." We met back by the bulletin board and they started calling up "things." I wrote each of their contributions on separate cards to use later in a closed word sort, similar to what we had done with transportation earlier in the year. Of course, they at first named objects which were solids. I then started probing to get them to name liquids, asking what were some things they could drink, where did they play in summer, and how did they clean themselves. Then we used a word sort to separate all the items into like groups. As I showed them how to separate the cards into groups, I asked them to think how all the objects under each label were alike so that we could start to develop tentative definitions for solids, liquids, and gases. Not a single gas had been offered, so only liquids and solids had listings. With all the examples in front of them, we came up with some tentative definitions for solids and liquids. First they said you could feel both, so I wrote that on a card beside each label. Then they told me that solids stayed in a certain shape and liquids were the shape of the container they were in. Those two definitions were written on the board. Good start! After listening to books and watching films with information about solids, liquids, and gases, they should have even more to add to the chart!

It became immediately apparent that "gases" had no items listed under it. Jim suggested that we write "gas" on a card and place it underneath the term "gases." Others said we couldn't do that because gas is a liquid. I must say, I ended the lesson with all of the children in a state of cognitive confusion! I gave them some homework to do. They were to talk with their parents, siblings, friends, bus driver, anyone to see if they could come to school with the name of at least one gas to add to the bulletin board.

Several children remembered to do this and came in with the name of a gas. Other children looked in the science textbooks for help. The problem with this unit is that the gaseous state children are most familiar with, air, is composed of several gases. I wrote the names of several gases, such as hydrogen, oxygen, and helium on the web. We talked about ways gases were used in everyday life, such as in oxygen masks and balloons filled with helium. Even though the children will not be expected to know the names of these gases, they are fascinated by having such big words in their room!

I decided to use cause/effect to help them see some relationships among the three forms of matter. For example, I asked them to listen as I read a section of a book to find out, "Why does a balloon have a shape if air (a gas) has no shape of its own?" and "What happens when an ice cube is left in a glass on the window sill?" Then they were ready to try some experiments on their own.

Cause/Effect

As we talked about each experiment, I made a content language experience chart for each, labeled with the number of the experiment we were performing. For the first experiment, I brought balloons to school. Here is what the chart looked like:

Content Language Experience

Air Is Something—Experiment One

Mrs. Klare gave us balloons (Dave).

Nothing was in the balloons at first because we checked and they were flat (Pat).

Mrs. Klare let us each blow up our balloon (Steven).

It didn't look like anything was in our balloons but they got big so something must have been inside and it was air! (David).

Mrs. Klare chewed an onion and then blew up a balloon (Michelle).

She make balloon go boom (Mariane).

We smelled what came out of the balloon and it smelled like onions. Yuk! (Jim).

Other experiments and charts were made to demonstrate changing solids to liquids (by melting hard candy in the electric skillet) and turning liquids into solids by freezing or cooking. Evaporation was shown by putting ice cubes into the skillet and boiling them into nonexistence. Cause/effect statements were easily generated with all these experiments. For example, "Why did the solid suckers become liquid?" and "What happens when ice cubes are boiled?"

Direct Experience

It's been quite a month! I, for one, am ready for R & R.

January:

I have always enjoyed January so much because the children and I are both glad to be back to school and into a routine again. January is one of our more exciting months because I do try to provide many types of interesting activ-

Content Journals

ities. By the end of this month, I found it hard to believe that children were writing so much or so well in their journals. I guess it makes sense that if they regularly write and get reactions to their writing, their composition skills will improve. The children have been writing twice a week about the science unit on animals, which will continue through February. Here are excerpts from several journals:

"We lerned that ther are meny kind of animuls. Some animuls have hare and some have fethers. Some have skals. Somtims babies are born from ther mommys and somtims they hatch from eggz" (Pat).

"All stuf is liveing or non-liveing. And anmals is part of the liveing ones. Anmals are liveing becus thay ned food and watr and ar and thay have babys" (Steven).

"aminls have baby amnls thay ned eet and dink wotr" (Dave).

Clearly, the children have been learning about many new ideas. It is also clear that they do not always take advantage of the word wall while they are writing in their journals. That is fine with me. Journals are a chance to get their ideas down. We can always work on editing the sentences when they turn entries from their journals into oral or written reports. So when I write a note by each journal entry, I only react to how accurate the information is, and I raise points which help elaborate their information: "Name some animals who are like this." "Why do animals need to eat and drink?" and "I

Revising

would like to know more about ——." Such querying causes them to think further about their entries. Occasionally I encourage them to rewrite entries to incorporate the points I have suggested. The longer entries that result are *usually* more accurate!

I used to have children make booklets to go along with the units we were studying. But to do the booklets, I either wrote sentences on the board for them to copy or asked them to tell me some things to write about and then again had each child copy what I had written. I am happier with the journals since each child is challenged to write at least two sentences per entry—and some write a whole page!—so that I can see clearly how well each is able to apply what they have been learning rather than how well they can copy my ideas. Content journals require students to call up, organize, connect, image, monitor, review, evaluate, and apply. Not too bad for one little old strategy!

Peer Response

I also put the students into heterogeneous groups every week or so and have them share what they have written in their journals with one another. I find that they all go away from those writing groups with more ideas to write about and with ideas, too, of ways to make their own entries better. As in all peer response groups, group members ask each other questions to elicit more information that will clarify the ideas stated. Some of the children have started keeping a journal for social studies, too. As you might guess, these are the children for whom writing is easier and more satisfying: Pat, David, Sharon, and John. Kazu and Mariane are also keeping their own journal for social studies so that they can improve their English language skills. Periodically they show me what they are writing and I react to it just as I do to the science journals. I wonder if I should ask all of the students to write about social studies, too? I need to think about that one for a little while.

Each time the students form themselves into peer groups, it gets a little bit easier; they are really beginning to know what to do and how to do it. I am well on the way to my goal of independence with this kind of organization for writing.

Independence

I introduced the one-paragraph report to the kids this month, too. Each report begins with a topic sentence, explained to the children as the one sentence that tells the most important information, followed by supporting details. After all our experiences before the holiday break with take two, the children finally understand what I mean by "most important." We once constructed reports after viewing a film for our social studies unit, "Needs and Wants." I used a version of focus to set the purpose, instructing the students to watch and listen to remember everything. After the film, children went to their heterogeneous groups (organized so that each group would have students who could model good thinking and language) and listed all they could remember. Then they sorted the statements into main ideas and supporting details. That way, they could select one main idea as their topic sentence for the one-paragraph essay, and could pick out several supporting details as well.

Reports

Comprehension Lesson

All groups then watched the film again to check the accuracy of their information. They made changes in their reports in their peer group sessions. Each group came out with a written report done on chart paper that was hung in the room, each group member's name listed on the paper. Children feel such pride in being part of a successful effort! Even though at this point Jim, Dave, and Ray would be unable to produce such a report independently, they can each be part of their various groups to complete the task.

Reports

To introduce the unit on wants and needs, I listed the two terms on separate pieces of chart paper and asked the students to talk about things they wanted and things they needed. We came up with an enormous number of frivolous and necessary items! For them, it seems that wanting and needing are the same thing. We talked about the difference between the two terms through a remember when activity in which I recalled things I needed as a child, how they were obtained, and why they were necessary. I then did a remember when with wants I had had as a child. After I was done (and did they listen attentively—children love to learn more about their teacher's personal life!), I asked them to tell me the difference between "want" and "need." Then they word-gathered wants and needs to put on the two charts. Sometimes we had to talk through where a word or phrase belonged because a child would insist it was both a want and a need. For example, Ray said pizza was both a want and a need. After discussion, it was decided that pizza belonged to the general category, "food." So we made a heading that included many kinds of food for the need list. Chocolate cake went on the want list, since you could get along without that kind of nourishment (couldn't you?). Toys all went over to the want list. It took a couple of sessions to get everything down

Remember When

Vocabulary

they wanted to list, but with my gentle guidance, we had examples of needs in each of the three categories: food, clothing, and shelter.

I have been feeling so tired lately that I am having a hard time keeping up with all that's going on here! I must need to up my vitamin intake.

February:

The wants and needs unit continued in social studies, as animals continued in science. I made one new addition: all the students now keep content journals for social studies, too. I have continued the holidays unit, which really picked up this month of presidents' birthdays and Valentine's Day.

Organizing Information

At the end of the month, the children constructed a web for animals that we placed on the back bulletin board. It was a great way to call up, organize, connect, image, and review information. I've put a sketch of it in my book so I'll remember it for future years.

Reports

To apply what they had learned about animals in an art activity, each student was to take one of the seven groups we had studied and create a new animal with the characteristics of that group. Dr. Seuss has definitely had an influence on these kids; they were undaunted by either the creation or the naming of their critters. They all had to write short descriptions of what their animal looked like (hair, scales, feathers, etc.), how its young were born, and what it ate. They used the data charts we had made for each of the seven animal groups as their source of information. All animals were put on display in the form of pictures, clay models, papier mâché, and so on, with cards that each child had written describing the animal. We invited the principal, our upper-grade student helpers, and the parents in for a tour of this unusual zoo.

Vocabulary

Our major review activity for wants and needs consisted of review sentences that students constructed from the key words I had listed on the word wall throughout the unit. Since I now put reading, science, math, and social studies words on the same word wall, I find that it helps to use color coding. All the green words are for science, yellow is math, red is reading, and blue ones for social studies. To write review sentences for social studies, students first had to locate all the blue cards on the word wall. For some, that was a task in itself.

In small groups—heterogeneous, of course—the children listed each word on small pieces of paper. With all the words in front of them, they were told to think of two sentences about what we had been learning, using at least two of the words in each sentence. After each group had had a chance to give one of their sentences, I asked if any other sentences had been developed that were not already listed. As they were given to me, I wrote the sentences and then circled the two words from the word wall. In this way, they could see which words had not yet been used, and constructed additional sentences using quite a few of the leftover words! Here is their final review sentences chart on needs:

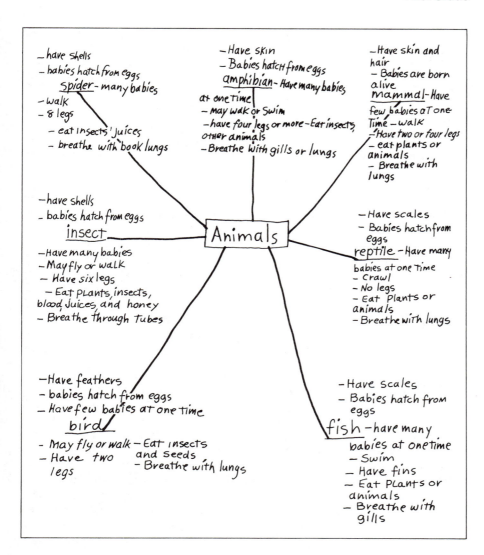

What We Need

We need and want many things (Stephanie).

We need clean air and water or we would get sick and die (David).

We need food so we don't starve (Jim).

We need clothing, shelter, and warmth so we don't get too cold and die (Jakeitha).

We need love and safety because people need more than just stuff to keep from dying because we need to not get hurt and to feel good about ourselves (Pat).

Needs take care of how you live and how you feel about yourself (Michael).

Math Unit   The children are studying money in math, so the yellow cards on the word wall are the names of the coins and the symbols of dollars and cents. The children have been writing some pretty hard word problems for one another with these new words, asking for some addition and subtraction beyond their required level in the math series (we're up to twelves in the middle group right now). What astounds me is that children who seemingly cannot add or subtract above ten, can in fact make change and therefore can do difficult addition and subtraction when money is involved. Children today seem to have more money and to have handled it earlier than my generation did! I helped Jim to see that what he was able to do with making change from a quarter was harder than what he was having trouble with in math. He couldn't believe it! All those numerals were related to money? He has really gained confidence in his math ability as a result of this little insight. He now makes all of his addition and subtraction problems deal with money and then it seems to make sense to him.

Well, I had my own little insight at the beginning of this month about the reasons for my increasing fatigue, and the doctor confirmed it. Long about July, Vera is going to have a new little brother or sister! Just wait until I tell the children!

March:

Near the end of the month, Kazu asked me if I was getting fatter! I thought it was a good time to break the news to the children, since I will only get fatter and fatter and I would rather they know why. They immediately wanted to pull out the webs and data charts we had put together for animals so that they could see where I fit. They had apparently forgotten that people are mammals, et cetera, et cetera. I pulled the charts out and we all gathered around them on the floor to see if I met the characteristics. The children were fascinated. What did it really mean that the baby would be born alive? Was the baby alive now? They seemed to be in more of a mood for the animal unit now than when we originally did it.

Science Unit   In response to their questions, I sent a note home to parents explaining my situation and the children's questions. Would they mind if I tastefully presented some basic information about how babies are created and develop? Some parents did object, of course, as is their right, and I arranged for those **Literature**   children to engage in an art activity out of the room while I shared *How Babies Are Made* and other books dealing with beginning sex education concepts. The children were fascinated and wanted to know if the same held true for other animals. Therefore, this month has included a review of the growth and development of baby animals in each of the seven categories. All of the children in the class found the information—presented in greater depth due to their increased questions—to be much more interesting the second time around. It's amazing what motivation does for learning. And I thought I had done a good job with motivation earlier. Just goes to show you!

I am glad that I took the additional time to go back to the animal unit. I think we teachers are probably afraid to do that, since we feel the pressure to continue marching through all the assigned units. But in this case I saw clearly that our review was really time well spent for the students. A bit serendipitous, but isn't that what it's all about—seizing the teachable moment?

Nevertheless, we did finally begin the science unit on plants. The children's **Science Unit** first questions were about how baby plants were made! So that is where we began our data chart. But the children quickly lost interest when they discovered that plant reproduction was not nearly as interesting (to them) as was animal reproduction. The rest of the unit then continued pretty much as I had planned it. We took field trips to the local plant nursery and the grocery store so they could see the real thing. Many of the parents who had begun seedlings **The Real Thing** for their home gardens were willing to contribute seeds for our experiments. **Organizing** Using the outline shown below, which I had first used when introducing an- **Information** imals, I was able to show the children how plants fit into the world around them. This outline is a little different because it shows one big idea broken down into successively smaller parts. The web we did on animals took that one section of the outline and developed it more; the same thing will be done with plants.

If plants are living things, I asked, what do plants need (to use a word from social studies!)? Children called up what they knew of plants and hypothe- **Direct** sized about plant needs. We then constructed a series of experiments as we **Experience**

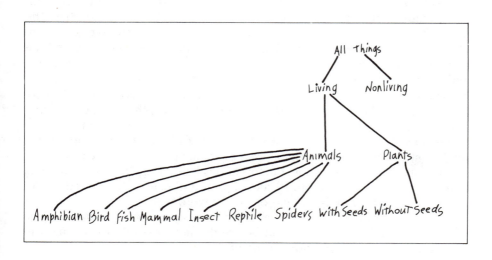

had done with solids, liquids, and gases. Each experiment concerned one of the plant's needs—air, light, water, or food. I had children predict what they thought might happen and listed the predictions on a content language experience chart. Here is the chart for one of the experiments:

Content Language Experience

Experiment #3: Plants Need Water
  Guesses: Both plants will grow if they have air and light.
        One plant will not grow if it doesn't have water.

We put two pots in the window and they both had seeds and dirt and we didn't cover them up (Ray).
I got to be in charge of one pot and I had to give it one tablespoon of water every day (Jim).
I was in charge of one pot and I wasn't allowed to give it any water at all (Michelle).
For long time it did not look like anything going to grow (Kazu).
But, presto bingo! One day we saw something green in Ray's pot and a plant grew and nothing grew in Michelle's pot (Sharon).
This must mean plants need water but how much is a very good question (Steven).

A good question indeed, so we got some seedlings and experimented with the amount of water and discovered that too much water will kill plants as easily as too little. A good lesson for me with my house plants!

Math Unit

Fractions was the math unit of the month as the middle group of children entered into computing with numbers up to fifteen. The top group has finished the book, and I am creating lessons for them based upon the second-grade math curriculum. I'll need to inform next year's teachers of that. The lowest math group is clicking right along with adding and subtracting to ten. They should be able to go through twelve by the end of the year, and the middle group should be finishing with the standard math curriculum of adding and subtracting to eighteen. I am glad that I have pulled out the units on measurement, time, money, and fractions for students to work on all at once. Even if some children cannot add or subtract very well, they may understand fractions, especially with all the cooking activities we have continued to do. "Interrupting the regularly scheduled program to bring them this important unit" is not only motivating but a great pick-me-up, since math can seem to be only number-crunching for students at this level. They love doing the real thing with objects we cut into fractional parts and playing be a mind reader with the fraction symbols and words on the word wall.

The Real Thing
Be A Mind Reader

March has ended and I am feeling a tad more energetic these days. Thank goodness the school year will end before the tiredness returns! It's hard to believe we are on the countdown months!

April:

April has always been one of my favorite months. The world becomes colorful again and the warmth is so welcome. We took some of our plants outside to see what might happen to healthy plants if they weren't kept warm enough. The black leaves on the tomato plants gave some indication, but students were puzzled about how the spinach had survived the same temperatures. That led into some research about when plants can be started outdoors and why. This has been a very interesting unit for the children, calling upon many research and writing skills.

Research

The children wrote twice a week in their science journals about the various experiments we were doing. Some children even proposed additional experiments, which would have impressed the National Science Foundation with their complexity! The emphasis this month has been not so much on plant needs for survival as on the different kinds of plants and the terms "root," "stem," and "leaves." We looked at the functions of these plant parts, and at food plants, sorting them by whether we ate their roots, stems, leaves, or several parts. Children were astounded to discover that we ate the part of the potato that grows underground. I used an old book that still has great information (how much can carrots change, after all?), Zim's *What's Inside of Plants.* I also used a more recent book on different food plants, *Hoe, Hoe, Hoe, Watch My Garden Grow.*

Content Journals

Vocabulary

Literature

At the beginning of the school year I always wonder how I am going to fill up all the wall and bulletin board space in my classroom. By this point in the term I am wishing for more. It seems that every available space is covered with content language experience charts, illustrations, webs, and word sorts. There are also displays of books and magazines for our current units in the appropriate learning centers. Every week during the scheduled library time (though of course children may go to the library at other times as well), we find another piece of information to bring back to the displays. During these weekly trips, I have been modeling how to search for a key word to locate information in the card catalog. The children have also gotten to know the names of some authors fairly well, too. "Oh, here's another book by Dr. Branley," someone may say as they locate another science book. Some of these authors are becoming as familiar to them as are story book authors Sendak, Seuss, Steig, and Mayer.

Literature

We have been taking data charts to the library for a couple of months now, so that when we find out something new, we immediately add it to the chart along with the source. Filling in the data chart at the library has really helped children learn to organize, connect, monitor, and review information. As we fill out the charts, they monitor where we have little or no information so that we can search for more.

Organizing Information

The children have discovered that some questions on the data chart are not as important as others. Thus we strike off some questions and write in substitutes. Students have also discovered that you cannot ask questions that are

Identifying Questions

too specific "Why is it colder at Aunt Ruth's house than it is here?") or too general ("What happens in January?"), as we have spent considerable time at the card catalog unable to find anything out about such questions. Then we talk about broadening or narrowing questions to make them more useful. For instance, we talked about where Aunt Ruth lives, posing such questions as, "Is the weather different in different places?" "What causes the weather to be different in other parts of the country?" "Which parts of the country usually have warm weather and which have a lot of cold weather?" I feel good about their developing research skills.

Social Studies Unit

The social studies unit this month was about rules and why they are necessary. I probably ought to start the year with this unit since discussing the reasons for rules has such an impact on their behavior. We began by talking about rules for different places, which are really sets of expected behaviors that allow all to do what they are supposed to with little interference from others. We had set some room rules together at the beginning of the school year, but they were just leftovers from expected behaviors in other situations. Children really had no idea why they should not talk too loudly in the room.

Direct Experience

To show them the alternative, I bravely (foolishly?) abolished rules for one morning in the room, having warned our principal, Mr. Head, what was coming! Children crowded into the most popular centers and didn't go near others; children talked very loudly and missed being called to math group time; children didn't finish their daily work; children interrupted one another or got up and left groups before they would have normally been allowed to. Dave and Jim thought that this day was wonderful; most of the others, however, did not like being uncertain of what was expected of them and did not like the rudeness of some of the other children. We had a discussion during the next social studies period on the reasons for our rules and on what makes a good rule.

Planning

We broadened this, of course, to playground and bus rules, home rules, and community rules. All the children came out of this experience with a greater appreciation for why societal rules developed. These discussions and brainstorming sessions were a prelude to each child making an oral report

Oral Reports

about a rule. They had to state the rule and explain the reason for it. I find that they can plan such short oral reports by making a few notes on cards so that they are not just reading a written report.

Another busy month ends, and I find myself concerned about the nearness of the end of the school year with tons more left to accomplish! I have this same feeling every year—when will it end?

May:

Parent conferences early this month took up an enormous amount of my time, both for preparation and for the actual conferences. However, both the parents and I gained a lot from the exchange of information. I always prepare the children for the conferences by telling them what I am going to tell their parents. Then I ask them to write down something they would like me to tell their parents that they are doing well. That's yet another way for them to monitor their learning, review what they know, and organize their thoughts.

In math the children were learning to tell time and in science they were studying what caused time to change, so we worked on the two units together. Time is such an abstraction. When you try to explain the passage of time, how the earth rotates around the sun while simultaneously turning on its axis, you are into heavy stuff. We showed how the earth moves (even though we can't feel it) by putting a stick outside and measuring the position and length of the shadow cast over time. This was a great way to apply their previous work with linear measurement to their new study of time. They began to predict what would happen as the day went on, predictions that I wrote on a chart so that they could test their hypotheses. Using the strategy, a picture is worth a thousand words, I chose films as the best way to help them grasp this unit. I also used books such as *What Makes a Shadow?* and *The Day We Saw the Sun Come Up*. We did a lot of one-paragraph essays to break the information into smaller bits for better understanding. Here is Kazu's first-draft paragraph on days:

Math Unit/ Science Unit

A Picture Is Worth A Thousand Words

> A day is 24 hour long. Each day earth go around pretty fast so we have day and night. In 24 hour we have dark and light. Seven day make one week, and many day make a year. That mean earth turn around and around many time and make many day and night time.

A combined social studies and science unit dealt with simple machines and how they make work easier. Children first met as a whole class to talk briefly about the reason for having machines (to make work easier through pushing, pulling, and lifting) and then to hear about six types of simple machines. I had them call up jobs they had seen their parents doing or which they had done themselves. Then I put them into small groups and asked them to go on a scavenger hunt to locate the machines used for each job, or pictures of the machines. When students brought their findings in, we examined each one as best we could to see how simple machines were used to make more complex ones. For some this was easy to see. A crowbar was a lever, a wheelbarrow used wheels, and a pulley was the simple machine on which an elevator was based. However, dishwashers were tough. We asked Steven and Stephanie's father, an appliance repairer, to come in and talk to us about how some machines work. That helped some, but I'm afraid I didn't prepare him well enough about how basic he needed to be. The only thing they really understood was that gears were used. Good enough, I guess.

Combined Social Studies and Science Unit

Scavenger Hunt

We constructed a web on one bulletin board to list the simple machines we were studying: gear, lever, ramp, wheel, pulley, and screw, also showing examples of the tools that used them. We made a picture of each simple machine and outlined where the machine fit into pictures of tools. We also made a feature matrix listing each simple machine on the left and characteristics along the top. As we examined various simple machines, we filled in the feature matrix.

Organizing Information

Content Journals

A Picture Is Worth A Thousand Words

Children wrote in their journals about the simple machines they saw used around them and how they made the work easier. All in all, I think the children are beginning to understand the need for tools and how people's lives have been made easier with the development of tools. I showed a film about Native Americans who had lived in our state long before Europeans came to America. One part of the film dealt with the tools that Native Americans had used. Children were very surprised to find that the Native Americans had not discovered the wheel, since it is such an important part of many tools. They saw how Native Americans' transportation development was limited by this lack. I had them brainstorm what we would not be able to do if the wheel had not been invented. We then did the same for the pulley and the lever. Finally, children wrote descriptions in their journals of life without these machines.

During independent work time, the students had to create a new tool using one or more simple machines. During art, they made a model of this tool from clay or wood. Then they wrote a card describing their tool, listing its name, what it would be used for, and which simple machines it used. Those descriptions were refined during their peer group sessions and we were finally ready to invite guests to examine the products of our learning.

A tough month with such hard concepts to work on. We are now only days away from the end of this school year and I can hardly believe that the time is over.

June:

As I looked back at my first entries about what I had intended to do this year, I was pleasantly surprised at how well I did. I discovered, for one thing, that I had been promoting many of the essential thinking skills with the units I had always taught and the methods I had always used. But I found myself getting rid of some activities that I realized were not helpful for developing the nine thinking skills nor student independence, and substituting in others that were. I guess that setting goals at the beginning of the year alerted me to be aware at all times of the value of each activity I used with the children. Certainly I can see great growth in both their content reading skills and their composition abilities. Requiring them to write about the content areas from the beginning was a new idea for me, and it really worked. I gave up using my language arts textbook about January because the children were so far ahead of the first-grade skills we were expected to cover. Just through regular writing activity and responses from me and their peers, children's writing was more organized and better developed than I had ever seen for young children. Part of this is due, I'm sure, to the fact that they have learned about topic sentences and the need for supporting details. Additionally, the children this year wrote more total words, more different and varied words, and longer, more complex sentences than have my students in previous years.

The children are far more independent in their learning strategies than any group I have ever had. I guess all the modeling with gradual fading to student independence paid off. Not only did I "cover the content," but I think that for the first time, the majority of students learned it, too. There is no doubt in my mind that next year I will include even more strategies to help children learn to think as well as learn facts.

Helping the children organize information was a big part of my lessons, since children at this level need to bring some order to all the random facts they are acquiring. I used many webs, data charts, and one-paragraph essays, and did a lot of modeling followed by guided practice, allowing them to extend their learning with personalized inquiry. What a great year!

And now, off for the summer, which, with July looming, is going to be a pretty busy one for me. Maybe I can work on some more strategy development while I'm in the hospital!

REFERENCES

Andry, A. C., & Schepp, S. (1968). *How babies are made.* New York: Time-Life Books.

Barrett, J. (1983). *A snake is totally tail.* New York: Atheneum.

Bulla, C. R. (1962). *What makes a shadow?* New York: Thomas Y. Crowell.

Edge, N. (1975). *Kids in the kitchen.* Port Angeles, WA: Peninsula Publishing Co.

Daddona, M. (1980). *Hoe, hoe, hoe, watch my garden grow.* Reading, MA: Addison-Wesley.

Green, M. M. (1960). *Is it hard? Is it easy?* New York: Young Scott Books.

Kraus, R. (1971). *Leo the late bloomer.* New York: Windmill Books.

Lansky, V. (1978). *The taming of the C.A.N.D.Y. monster.* Wayzata, MN: Meadowbrook Press.

Lionni, L. (1967). *Frederick.* New York: Pantheon.

Mayer, M. (1968). *There's a nightmare in my closet.* New York: Dial Press.

Parents' Nursery School. (1972). *Kids are natural cooks.* Boston: Houghton Mifflin.

Peterson, J. W. (1977). *I have a sister—my sister is deaf.* New York: Harper & Row.

Shriberg, L. K., & Nicholas, C. (1980). *Kids in the kitchen.* New York: Wanderer Books.

Spier, P. (1979). *People.* New York: Doubleday.

Seuling, B. (1980). *The triplets.* Boston: Houghton Mifflin.

Zim, H. (1952). *What's inside of plants.* New York: William Morrow.

CHAPTER 9
Fifth Grade

August:

Next week the students will arrive and as always I am not ready and anticipate the year with my usual feelings of fear and excitement. Finding out last week that I would be teaching fifth grade rather than fourth was a shock and a disappointment at first. After two years in fourth grade, I was finally getting a good handle on what needed to be taught and I had developed some good units. But when Ruby died so unexpectedly, Mr. Head asked me to move to fifth grade. "Connie," he explained, "Miss Stone was the Rock of Gibralter and we need that kind of experience and stability in fifth grade. I know you are just starting your third year of teaching but you are so stable and creative. I know you can fill the void left by Miss Stone's tragic death." I am not at all sure Connie Tent can even begin to replace Ruby Stone but I am glad Mr. Head has such confidence in me! I will just have to learn some new content and develop some new units. Fifth-grade science content is interesting and I know the kids and I will enjoy learning all about our country, Canada, and Latin America. I have traveled in most of the United States and some of Canada, so I should be able to help make that study real for them. Teaching health will be a problem. There is no curriculum guide to work from and the textbook looks very hard. I will have to figure out how to make that material understandable and exciting when the time comes.

Schedule   I have a schedule and an overall plan for the year which I hope will result in a less choppy day, week, and curriculum. I was bothered both years I taught by the lack of time to study anything in depth and by the fact that we teach people the skills of reading, writing, and computing but never relate these skills to learning about the world. It is so difficult to integrate reading, spelling, language, and math with the other subjects when each uses a separate textbook and an unrelated set of skills. I'm not comfortable just making up a whole skills curriculum and chucking all the texts (although that is tempting!). So, being a typical Libra, I have worked out a schedule that seems a good compromise between the need for systematic skill development and the need to integrate those skills into the content areas. On Mondays, Tuesdays, Wednesdays, and Thursdays, I will teach the separate skills. We will begin each morning with math instruction, during which I will model for the students how to solve problems, guiding their practice in small groups, pairs, or individually at the board. I will then assign them approximately 15 minutes of independent practice that they can complete later in the morning while I work with reading groups. Later in the morning I will teach spelling and language, again modeling, providing guided practice, and assigning independent practice to complete during reading group time. Then I can meet with my three reading groups for 20 minutes each. Although this is a short time, I will have them prepare for the group by doing silent reading and workbook activities, using the group time to teach and provide feedback. We will take our morning break between the second and the third group meeting, which will give me time to see that everyone knows what to do and is proceeding with the morning's assignments. After I meet with the third reading group, I will convene the whole class to follow up on math, spelling, and language arts independent practice. We can check some of the work together and I can see how well they are doing.

I hope this schedule will allow me to solve two problems that I had during my first two years. On the one hand, I never had enough time to teach everything I wanted to; on the other hand, I had to create "meaningful" seatwork to keep students busy while I worked with reading groups. With this new plan, math, spelling, and language arts practice plus silent reading and workbook practice should keep my students busy, and will allow me to shorten the actual instructional time since I won't be waiting for them to complete assignments. Anything students cannot complete in the morning, they can do as homework. That requirement should motivate them to keep working, and it also addresses the fact that children work at different rates and that different assignments require different amounts of time.

We will go to physical education just before lunch. After lunch, the students will have 10 minutes for USSR—Uninterrupted Sustained Silent Reading—in anything they choose to read. I, of course, will read during this time also to provide a good model and to make sure I am not moving around the room distracting my students. Last year the students really came to look forward to this quiet interlude in our day, once they got used to it.

After our ten minutes of silent reading, I will read to them for 10 or 15 minutes. I have read to students both other years and my fourth-graders loved it. I hope my fifth graders will, too. I am going to try to read books that are in a series or whose author has written several other books, because I know that will motivate students to read the other books. I am also going to read some of the good fiction, biographies, and informational books that complement our science, social studies, and health units.

We will then spend 80 to 85 minutes on a science, social studies, or health unit. I have decided to work on one unit at a time for several weeks, using large blocks of time to really focus on what we are learning. Nothing was more disorienting to me and my students last year than trying to do 30 minutes of science, 30 minutes of social studies, and then fit some health in. Just when we were getting into something, I had to say, "Now, put away your science book and take out your social studies book." I think this short time and these quick transitions were the main reasons why the students and I did not get as interested in what we were studying as we could have. Still, I have tried to follow state guidelines about how much time to spend on each subject area. During each nine-week grading period, we will do two two-week science units, one one-week health unit, and one four-week social studies unit. Health is not really getting as much time as it needs but several of the health units can be combined with our science unit on the human body. Then we can spend all day Friday learning about our current unit. Friday will be my integration day!

On Friday, we will not use any textbooks. Rather, we will spend the whole day reading, listening, writing, speaking, and computing problems relating to our unit. We will also do art and whenever possible will relate music and P.E. to what we are studying in science, social studies, or health. I am very excited about this plan. I hope that by taking all day Friday to do content area work, we will be more excited about our units, learn more, and better apply the skills we learn the other four days. Here is my schedule as I hope it will work:

	Monday—Thursday
8:15–8:30	Get morning started
8:30–9:00	Math instruction/guided practice
9:00–9:30	Spelling/language instruction/guided practice
9:30–10:10	Two reading groups with me (20 minutes each) Independent practice as seatwork
10:10–10:25	Morning break
10:25–10:45	Third reading group/independent practice
10:45–11:10	Follow-up independent practice Assign unfinished for homework
11:10–11:40	P.E.
11:40–12:10	Lunch
12:10–12:20	USSR
12:20–12:35	Read to class
12:35–2:00	Science, social studies, or health unit
2:00–2:30	Monday and Thursday—classroom meetings Tuesday—Music Teacher Wednesday—Media Center Instruction
2:45	Dismissal Friday—Integrated Day

Thinking Processes

In addition to my new schedule, I have established some new goals for myself and my students this year. At the top of my list is to help students develop their thinking skills. Of course we will focus on these as we learn the scientific processes of observing, predicting, experimenting, controlling variables, etc. But I also want to help students use their thinking processes as they read and write. To this end, I will try to assure that they are practicing the nine essential thinking processes: call up, predict, organize, connect, image, monitor, review, evaluate, and apply. I have therefore developed a checklist to use each time I teach a comprehension or composing lesson.

Another major goal is to emphasize meaning vocabulary. It is clear to me that the major reason students cannot read, write, or learn in their content subjects is that they lack appropriate meanings to link with the new words they must learn. I am going to have a word wall for each unit and will try to provide real and visual experience from which they can build new meanings. I will also help them connect their experiences to new concepts, using many analogies as I help them develop their own analogies. **Vocabulary**

Helping students to become good writers and researchers is my third major goal. One of the major reasons for devoting Friday to integration is so that we have time to go to the library, locate resources, learn information, organize and report it. You simply can't do this in 30 minutes and I know I was never taught these important skills. I just had to figure them out as I went along. My students will get a better education than that. **Research**

Finally, I am going to work toward making my students independent learners. This will be hard: I tend to want to spoonfeed them information to be sure they all get it. But I know that they won't always have me there to do that. I shudder to think of how much those middle-school teachers will expect them to do and feel an obligation to do everything I can to prepare my students. This goal of independence is one I will work on all year, but I have dedicated March, April, and May specifically to this purpose. I even wrote it in big red letters on these months in my calendar. **Independence**

Well, as always I have high hopes. I know I won't accomplish everything I want—but I will accomplish more with this schedule and with my four goals of developing thinking skills, meaning vocabulary, writing and researching skills, and independence clearly established. I just wish someone had shown me how to do this before I started to teach. I could have done so much better my first two years. Maybe someone did try to teach me and I just wasn't ready to learn it?

September:

I survived September! To anyone who hasn't taught, that may sound like an overstatement, but to teachers, September is the hardest month. You have to set up all the classroom routines and expectations and get to know a whole new group of students. This year, I also had to learn about fifth grade, get my new schedule working, and begin work on all my ambitious goals. Too ambitious, perhaps.

My new schedule does seem to be working. I find it very hard to keep my reading group instruction to 20 minutes but the time limit does keep both me and the children on task. It also forces me to establish priorities for which of the manual's activities are most important and which things the students actually need me there for. Because I have given them more to do independently, the kids are working more diligently during seatwork time. They waste almost no time now that they know that what they don't finish in the morning becomes their homework.

SSR   SSR is now running smoothly. It took a few weeks for the students to realize what Sustained Silent Reading meant. I had to be quite firm in making sure they all had a book—two if they thought they would need two for ten minutes—and that they sat right down to read. I then sat down too and set my timer for ten minutes. The first two weeks it took almost ten minutes to get everyone actually sitting down with a book. That meant I had less time to read aloud to them and our unit work started a little late. But now they walk in from lunch, pick up their book from our classroom library if they don't have one in their desk (which most do), and immediately begin reading. It just goes to show you what determination and routines will accomplish.

I did have a problem with Dave and Jim not reading the first day. We had all settled down with our books and the next thing I knew they were laughing and talking with each other. I let them see how shocked I was. I walked right over to them, looked them straight in the eye, and delivered my lecture. "Perhaps you didn't understand," I began. "This is sustained silent reading time. It is the special 10 minutes we take out of a busy schedule each day just to enjoy a good book. You have just interrupted me and everyone else. I don't expect to be interrupted again. You have your books. Open them and read them." I then returned to my seat facing the class and resumed reading. They were shocked enough to be quiet for the rest of the ten minutes. But the next day, they tried it again. This time I went one step further. I moved two chairs on either side of my chair and put Jim and Dave with their books into them. Dave was scarlet with embarrassment. Jim tried to look unconcerned but I could tell he was embarrassed, too. The next day, without saying a word, I moved two chairs on either side of mine before we began SSR. I think Dave and Jim got the hint because they did not disturb us and the chairs remained vacant. I don't think Dave and Jim actually read during SSR. They are very poor readers and I think they try to defy me by just sitting with their books open and not reading, but I ignore them as long as they are quiet. They have not interrupted us since (and neither has anyone else), and I noticed them actually turning pages recently. You may not be able to make a horse drink, but if you lead him to water regularly and don't allow him anything else to drink, the chances are pretty good that sooner or later, he will drink! So, SSR is now established and I don't expect any more problems as long as I do it each day and read as the students read.

This is a most unusual group of kids. Bo says I say that every year. But, this year it is verifiable. I have not one but two sets of twins. Michelle and Michael are both delightful. They don't seem to compete with each other; indeed, they're quite supportive. Steven and Stephanie, on the other hand, should have been separated. Dee Klare tells me that she wanted them separated way back in first grade but the parents wouldn't hear of it. They want them together so that Steven can help Stephanie. "Help" is not the word I would use to describe what Steven does to Stephanie. Poor Stephanie is just a slow student and Steven always picks on her when she does not catch on right away. I try to stop it but it is difficult since this appears to be a long-established pattern. I have already requested a conference with their parents. Then, there are Kazu and Che, both Korean. Kazu is a top student. Che only came to our country recently. He will be another top student once he learns English, but is currently struggling. At least Kazu can help him. Hernando also knows very little English and no one here speaks Spanish. I am learning a little and I have some Spanish books for him to study reading—although none for any of the other subjects. I never realized when I was in school how many children I would teach who knew little English and how difficult it is to make adjustments for them.

I worry about Ray because he is so quiet. I can never get him to speak, even in reading group. He has little confidence and is always sure he will be wrong. Unfortunately, I think his perception is usually true! I am looking for some strength I can capitalize on but haven't found one yet. He is very uncoordinated and the kids never want him on their sports teams. He appears to have no talent for art or music, either. Surely, there must be something he does well!

The rest of the children seem quite average—although David, John, Sharon, and Pat seem to be unusually intelligent. I wonder if they need some kind of special gifted instruction. I will have to refer them and see. As always, I have a class full of the complete range of intelligence, motivation, and talent and it will be a real challenge to see that all—both the brightest and the slowest—make some progress in knowledge and skills!

I am especially enjoying our Fridays, as are the students. We did a social studies unit on the geography of the United States, Canada, and Latin America this month. We made a word wall, which was hard to limit to only forty words since there are so many terms they need to understand. I had to decide on the basis of which words educated adults knew and so included words like *latitude, longitude, continent,* and *equator.* I used many films and filmstrips to provide visual experiences from which to build meaning. Of course, we became experts at maps and globes, constructing a variety of maps during the course of the unit. We did a listening comprehension lesson in which I set the purpose by using a problem/solution format. The magazine article I read to them talked about problems that people living in North America must work together to solve. Before I began, I had them write down three major problems on one side of their notebook; as they listened, they filled in the proposed solutions on the other side. After I finished reading the article, they told me their proposed solutions. Then, there were several disagreements and I had to reread parts of the text. It appears that they can understand well if facts are stated explicitly, but have difficulty when a concept requires them to make an inference. As I reread the parts of the text, I tried to explain how relating the text to prior knowledge allows you to make certain inferences but I know not everyone understood. I will have to work on this.

We have done some writing and the results are not good. Most of my stu-

Social Studies Unit

Comprehension Lesson

dents don't like to write and don't write well, so my goal of making them good writers and researchers may be a little ambitious. But I am not going to give up trying to improve their writing. We probably just won't get as far as I had hoped. I plan to teach them to write paragraphs next month, since it appears that no one but Sharon and Pat has that skill. These students may indent from time to time, but where they "push it in" bears little relationship to where new ideas begin.

Thinking Processes

This month I am proudest of the progress I have made toward improving their thinking skills. My checklist for the nine thinking processes has many entries. I have found that it is quite natural to have students call up their past experience and make predictions based on it if you only remember to do so. It also seems to generate more interest to start from what they know and think. We have classified our word wall words and outlined several topics as a way of organizing information. I am also getting better at helping students connect the new things they are learning to what they already know. "Remember what we learned last Friday . . ." is becoming a normal part of my repertoire. Having students image is also fairly normal, once you start to do it. "Now, close your eyes and picture yourselves on that mountain in western Canada. It is 6000 feet up and covered with snow. . . ." I find that the students like to image things both before and after they have learned about them from listening, reading, or viewing. Monitoring happens most frequently when students have had a breakdown in comprehension and we must reread part of the text to clarify a point. I also take a few minutes each day to review what they have learned and have them remind themselves and each other of the important information. I have done three to a customer twice and they seemed to enjoy it.

Evaluate and apply are harder processes to teach, although I do try to remember to ask evaluative questions such as, "Do you think this is a good solution?" and "Would you like to live in this part of the continent? Why? Why not?" We did apply our knowledge when we made maps, and when we described various geographic features of different countries and had imaginary space invaders decide what they should pack if they were going to settle in that region. I must continue to think of ways to incorporate these two thinking skills on a daily basis. My checklist shows we are not practicing them nearly as often as we are the other seven.

Now that we are off and running, I expect to make great progress toward meeting my goals in October.

October:

Science Units

"Energy" and "Our Solar System" were the two science units we did this month. The students loved the energy unit because we learned many of the basic concepts during P.E. We played soccer and related the energy source and energy receiver to the players. Transfer of energy was easy to understand once the students grasped that the food they ate gave them energy which they then transferred to the ball when they kicked it.

The solar system was also fun to study. We led into it from our energy unit by beginning with the idea that all energy in our solar system originates from our sun. The most important concepts that I wanted them to learn were the following: how our planets orbit our sun, the various size and distance relationships in our solar system, and some of the distinguishing characteristics of each planet.

Before reading about planets in our science book, the students created two models of our solar system. We used reference books (*The Planets in our Solar System, How Did We Find Out About the Universe?*) to find out each planet's size and distance from the sun. One model showed the relative size of each planet, using assorted round objects to represent size. The students were amazed to see Mercury represented by a tiny marble and Jupiter by an enormous beachball. Another model showed the distance of each planet from the sun. We had to use the hall to represent how far away Neptune and Pluto were. These two models helped the children image the size and distance represented by those huge and abstract numbers. It also helped generate interest in learning about the planets.

When looking at the science chapter in our text, I realized that the way the various planets were described fit very well into a feature matrix comprehension lesson. I listed the planets down one side and their major features across the top and had everyone copy this pattern into his or her science notebook. Here is the feature matrix they copied:

Comprehension Lesson

Planets in our Solar System

	Closer to sun than Earth	Larger than Earth	Has moon	Has rings	Orbits the sun	Inner planet	Smallest	Largest	Has life as we know it
Earth									
Jupiter									
Mars									
Mercury									
Neptune									
Pluto									
Saturn									
Uranus									
Venus									

Ray's Feature Matrix:
Planets in our Solar System

	Closer to sun than Earth	Larger than Earth	Has moon	Has rings	Orbits the sun	Inner planet	Smallest	Largest	Has life as we know it
Earth	−	−	+	−	+	+	−	−	+
Jupiter	−	+	+	−		−			−
Mars	+	−	+	−	+	+		−	−
Mercury	+	−		−	+	+			−
Neptune	−	+		−		−	−		−
Pluto	−	+		−		−	−		−
Saturn	−	+		+		−			−
Uranus	−			−		−	−		−
Venus	+	−	+	−	+			−	

Based on what they already knew, I told the children to put a "+" or "−" to indicate whether or not a planet had a particular feature. If a child was unsure about a particular feature, the space was to be left blank. "If your mind is blank, leave the space blank," I explained. Here is the feature matrix that Ray filled out before reading the text. As you can see, his mind is blank on many facts. I was particularly amazed to see that he is unsure whether Jupiter, Neptune, Pluto, Saturn, and Uranus orbit the sun!

Next, the children read the science text section on planets. The children were clear about their purpose for reading: to confirm or change the pluses and minuses on their feature matrix, and to fill in blank spaces. As the children read, erasers were used liberally and quiet cheers and groans indicated that the children were actively comprehending rather than passively getting through the pages. When the children had finished, we performed a group task: to correctly fill out our class feature matrix. For every space, I had the children signal thumbs up if they had a plus and thumbs down if they had a minus. If I got a close to unanimous reply (a few are always too lazy to raise or lower their thumbs!), I put the plus or minus in the appropriate space. No response meant that we still did not know the answer, even after reading. For some spaces, there was still disagreement, so I had the children return to the text to argue their points and I again discovered the problem they have making inferences. Many children believed that the text did not say whether Pluto was larger or smaller than Earth, so I had David read the sentence that states, "Pluto is probably the size of Mercury." David explained that since we know that Mercury is smaller than Earth, we can infer that Pluto is, too. While the

Planets in our Solar System

	Closer to sun than Earth	Larger than Earth	Has moon	Has rings	Orbits the sun	Inner planet	Smallest	Largest	Has life as we know it
Earth	−	−	+	−	+	+	−	−	+
Jupiter	−	+	+	−	+	−	−	+	−
Mars	−	−	+	−	+	+	−	−	−
Mercury	+	−	−	−	+	+	+	−	−
Neptune	−	+	+	−	+	−	−	−	
Pluto	−	−			+	−	−	−	
Saturn	−	+	+	+	+	−	−	−	−
Uranus	−	+	+	+	+	−	−	−	
Venus	+	−	−	−	+	+	−	−	−

text did not directly state that there is no life as we know it on Jupiter, the text does state: "There is no water on Jupiter." I had to explain to the children that since life as we know it requires water, and since there is no water on Jupiter, there cannot be life as we know it on Jupiter. This "since . . . therefore" reasoning is always required for comprehension, but for many of my students, if the text doesn't say something explicitly, they don't get it! At least with this lesson and task afterwards, I could see where they were not making inferences and so could lead them back to the book and explain the reasoning.

Here is the feature matrix as we finally completed it. As you can see, several spaces are still blank, even after reading. Pluto is so far away that we don't know if it has a moon or rings, or if it might have life as we know it. We are also not sure about life on Uranus and Neptune. Jim was disturbed by these blanks and wanted to vote on what to put there. I don't know if he was serious or just putting me on but I tried to explain that you can't make truth by voting on it!

On Friday, we went to the library to do some more research on planets. I **Research** chose Venus and showed the students how I used the card catalog and other resources to find more information about Venus. I then divided them into groups for the other eight planets and helped them as they found information. Each group decided on three facts besides those we had read about in our text and one person in each group wrote these three facts on a chart to display in our room. Of course, I had showed them how I selected three facts about Venus and wrote these on my chart. They were very proud of their charts and of their burgeoning research skills—as was I!

Writing Lesson   Finally, I used their interest in planets to do a guided writing lesson on how to write a paragraph. Of course, I began by modeling for them as I wrote a paragraph on Venus. First, I reviewed what I knew about Venus from our feature matrix. Then I read the three additional facts from my chart. I told them that there were many different ways to construct paragraphs but that today, we were going to write paragraphs with a topic sentence, three detail sentences, and a concluding sentence. I pointed to the title of our feature matrix, "Planets in our Solar System," and explained that their paragraphs' topic sentences should get the planet into its topic—which in a feature matrix is the title. The next three sentences should describe some details about the planet from the feature matrix or chart. The final sentence could do many things; often it gave a fascinating fact or an opinion. As the children watched, I talked through my construction of topic sentence and my selection and construction of detail and concluding sentences and wrote the following paragraph on the board:

> Venus is one of the planets in our solar system. Venus and Earth are about the same size. Venus is hotter than the Earth because it is closer to the sun. Because there is no water on Venus, it can't maintain life as we know it. Venus is called the evening star and is the favorite planet of many people because it can often be seen on a clear night.

Having modeled how to write a paragraph, I had each child choose his or her favorite planet and write a paragraph about it. I reminded them to have their first sentence tell how their planet related to the larger topic of the feature matrix. Three sentences should then give specific information about their planet, based on the feature matrix, the charts, or any other information they knew. A final sentence should end the paragraph in an interesting way. "Remember, you can't include everything you know in just one paragraph. Just include what you believe is most important and interesting," I reminded them.

As the children wrote their paragraphs, the model paragraph, the feature matrix, and the charts were all available to them. When the paragraphs were written, I let several children read theirs to the class. I was amazed when Ray volunteered. His paragraph on Mars was a lot like mine in form, but it was all correct, and most important, he had volunteered to read! This was a most successful writing lesson. The children actually seemed to enjoy it. I guess when you know the information, have the correctly spelled words in front of you, and have seen the form modeled, writing is not so arduous. In fact, I overheard Kazu comment, "The paragraph just wrote itself!"

Literature   I encouraged the students to read science fiction related to outer space this month. Among the most popular books were, *Planet out of the Past, The Deadly Hoax, The Doors of the Universe,* and *Another Heaven, Another Earth.*

November:

Health Unit   Our first health unit was a success. The topic was "Your Emotions," and the major idea being that we all experience a range of feelings, some happy and some not. In looking at the text, I thought the information was fairly trite and was unprepared for the response of my students. Many of them clearly thought that fear, anger, and inadequacy were emotions unique to them. They were amazed to read that we all feel these emotions—children and adults alike—and there are healthy and unhealthy ways to deal with them. We did many skits and a lot of talking. I put them into small groups, gave them a description of some events in a child's life, and had them decide which emotions that child would probably feel and how best to deal with them. They worked well in their groups, better than I had expected. I think their concentration and the strength of their discussion stemmed from the immediacy of the topic to their own lives. I had a time limit for the groups and had each group prepare a summary of their discussion. I think this structure also helped to keep them on task.

Group Work

In the weeks before our unit, I had read them *Bridge to Terabithia* and *Ramona Forever*. I was able to refer to these characters and their emotions as we worked in our unit. Finally, I assigned each student to find a book in which the character experiences some strong emotions, and to prepare a short report listing the emotions, the reasons for them, and the way they were handled. They all did a good job with these reports—even Dave read *The Flunking of Joshua T. Bates* and reported on it. I know the unit was a success because I have heard the children use the terminology in talking among themselves. I think they now have more empathy with each other when they are experiencing strong emotions. They also seem to have a better idea of how to handle emotions. I heard Jim say to Bob, "I'm angry at myself right now, so you and me will both be better off if you just stay clear for awhile." I think before our unit, Jim might have just hauled off and hit Bob. Next year, I think I will start the year with this health unit.

Literature

Our social studies unit took most of the month. We learned about the European settlement and expansion of the United States and did our first scavenger hunt. To prepare for the scavenger hunt, I read through the materials I wanted the students to read or listen to and wrote down all the interesting things that students might find either an object or a picture for. Here is the list:

Scavenger Hunt

prairie	Rocky Mountains	wagon train	gold
canal	mission	textile	immigrant
pioneer	cotton gin	trains	Indians
totem pole	sod house	lantern	spinning wheel
basin	grub hoe	broad ax	iron skillet

We did the scavenger hunt during the week that we worked on our health unit. I had hoped that by the time we actually started the settlement and expansion unit, the students would have been motivated by the search. Before I started the children on the scavenger hunt, I asked them to call up their experiences with scavenger hunts. Many had been on them and explained how you had a limited time to find a bunch of things. I helped them to see that no group usually found everything but that the group that found the most was the winner. I then divided the class into six groups of four and gave each group the list. I appointed a leader and recorder for each group. We read over the twenty items on the list and discussed what they were. If the group was unsure about something, I suggested they would have to find out for sure if they were to find the correct object or picture. To my question "Where can you find out more about what these words mean?" they responded, "Dictionaries, encyclopedias, and other library books." "Right," I said, "and I will let each group go to the media center for 15 minutes this afternoon to look up the things you are unsure about." I then explained that real objects or models counted two points, while pictures—photographs, magazine pictures, tracings, or drawings—counted one point. I warned the students that I would not count any "thrown-together" drawings or models. They would have one week to find and make what they could. I also asked them not to bring anything to class that they could not hide in their desks until the appointed day—next Friday. "You don't want the other groups to see what you have," I chided. Finally, I told them that just as in real scavenger hunts, I was sure that no group would be able to find an object, or even a picture for each word. The knowing glances that passed from Sharon to Pat and from Dave to Jim let me know that my challenge was going to be met.

I let the groups meet several times for just a few minutes during the next week. I emphasized whispering and secrecy and the children soon got into the mood of the hunt. I gave them tracing and drawing paper as needed and granted their requests to go to the media center alone. I knew my effort to get them interested in our unit was working when I ran into my old friend, Lib Booker, a librarian at our public library. She remarked on how many fifth-graders suddenly wanted books on our country's discovery and expansion!

On Friday morning, there was much excitement. I let each group display what they had scavenged and then had each group tally their score—two points for each object, one for each picture. Most of the groups had pictures of almost everything, and objects for common things such as gold and lantern. After the groups had done their own tallies, I double-checked the points of the winning group, Sharon, Michelle, Bob, and Ray. They had made a papier mache model of the Rocky Mountains, a small wooden totem pole, and a sod house out of mud. They also had a miniature wagon train. The others were amazed. I can tell that there will be a lot of models constructed for the next scavenger hunt.

As their prize, I let Sharon, Michelle, Bob, and Ray have the rest of the morning off to put up their bulletin board. Sharon very neatly lettered cards for each word and they all arranged and stapled the pictures collage style. They put the labeled objects on a table which they pushed under the bulletin board. A title and credits, "The Settlement and Expansion of the United States by the Scavenger Hunt Winners—Sharon, Michelle, Bob, and Ray," completed the display which would serve as a springboard for our study. This first scavenger hunt was a success but I believe the next one will be even better now that the children understand what to do. I already heard some groans and comments like, "We could have made those things, too."

We finished this unit with a research day. During our unit, we had developed a list of explorers. I added a few names to this list and then assigned each child a partner. The partners picked one explorer that they wanted to learn more about. Then we made a list of *wh* questions to which we might seek answers. Here are the questions the students came up with: **Research**

What did the explorer explore?
When did the explorer explore?
Where did the explorer explore?
How did the explorer get here?
Why did the explorer come here?
Who was in the explorer's family?
Who did the explorer find while exploring?
How were the explorers treated by the people they found?
How did the explorers get the money to explore?

To model for them how to locate and organize information, I picked an explorer that no one else had picked and showed students both how to locate sources and how to find information within those sources. I read aloud from the information I had found, with the students stopping me when I read the information that answered one of our questions. I recorded each answer next to its question. When we found some fascinating information that didn't answer any of our questions, David had the idea of adding P.S. at the bottom for miscellaneous facts. The children then worked in pairs under my direction. I had paired the better and the weaker students so there was a lot of one-to-one-teaching going on. I have decided that only one teacher cannot possibly teach twenty-four individuals, so I must maximize partner and group work for my students to teach each other. I no longer feel guilty about these pairings since Dee told me that research shows that the child tutor often learns more than does the tutee!

December:

To me, December, not February, is the shortest month of the year! Between doing holiday things with the children here and preparing for the holidays myself, I find it very hard to accomplish any of my normal academic tasks. I did unexpectedly add another word wall to our room. Of course we have one on the side bulletin board which changes as our unit changes. But when I discovered recently that many of my students did not really understand many of the words in their math books nor its symbols and abbreviation, I turned the space above the front chalkboard into another word wall for math items. Since I began it so late, I added five terms each day this month until I got them all up. We spent a good part of our math period learning these symbols and attaching appropriate meanings to them. From now on, I will add new **Vocabulary** terms gradually as we begin a new chapter in math. I select the terms from the fifth-grade textbook, but there is much overlap for my group working in the fourth-grade book and I know it will help them next year to have learned the essential fifth-grade math vocabulary. Here is the math wall as it currently looks. As you can see, I have translated the symbols and abbreviations.

hundreds	cent (¢)	ray (→)	degree (°)
billions	angle (→)	tens	millions
right angle	thousands	prime number	acute angle
sum	average	digit	addends
kilometer (km)	obtuse angle	estimate	meter (m)
round off	regroup	centimeter (cm)	difference
common	ones	factors	multiples
multiples	product	even numbers	odd numbers
greatest	quotient	remainder	common divisor
common	divisor	less than (<)	greater than (>)
denominator	dollar ($)	percent (%)	line (↔)

Each day at the beginning of our math time, I have the students number a sheet of paper from one to five as I call out the definition of five terms or write something on the board to express them. The students write the word for each term and then we check. Here are some meaning cues I gave them, followed by the answers in parentheses:

1. 2, 4, 6, 10, and 106 are examples of this. 1, 3, 5, 107, and 409 are not. (even numbers)
2. The symbol for ray (→)
3. The abbreviation for kilometer (km)
4. When I do this problem (64 X 35 = 2240), the numbers 64 and 35 (multiples)
5. For the same problem, the number 2240 (product)

Be a Mind Reader

I also use a game called be a mind reader that students particularly enjoy and that helps us review the meanings for these terms. Again, students number their paper from 1 through 5, but this time I think of only one term and give five clues for it. The first clue is always the same, "It is one of the words, symbols, or abbreviations on our math wall." The children always moan, but I tell them to try to read my mind and guess what I am thinking of. They write their guess on the first line. The remaining four clues narrow down the problem until by the fifth clue, only one answer is possible. As I give successive clues, the children continue to write the same one unless my clue tells them that theirs can't be right. Here is one set of clues I used:

1. It's one of the words, symbols, or abbreviations on the math wall.
2. It is a symbol.

3. It is not "<" or ">."

4. This symbol refers to money.

5. This symbol means dollar.

Jim guessed this one on the first clue! He was so proud! "How did you do that?" everyone asked. "He read my mind," I responded. Jim beamed and I was delighted he was getting some positive attention. Some children need a little luck to shine and be a mind reader allows the chance for that lucky guess.

I wish I had started the year with work on these math terms but it just didn't occur to me until recently that not understanding what the book said was a part of my students' problem with math. It is clear from their improved work that this vocabulary work is helping. Next year, I'll start a math wall the first week of school!

We did manage to complete a science unit on the ocean this month. Many children had not been to the ocean and it is a hard concept to explain to someone who has never experienced it. I relied a great deal on visuals. I got two good films from the state department media center which helped the children to see the ocean's enormous size and to build concepts for terms like "low tide" and "high tide." I did a prediction activity to set the purpose for a viewing lesson on a filmstrip that showed the various parts of the ocean bottom. I gave the students the following list and asked them to guess which things we would find on the ocean bottom:

Science Unit

Comprehension Lesson

mountains
shelf
roads
floor
treasure boxes
ridges
slope
fences
cracks
oceanographers
plains
continents

Of course, many of the students didn't know the ocean bottom is called the *floor* or that there is a continental shelf there. They accused me of tricking them and I protested, "You know I would never do such a thing!" We talked about the different meanings of *floor* and *shelf*. I also had to allow that although our filmstrip hadn't shown a treasure box, you might indeed find one on the ocean's floor.

Prediction has been quite a successful way to help the children have clear purposes. Sometimes I use prediction in an open-ended way. I might have said, for example, "Name some things that you think our filmstrip will show at the bottom of the ocean." Other times, I give them a list of things or of true/false statements, have them make guesses about them, and then they read, listen, or view to confirm their predictions. It is amazing how much more actively they read after making that small investment of guessing or predicting. They attend very carefully when they want to find out how they did! I guess this is a normal part of human nature and I am glad I can capitalize on it to help them become more active learners.

I suppose the high point of the whole unit was when Bo brought in his scuba diving equipment and some things he has collected in and near the ocean. The children seemed to hang on his every word. Bo has never had much experience with children and had been a little nervous about coming. He really got into it and even expressed regret that we couldn't take the whole crew with us when we go to the shore for the holidays. I must admit that I am attached to my children—but not that attached!

January:

Health and Science Unit

We spent this entire month on a combined health and science unit on the human body. The four chapters of the health book and the one in the science book covered much of the same information. I borrowed some bones and a lot of models from Annie Mull who teaches at the high school. I had an X-ray technician and a pediatrician come in and talk to us. We have become more health-conscious since we began our study. We kept charts of the food we ate and the exercise we've had and we evaluated how well we were nourishing and exercising our bones and muscles. (The children were amazed to learn that I go to a health spa several times a week. I brought my sweat suit and my tape one day and taught them a few aerobics routines. They loved it!)

Word Problems

Math has once again been the focus of much of my creativity. The math wall vocabulary activities have definitely helped, but I noticed the children are still having a great deal of difficulty with word problems. I know that computation is not their main problem because I set up the computations for some word problems that many of them had missed and the children breezed right through them. Their difficulty seems rather to be a lack of understanding of what they are trying to find out and an inability to figure out which operations to perform. I have been taking them through a set of steps that I hope will improve their ability to think through word problems. I have listed these steps on a chart and each morning we work through several problems following these steps:

1. Decide what question the problem asks you to answer.
2. Decide what facts are given.
3. Estimate your answer.

4. Decide which operations to do in which order.

5. Do these operations to get your answer.

6. Compare your answer to your estimate.

Coming up with the steps and writing them on the chart was the easy part. The hard part is teaching the students to follow the steps! As with everything, I began by modeling what to do. I made up a word problem related to members of the class. (They are always more motivated and attend better when the problems are about them.)

> Sharon, Pat, and Sarah all want to make cheerleading outfits. It will take 3 1/2 yards of cloth for each and the cloth costs $4.99 per yard. How much money do they need to buy enough cloth for all three outfits?

I wrote this problem on the board as I read it to the class. I then modeled how to go through the five steps. (Modeling is just a fancy term for thinking aloud as you do something, so the kids can figure out what you're doing and why you're doing it.) "Well," I began, "I have to figure out what the question is and it is a little tricky. The question is not how much cloth they need, although I will have to figure that out, too. The question is how much money they need in all." I then wrote, "How much money in all?" next to step one. Next to step two, facts, I wrote, "3 1/2 yards for each outfit; 3 outfits; $4.99 per yard."

"Estimating is important," I mused aloud, "so that I can tell if my answer makes sense or if I misplaced a decimal point or did something else dumb like that." (The children tittered at the idea of their teacher making dumb mistakes.) "If the material costs $4.99 per yard, that is close to $5.00. There are three of them, so if it only took one yard each, that would be $15.00 but it takes 3 1/2 yards each. Three times $15.00 is $45.00. The answer will be a little more than $45.00" I then wrote "$45.00" next to step three.

For step four, I reasoned that since I knew how much one yard cost and wanted to know how much 3 1/2 yards cost, I would have to multiply. I would then know how much it would cost for one girl, and since there were three girls, I would have to multiply again. I wrote, "multiply $4.99 X 3 1/2; multiply that times 3" next to step four. Finally, I did the calculation, compared $52.40 to $45.00 and decided my answer was indeed "in the ballpark."

After modeling the whole procedure for the students, I took them through several other problems and let them help me decide what to write and why. Then I had them turn to a set of word problems in their books (those working in fourth-grade math used their book) and had each student write down only the question he or she was trying to answer. I went around and gave help as they worked. It became very clear that deciding on the question was not easy or automatic for many of them.

On the following day, we worked together on just that step—deciding the question. I gave them many problems that used their names and we decided what questions was being asked. I then assigned them a page of word problems they had already worked on (not very successfully) and had them write the question for each one. We continued to work on determining the question for a few days and then went on to step two, determining the facts. This was easier for them. Step three, however, estimating the answer, continues to be a problem. Many of them still can't come up with a reasonable estimate. This worries me, because the people who are good in math always have an estimate to provide them feedback. I hope that if we continue to work on this skill all year, they will get better at estimating.

Step four, deciding which computations to do in which order, is also difficult but we are continuing to work on it. The last step, when we finally get to it, will be easy. If computation were all there was to word problems, my students would be home free! At least the children and I now have a systematic way of attacking these problems and I understand how much complex thinking goes into them. Bo has heard me talk all month about word problems and he says the steps I am teaching—determining the problem, gathering facts, considering a reasonable solution, deciding what to do in what order, and then actually solving the problem and seeing if your solution works—is how we solve not just word problems, but life problems. Perhaps the process I am teaching my students has a wider application than I realized!

February:

Social Studies Unit

Canada was our social studies adventure this month. We pretended all month that we were actually there to explore this vast and diverse land. Several of the children had been to Canada and they became our guides. Pat's grandmother had emigrated from Canada and Pat shared the stories she had heard. We learned a little French and a lot more geography. This was also a month to do a lot of writing. Developing good writers has been one of my goals all year but I have not given it as much time as I think it deserves. For this unit, I decided we would write every day. One way I accomplished this

Content Journals

was to have the students keep journals. This fit in with our idea that we were not just learning about Canada but actually imagining ourselves there. We kept journals—my boys would object to their being called diaries—of the major things we had seen and what we had learned. Each day, at the end of our social studies time, we had 5 minutes to write in our journals. Just as for USSR, I stuck firmly to the idea that this 5 minutes is uninterrupted, sustained time for silent writing and I wrote too. At first, the children were unsure about what to write but I assured them that they were recording personal remembrances, impressions, and questions, with no particular form or content that they needed to include. They were their own audience, and the only restriction was to relate their writing to our study of Canada. As the month went on, the children became used to this time and, as with USSR, they seemed to enjoy it. I did not grade what they wrote, but I did check to see that there was an entry for each day and that the entry related to Canada. The daily points they got for recording their thoughts accounted for a small portion of their grade.

Grading their work has been a problem all year. In skills subjects like math, spelling, language, and reading, it is fairly easy to give a grade. The children are working on their own levels. Once I have modeled and provided guided practice with the skills, I feel comfortable testing their ability to perform them independently.

Grading their work on the units, however, is much more difficult. I believe that a grading system should motivate all students to work hard. This is easy to say and not nearly so easy to do. Many of my students—Dave, Jim, Hernando, Che, and Ray most particularly—have very limited prior knowledge of the subjects we are studying. They are also limited by lower reading ability and, for Hernando and Che, limited command of English. If I simply taught the fifth-grade content and then gave them a comprehensive test, they would fail. Some teachers think they should fail if they can't do "fifth-grade" work, but I know that children come with different abilities. Just because they are all in fifth grade does not mean they all have fifth-grade ability.

Then, there are those on the other end of the spectrum, specifically Sharon, Pat, David, John, and Kazu. These children bring huge stores of prior knowledge, motivation, and intelligence to our units. They probably already know most of what we are supposed to learn in fifth grade. My grading system must motivate them, too. I can't let them think that they don't have to study but can just slide by on what they are fortunate enough to know.

The problem is complex and I am not totally happy with the solution I have worked out. For each unit, I set up several parts that count toward total grade points. I give points for daily assignments, such as the journals and homework, which I never grade, but simply check to see that "a good effort was made." Of course, a good effort from Hernando is not of the quality I expect from David but I can determine this fairly easily. By now, all the kids know what it means to see, "You just threw this together—no way!" on their assignments. Knowing that life is not perfect and that no one can complete all assignments every day, I always have more assignments than can be counted for points. For the Canada unit, for example, I had 35 assignments, short daily and homework activities including the daily journal entries. The children could get up to 30 points out of the 35. Thus anyone who was there every day with the first 30 assignments did not have to do the last 5! The children loved this and tried to get all the first ones done so they could "lay back" later. I had already planned to make the last five assignments less crucial than the others because I knew that many of the children would not need to complete them.

The second part of the grade comes from the unit tests. We had three tests on Canada and they were all worth 10 points, plus 2 bonus points. The 10 points part of the test was taken by everyone and included the most important information, which we had learned in class and reviewed. The other 2 points was based on any other information intended to challenge my really top students. Only children who chose to took the bonus part of the test.

Finally, I gave my students credit for up to three projects. These projects ranged from library research projects to reading additional books on Canada

(*Canada's Kids* and *Take a Trip to Canada,* among others) to creating models, maps, visuals, or realia. For the most part, students did these projects out of school, although we did have some time to work on them on Fridays. These projects were each worth 10 points if they were done well. Again, "well" differed for different children but all children knew I didn't accept sloppy work.

Thus for the Canada unit you could get 30 points for daily assignments, and anyone who was making a good effort should have gotten these. The test on the most important concepts accounted for another 30 points, which again everyone should have gotten. The bonus tests and projects were there to motivate my top students, although most children did at least one project per unit. For Canada, two of the slower students—Che and Bob—did three good projects.

For the most part, I am happy with this grading system because it does seem to motivate my slow students to work with me and learn the most important information, and my top students to do projects and bonus test points. Of course, not everyone is happy with this system. John's mother complained about her son's C in social studies. I had to show her that he just hadn't put out much effort. He had not attempted any bonus test points and had done only one project. "He must learn that he must earn his As," I explained. She agreed to see to it that he made a greater effort during our next unit.

In addition to our journals, we did other writing activities this month. I have been saving the free postcards I get at motels and the children learned the postcard form, which they enjoyed. We also wrote pen-pal letters to children in a fifth-grade class in Canada. I had met Kay Beck at a meeting I attended last May and when I realized I would be teaching fifth-graders about Canada, I wrote to set up this pen-pal arrangement with her. The children love having real friends in another country and we will continue our letter writing for the rest of the year. Who knows? Some of them may remain pen pals for the rest of their lives!

March:

Independence

It's a good thing I wrote the word "Independence" in big red letters on my March, April, and May calendar months way back in August, or the year might have ended before I realized that I needed to move my children (I must stop thinking of them as children—they will be big middle-schoolers in five months!) toward becoming more independent learners. This month, I have tried to

Vocabulary

show them how they can independently learn new word meanings. Instead of me previewing the unit on plants and selecting the key words, I had the students look through the science chapters and write down words which seemed important to them of whose meanings they were not totally sure. I gave them about five minutes for this, then I made a list of all their words. I chose those I considered most important and least known and we pronounced them and talked about what they might mean. Of course, some students knew some words. But no one could tell me the meanings of words such as monocot, dicot, and photosynthesis. I told students that as we studied plants, I would help them see how they could use their texts, our dictionaries and other reference books, and their own common sense to learn meanings without my telling them or showing them. Some of my students looked a little skeptical and so was I, but I knew that I must attempt to move them toward independence since they were sure to meet some "sink or swim" teachers in the coming years.

Fortunately, most of the words that the students had identified were also the words that I had deemed most important for them to learn. I added two words—*vascular* and *nonvascular*—and left the rest of the list as they had written it. That meant we had more words than I usually allot, twenty for a two-week unit. But they had chosen some words that I thought most of them knew and others that were so obscure, I didn't intend to focus on them much. So I left their list intact. That night, I divided their list into words for which I thought they had no meaning and words for which they had experienced the meaning but did not know the technical term. Fortunately, there were only four words for which I thought they might have little or no experience—chlorophyll, photosynthesis, carbon dioxide, and stomata. All the other words, though unfamiliar to the children, represented something they had experienced. They had all seen ferns, but did not know the leaves were called fronds. They had all seen vascular plants—trees, tulips, and carrots—as well as non-vascular plants—mosses. Likewise, they knew some plants only lived one year—annuals—and others lived a long, long time—perennials.

I then looked through the chapters in their science book to find pictures from which students could build or call up their experience, and to see what context clues were provided by the words. Finally, I looked at the list to see what morphemic clues the new words contained. For all the words for which the students had meaning, I found that the pictures, words, and morphemes would help the students call up their experience and connect it to the new words. The problem came, of course, with the process of photosynthesis and its related words, *chlorophyll, carbon dioxide,* and *stomata.* I knew that the text explanation of this process would make no sense; even though the children could read the words, they would not understand what was actually meant by them. I decided to follow the suggestion in the teacher's guide providing for direct experience through an experiment: we would deprive some plants of light, others of water, and others of air, by smearing petroleum jelly on both sides of the leaves. Still other plants would be given light and water and not smeared. Over the two weeks of our science unit, we watched the deprived plants grow. I helped them connect this experience with photosynthesis by explaining that light, water, and air, from which plants get carbon dioxide, are all required for plants to make their own food. I further explained that all green plants got their green coloring from a chemical called chlorophyll, and that the air enters the leaf through stomata, the tiny openings that we had clogged when we smeared petroleum jelly on the leaves. The plants that died had chlorophyll, as we knew from their green color, but because we had deprived them of light, water, or carbon dioxide, they could not make food and they died. This process of making food, I explained, can be done by all green plants, and it is called a big word—photosynthesis.

The experience I provided for the children allowed them to build meaning to associate with photosynthesis and the related words. I used pictures, context, and morphemic clues to help them call up and link their experience with the unfamiliar words. I have been using these clues all year, but this month I focused more on the pictures and context in the textbook and tried to get the children to discover the morphemic clues themselves.

To begin my lesson, I circled the words vascular, nonvascular, botanist, biennials, conifers, monocots, dicots, and life cycle on the chart of words the students and I had selected to learn. I then had each child write a definition for three words of his or her choice. By now, the children know that they can write whatever they think, even a silly definition or something the word sounds like, and that we then compare these guesses made without context to our more probable guesses made from context. I let the children share a few of these guesses and the class hams always have a good time. Dave said that vascular was what you had left after the vase had shattered. Jim suggested that a botanist was a scientist who studied bottles. Sharon said that life cycle was a new kind of bike you didn't have to pedal. The children enjoy their silly guesses, but the guessing serves a serious function, too. When we read a word in context or see a picture, sometimes we think we knew all along what the word meant. The guessing focuses the children's attention on the words and lets them see that they don't really know what they mean. After guessing, they are curious to find out the real meanings and they see clearly how much the context and pictures help.

I directed the children's attention to certain sentences and pictures in their books and asked them to explain the words' meanings based on what they read and saw. In previous units, I had written context sentences on the board or provided pictures from magazines, books, or filmstrips. But now I wanted them to utilize the resource in which they were most apt to encounter unfamiliar words, their textbook. As the children explained their meanings based on the text, I probed to get them to explain their reasoning, since often the book doesn't come right out and say, "This means that." I also helped the children to connect their own experiences to the words. "Can you name some vascular plants you see on the way to school?" I asked. "Some nonvascular plants?" I let a few children look up some of the words in our encyclopedia to give us other examples of the meaning. Finally, I had each child write the words on a page in their science notebook along with our class definition, an example, and, if they liked, an illustration.

To help children use morphemic clues, I directed their attention to the word conifer and asked them if there was anything about the word that would help them remember that conifers are plants that produce seeds in cones. With my help, they noticed the cone-conifer relationship. I then asked them what word we could use to describe someone with courage? To describe something associated with danger? I wrote their responses on the board next to the root word (courage, courageous; danger, dangerous). I then wrote *conifer* and *coniferous* and the children saw that coniferous was a word used to describe conifers. In a similar way, I helped them to see that bicycles have two wheels, to bisect is to cut in two parts, and biennials are plants that live two years. I also pointed out that many words that start with *bi* have nothing to do with two, reminding them about *biographies.* Morphemic clues are helpful, but in English, they can mislead you. I try to remind my students to check morphemic clues against the other information in context and pictures.

We did many other activities in our unit on plants. We created a class horticultural guide to which each child contributed by researching and writing a one-page illustrated report on a selected plant. The books *Being a Plant* and *Plants up Close* were most helpful. We took on a beautification project, planting some lovely shrubs donated by Hernando's dad and some pachysandra and ajuga that we dug up at my house. **Research**

We even wrote some poetry, plant cinquains. Cinquains are poems for nonpoets. There are many different ways to create these five-line poems. In this unit we brainstormed ideas for each line as a group. Then each child selected from the brainstormed list or came up with more ideas of his or her own. We wrote cinquains about monocots, dicots, conifers, annuals, and perennials as a way to review their important characteristics. The first and last line of the cinquain were the same for everyone—the topic of our cinquain. For the second line, we brainstormed a list of *-ing* words that described the topic. For the third line, we brainstormed examples of the topic. For the fourth line, we brainstormed four-word phrases and sentences that summed up the topic. Each child then chose or made up two *-ing* words, three examples, one four-word phrase or sentence, and created his or her own unique cinquains. Here is Ray's cinquain for dicots. I am so proud of him!

Dicots
Blooming, growing
Pines, roses, beans
Two seed leaves each
Dicots

April:

Well, April was Latin America month! I feel like I have been on one of those "see six countries in four days" tours. I am sure that we could have studied Latin America all year and still had more we wanted to learn. There is just never enough time! At least, I think we accomplished the major goal of the unit: to give our youngsters some understanding of the similarities and differences between us and our southern neighbors. **Social Studies Unit**

I have tried to use more generic purposes in my comprehension lessons **Comprehension Lesson** this month in my continuing crusade to move my students toward indepen-dence. In earlier units, they completed many partial outlines, feature matrices, webs, and timelines which I set up for them. This month, I had them make outlines, webs, feature matrices, or timelines from their reading assignments, but I did not give them the headings or categories, or tell them how many boxes or slots to fill in. This was hard for all of them and Hernando, Dave, Jim, and Stephanie did not write much down after reading. We had to spend far more time following up the reading and constructing the outline, feature matrix, web, or timeline. But most students did get better by the end of the month and if I can teach them to preview text and decide on a notetaking structure—which is really what outlines, features matrices, webs and timelines are—they will be able to determine and note the most important information by themselves.

Research We have also continued to work toward becoming independent writers and researchers. This month, we created a travel book and I typed all the articles on my microcomputer (Never again!) and then had the children il-lustrate the book. We duplicated it, so that everyone could take a copy home and take his or her family on an imaginary journey to Latin America. I must admit that the children worked as hard as I did and they were very proud of their creation, as was I. I have tried all year to give them real audiences and purposes to write for, but this was my most successful attempt. Creating a real book to share knowledge about Latin America with their families was indeed a real purpose for a real audience.

We spent the first week with maps, globes, and other resources studying the geographic, cultural, and political boundaries of Latin America. The chil-dren were amazed that there are over 30 countries to the south of us ranging from tiny Trinidad to huge Brazil. During the next week, we did an in-depth study of Mexico which I used to model the research and writing process we would use to create our book. First, I had them generate questions about Mexico. Then we tried to organize them. We decided that there were ques-tions about people (How many people live in Mexico? Why do people from Mexico come to the United States? Where did the people in Mexico come from?), customs (What do they like to eat? Do they go to school in summer? Do they have Christmas too?), government (Who is their president? Do they have a good government?), and the economy (Where do people work? Why are so many people poor?). We put two questions into our all-important mis-cellaneous category.

I put each category of questions on a transparency and we trooped off to the library to locate sources likely to contain the answers. Using the card catalog, *Reader's Guide,* and indices of reference books, we collected quite a few. We found seven books devoted entirely to Mexico! How could we find our answers without reading everything? Of course, we brainstormed some key words to find the information more efficiently. For some questions, it was easy to come up with a useful key word. *Food* helped us find information about what people eat. For other questions, it was more difficult. To answer the question about why people come to the United States, I had to suggest that we look under *emigration* and *economy*.

As we were finding our answers, we also found other information, so we added some categories. Our question about where people came from led us to information about Mexico's early history, creating an early history category. We also decided that since we were writing a travel book, we needed information about recreation and good places to visit—another category. Eventually, we had transparencies with information about the people, early history, the government, the economy, customs, things to do and places to visit, and of course, miscellaneous. The children wanted to write down everything they had found, but I tried to show them that in our one travel book, we could not duplicate the information in many books devoted solely to Mexico, especially since we wanted to cover all of Latin America. I modeled for them how I decided what seemed most important, but when they got started on their own work, it was clear that setting priorities and limiting your notes is a skill they won't master this year!

During the third week, the students researched their chosen country. Previously, I have had them do this research in small groups or pairs but, keeping my independence goal in mind, I decided they should try it on their own. I did assign smaller countries, which have much less information to plow through, to my slower children. I don't think anyone noticed this and it made the task more manageable for everyone. Each child had one sheet of paper for each category, with some questions and key words. With the help of our librarian, we located sources for everyone and helped students to find the information within. Of course, Dave, Jim, Hernando, Stephanie, and Ray required the most help, but even they put out a good effort and found some information. Much of what they found was very hard for them to read, so I read a little to them and helped them write down the important facts. It is at times like this that I wish the pupil-teacher ratio were about five to one! Fortunately, some of my better students finished their research and helped the slower ones to make workable notes.

Finally, we got ready to write the reports. We decided to use a standard form with one paragraph for each subtopic. I pulled out my transparencies on Mexico and showed the children how to combine the information into paragraphs on the people, early history, etc. By now, most of the children have a good idea about how to construct a good paragraph. The fact that the notes were organized on separate sheets of paper around subtopics helped them keep their paragraphs on track. We used miscellaneous information in our concluding paragraph if appropriate. We had to make some return trips to the library for missing information or to check contradictory facts. I had shown the children how to write the source for the information in the margin in case they needed to find that information again, but I think most of them forgot this little detail! In some cases, we simply could not find the source so we found another one or deleted the information.

Once the first drafts of the reports were written, I paired the children to   **Revising** read theirs to each other. They were to listen for information only at this point, to help the writer make the piece clearer or more interesting. I myself sat down with Dave, Jim, Hernando, Che, and Ray and helped them finish sentences and clarify what they meant as much as I could. Once the children had revised for content, we began the editing process. Again, I had them work with their partners first. This time I had the partner read the piece aloud as the writer looked on. I have been having them edit like this all year and it is most helpful to the writer. Writers cannot generally proof their own writing since they read what they meant to write, not what they actually wrote. Bob wrote, *"Were did the erly peoples of trinidad come from."* When Kazu read this, he noticed the misspelling of *where,* the unnecessary *s* on *peoples,* and the need for a capital T on Trinidad. Once Kazu pointed these out, Bob saw them too and fixed them. They both missed the fact that *early* was misspelled and that the sentence should have ended with a question mark, but three out of five is better than none.

Once the partners had worked together to edit the papers, each child copied his or her report in best handwriting. "I am not going to type anything hard to read," I warned. As the children finished copying their reports, they brought them to me. I checked them over quickly, correcting whatever mechanical problems remained, and then typed each on my microcomputer. I had brought my printer to school and the children were most impressed with watching their words appear on the screen and shortly after be "magically" printed. I processed as many as I could at school as the children watched in fascination, or began their ink drawings to be copied for our book. I finished the rest over the weekend, sure I would never do this again, but the parents were so impressed and the children were so proud, perhaps just once more! Several parents have access to word processing equipment, so maybe I can get some volunteer help next time. In fact, Sharon and David say that they type on their computers at home. I think I need to get organized if we are going to do a book on animals next month!

May:

Science Units This month, we finished our final two science units: "Matter" and "Animals." The children already had a tremendous amount of prior knowledge about animals; from what I can tell, it is part of the science curriculum at every grade level. I know I taught an animals unit in fourth grade and Dee teaches one in first. Matter, on the other hand, was another matter! Jim even showed his language prowess when I got frustrated with their inability to keep mass and weight distinctions straight: he asked, "But Miss Tent, what does it really matter?"

We continued our push for independence and they are actually acting more like middle-schoolers. Once again I let them preview their textbook for vocabulary words and tried to focus their attention on picture, context, and morphemic clues as well as show them how our dictionaries and reference books could help them develop meanings for unknown words. As I mentioned, we had a great deal of difficulty making the mass/weight distinction. Of course, children think of weight as how many pounds they are, which is in fact their mass. Weight, or the amount of pull between objects, is a concept many of them never did understand. It helped to have them view films of astronauts and to realize that the astronauts still had the same mass but were weightless because of lack of gravity. We used a balance scale to measure mass and made a simple pulley scale to measure weight. I do believe my more able students understood the difference by the time we finished.

The conceptual difficulty of the unit on matter was balanced by the ease   **Research**
with which my students approached the unit on animals. Even my slower students knew most of the information in our textbook, so we read it quickly to remind ourselves of what we knew and reestablish the terminology. Then we spent our time researching various animals and their habits. I divided the class into five groups, each to become experts about one class of animals. One group learned about invertebrates. Another group studied both amphibians and fish, because there are so few amphibians. The other three groups studied reptiles, birds, and mammals. We decided that each group would create an ''encyclopedia'' for their class of animals and that we would donate these to our school library as this fifth grade's graduation present to the school. The encyclopedia would include a general introduction giving characteristics of the animal class and illustrated pages for as many different animals as we had time to do.

Of course, we brainstormed a list of questions about each animal, classified the questions, and decided on key words to help us locate information. We then set up a data chart with the questions along the top and room to list the various animals down the side. I also had the children keep a list of sources, each of which they numbered as they added it to their list. They then put the number and page number next to the various pieces of information they found. This was not perfect but they did note more source information than they had last month.

In addition to everyone's main function of finding and recording specific information, I gave each child an official duty. In each group, one child was the leader, keeping all the group's information and making sure everything got done. I tried to put good organizers in every group and appoint them leaders. Another child in each group was appointed reference librarian, taking primary responsibility for locating sources and keeping information accurate. I appointed an art director for each group, although all the children could do art and I provided tracing paper for the less artistic. The art director was to oversee the production of the art , however. I also had an editor, who looked at each article before it came to the editor-in-chief (me!). Finally, each group had a production manager whose job it was to put the finished pieces into the book and see to pagination, binding, cover design, index, etc.

It is hard for me to believe even now how hard all my children worked. They took their individual responsibilities very seriously and were determined that their group's encyclopedia would be the best. Parents told me stories of weekend trips to the public library and of hours their children spent reading, drawing, checking off what was there and what was needed, designing covers, and editing. I did not type the books this time but let the children write the pages in their neatest handwriting. I had no idea some of them could write so well.

The idea of giving every child some special responsibility worked out much better than I had anticipated. It used the strengths of all and made each child feel that his or her contribution was critical. The groups—which contained bright and slow, industrious and lazy, impulsive and reflective children—all worked well and developed a strong sense of cohesion. Next year I shall have to find more ways to assign groups in which each has a special responsibility.

June:

Why is it you think the year will never end and then it ends before you are ready? This year's students are grown-up middle-schoolers now and I am looking forward to a super fifth-grade year next year, knowing so much more than I did when I began this year.

We did our final health unit in the final week of school. This was a required unit on drug abuse. I still contend that fifth-graders are too young to be considering this sophisticated topic. I was surprised, however, at how much some of them knew. Jim suggested we have a scavenger hunt, but I demurred.

Thinking Processes   In looking back over the year, particularly at my ambitious goals, I am "cautiously optimistic"! My checklist demonstrates that, for the first time in my illustrious teaching career, I paid more than lip service to helping students learn the thinking skills that seem to be the foundation for all other learning. The two I always found hardest were, of course, the highest-level ones, evaluating and applying. But as the year went on I did learn how to phrase questions so that students would have to evaluate and apply what they were learning to new situations. And I finally got in the habit of saying, "This question requires a lot of brain power. You will have to think and decide what your answer will be. I don't want to see any hands until I have counted slowly to five." This five seconds of wait time was crucial to the students' ability to develop thoughtful answers and, as research suggests, improved the quality of their answers dramatically. I also tried to assign projects that required evaluation and application.

Meaning vocabulary was probably the area in which I felt most satisfied with the progress we made toward our goals. I was particularly excited to see that students could select their own words to learn, and could independently apply the strategies I taught them to learn the appropriate meanings.

My students made tremendous progress in writing and researching, but they are still a long way from where I would like to have had them when they went off to middle school. I guess these are such complex processes that they take a very long time to develop. Some children, Sharon and Pat particularly, are indeed independent writers and researchers. My slower ones made some progress and seemed to learn a lot of content as they engaged in writing and researching, but their skills are still very rudimentary. Many of my average children also made progress in learning how to write and do research, but they continue to need a lot of guidance. I always wonder how much real teaching they get once they leave elementary school. My friends who are high school teachers are always ribbing me about my "misguided" beliefs that the only real instruction goes on at elementary school. I hope in this case that they are right because, even with good elementary instruction, these kids still have much content to learn as well as independent learning strategies.

Next year I plan to use the same schedule as this year, with one exception. I am going to use both Thursday and Friday for integration days. I found that I could integrate the teaching of the language arts and mathematics skills with all my units and students got opportunities to apply these skills to real problems. It was not as hard as I thought it would be to cover the textbooks in four days, because I chose what was most important. Mr. Head, who was skeptical about my Friday integration at the beginning of the year, was actually very pleased with what he saw on Fridays and sent other teachers to observe. He even suggested I might want to consider two days of integration. I didn't tell him I had already decided to do so!

All in all, a quite successful year! Now, if I can just stay at the fifth-grade level another year or two, I think I could get quite good at this. This summer, I plan to become proficient in Italian and French as Bo and I take our rail-passes through Europe!

REFERENCES

Asimov, I. (1983). *How did we find out about the universe?* New York: Walker and Co.

Branley, F. M. (1981). *The planets in our solar system.* New York: Crowell.

Cleary, B. (1984). *Ramona forever.* New York: Morrow.

Collier, J. (1983). *Planet out of the past.* New York: Macmillan.

Corbett, S. (1981). *The deadly hoax.* New York: E. P. Dutton.

Engdahl, S. L. (1981). *The doors of the universe.* New York: Atheneum.

Holbrook, S. (1983). *Canada's kids.* New York: Antheneum.

Hoover, H. M. (1981). *Another heaven, another earth.* New York: Viking.

Lyle, K. (1983). *Take a trip to Canada.* New York: Franklin Watts.

Paterson, K. (1977). *Bridge to terabithia.* New York: Crowell.

Pringle, L. (1983). *Being a plant.* New York: Crowell.

Rahn, J. E. (1981). *Plants up close.* Boston: Houghton Mifflin.

Shreve, S. (1984). *The flunking of Joshua T. Bates.* New York: Knopf.

CHAPTER 10

Social Studies and English

August:

My name is Hugh Mann, and this is my second year of teaching. I've been hired primarily to teach social studies and some English; I'm also the head varsity baseball coach. I probably know more about baseball than about the school subjects I'm hired to teach, but I actually enjoy both. Sports and books have always been a part of my life. I even read for fun in high school, when most of my friends barely touched a book—unless it had especially interesting pictures.

This year's teaching assignment is the same as last year's. I have two sections of American history and three sections of English II. Both courses are intended for sophomores. My department head said that he typically assigns first- and second-year people just two courses, but that the load will go to three or even four preparations as experience is gained. I appreciate the relatively light load because I'm still getting a handle on how to teach effectively. My student teaching and my first year of teaching were largely matters of staying alive. The students and I got along well and they seemed to learn something, but I frequently was at a loss while planning lessons. I've given some thought to my teaching over the summer and I intend to try some new things this year. One of the guys I played baseball with this summer teaches also, and he gave me some tips I intend to try out.

My reaction to the textbooks for my courses still is near panic: "How can I ever cover all this stuff?" The history text contains twelve units, which consist of three to five chapters each. The chapters are long and just stuffed with facts! There are two books to teach for English, a literature anthology and a language arts text, which presents mechanics such as grammar, spelling, and writing conventions. Needless to say, the English texts also are rather imposing. I want my students to spend time with materials other than the textbook, so right now I'm still not sure how to get everything covered.

My other big concern is managing approximately 130 students each day. Maintaining discipline and keeping the students interested in the subjects can be big problems, as I remember from my own high school days and from my brief teaching experience to date. Stay tuned, and as I report my teaching adventures each month in this journal, we'll both find out how I do.

September:

One of my first activities in American history was to take my classes through a "tour" of the book. I pointed out the table of contents, the glossary, and the index. Within each chapter I directed the students' attention to the intro-ductions, conclusions, bold-faced headings, footnotes, illustrations, maps, graphs, and review sections. I wanted to accustom the students to the text so they could better predict, organize, and review while moving through it. When I recommended reading the end-of-chapter questions before reading the chapter, several students spoke up. One student, Ken, thought my recom-mendation sounded like cheating; Judy informed me that she did it all the time because her honors English teacher in junior high had suggested it; and Lonnie sullenly announced that if they had to answer the questions, then it only made sense to go to them first, find the answers, and be done with it. I responded that the special features of a book were intended to help people learn, and that I did not plan to have students merely copy down answers to sets of questions. "I want to develop your abilities to think, not to regurgi-tate," I rather pompously declared. "Use the special features of the books in order to learn what is presented. We'll spend most of our class time discussing what you've read."

Well, we discussed our way through the first unit of the American history text, "Early Years in America," and, frankly, the discussions weren't very pro-ductive. The unit consisted of about 100 pages with chapters on Native Amer-ican culture before Columbus' arrival, the European age of discovery, and England in the New World. Our discussion of the first chapter typifies how the other discussions have gone this month.

The students came in on Monday, having been told to read the chapter on early Native Americans over the weekend. I was ready to go. "What did you think of the chapter?" I asked. When nobody responded right away, I called on Ken. "There sure were a lot of tribes," he answered. Nobody else had anything to say. I could see some of the students in the back begin to put their heads down for a nap or to whisper to each other, so I immediately asked another question, "What did you learn about the tribes?" Judy piped up that they played different ball games. "Mr. Mann, the Eskimoes played some kind of kickball, and I think the book said the Algonquins invented lacrosse." Rod, this year's football quarterback wanted to know how lacrosse was played. I told what I knew, and the discussion picked up as comparisons were made between lacrosse and the various other sports the students knew. I chimed in to explain in some detail how catching and throwing a ball with a lacrosse stick differed from catching a baseball and either hitting it with a bat or throwing it. Before I knew, the hour was over and our discussion of the chapter had ended. I felt uneasy about what had been accomplished, but the next class came in and I didn't have time to sort out where I had gone wrong.

In order to help develop vocabulary, I reproduced word puzzles from the teacher's resource book. The puzzles consisted of words with their spelling scrambled accompanied by definitions. For instance, *UTRIPSAN* was next to "Fundamental religious group that established a colony under the auspices of the Massachusetts Bay Company." When I passed out the first set of scrambled words, Judy completed it in about 10 minutes and asked if she could make up her own for the class to do. At the other extreme, Ambrose never turned his in. I asked him about it, and he reported that he never was good with "them kind of things." In general, the classes worked busily completing the worksheets; the sharper students got all the items correct, and the duller students missed some. I wonder if the puzzles are producing any new insights into the words and their meanings?

Sophomore English began about the same as American history. One assignment dealt with book reports. Since our anthology kept everyone on the same track, I wanted to give students a chance to branch out on their own. There are terrific books written specifically for teenagers, and some of my sophomores could easily handle materials intended for adults. Thus, the assignment was for each student to read at least one book per month and turn in a written summary as well as a statement about whether they would recommend the book to a friend. I heard some grumblings like, "We've been doing book reports since third grade," but when I reassured the class that they could choose any book they wanted, they seemed to accept the idea.

Language arts probably should be called "language skills" because it covers topics such as parts of speech, sentence construction, and report writing. There is very little about the artistic, creative side of language in the text. I decided to cover language skills Monday through Wednesday and do literature on Thursdays and Fridays. Language skill work mostly consisted of me explaining various rules and definitions ("Proper nouns name particular persons, places, or things.") followed by exercises in locating the item that had just been defined ("Underline the proper nouns in the following sentences."). I usually also have the students make up sentences containing the items being studied.

The literature anthology is focusing on theme. The passages are pretty interesting, so most of the students read them. After reading each passage, we discussed its theme.

All in all, I'm not really satisfied with how my classes went this past month. My routines are functioning smoothly enough, but my students seem like automatons going through the motions. I don't get it! I'm running my classes the way I remember them being run when I was a student. Isn't this the way it's supposed to be?

October:

Our discussions in both classes of American history moved this month from very loose to very structured. I was getting concerned about the students coming in unprepared and leading me off on tangents, so I resolved to hold the class closer to the text. This month's unit was on the American Revolution.

One day we were talking about the early events in Boston. After dealing with the Stamp Act, the Quartering Act, and the Boston Massacre, we got to the Boston Tea Party. Lonnie wanted to know why it was called a "party." After I stated that some words have several different meanings, Rod interjected that the Boston Garden, home of the Celtics basketball team, really wasn't a vegetable or flower garden. "Who are the Celtics?" Ambrose wanted to know. Well, Ken eagerly began explaining the past triumphs of Larry Bird, Bill Russell, and Bob Cousy when I interrupted forcefully, "No more talk about words with multiple meanings! What did Lord North and King George do after the tea was dumped into the harbor?" As soon as I got the answer that I wanted ("passed the Intolerable Acts"), I asked "What did the Intolerable Acts consist of?" After Judy finally supplied the correct answer, I continued with questions such as, "When did the First Continental Congress meet?" "What actions did it take?" "Why did General Gage order a march on Concord?" and "Where did the Second Continental Congress meet?" Answering these questions kept all my students on their toes and we moved efficiently through the chapters, although I must confess that I began feeling like a prosecuting attorney. I also began to wonder if I were promoting only rote memory in my students.

A high point in history this past month was the arrival of the first edition of the weekly magazine we'll be receiving during the year. The magazine is quite appealing! It has many visuals, lots of color, timely articles, and features such as crossword puzzles that the students really like. I pass the magazines out each Friday, and the students either read them on their own or complete assignments that are due by the end of the following week.

The scrambled word puzzles began losing their appeal by the end of September, so I began setting aside about 30 minutes a week for vocabulary work using the dictionary or the textbook. I wrote a list of important words on the board, and the students copied the words and looked up their definitions. This started off about as well as the puzzles because everybody kept busy and almost everybody turned in completed papers. The students worked with abstract terms such as *sovereignty, loyalist, representation, inalienable right,* and *confederation*; the list also included names such as *Lafayette, Greene, Adams, Hamilton,* and *Jefferson*.

American history still doesn't seem to be grabbing my students' attention the way I want it to. As in September, we're moving through the material, but the students don't seem to be connecting anything they're learning with their present lives. Something else is going to have to happen!

In English I implemented a rather successful grouping system to help with **Group Work** our boring study of the parts of speech. Working in groups to solve problems seems to improve the acquisition of information as well as social skills. And since one assignment per group rather than one assignment per individual certainly decreases the paperwork, it was worth it to spend some time figuring out how to get my students to cooperate with each other.

I introduced the grouping system by informing the students that they could work with another person or two on the next set of assignments. I emphasized that they could work by themselves if they wanted, knowing that some students have extreme difficulty interacting with others. For instance, Theresa, in one of my English sections, has not yet spoken to another class member. She invariably enters and leaves class by herself. I didn't want to force her to work with others or force others to work with her. The groups broke down according to predictable lines. Judy got together with two other college-bound types, Rod and another athlete teamed up, and Ken formed a group with two other friendly, gregarious students. I told them that their groups needed to last for one month before new ones could be formed and that they should always meet in the same spot during group work time. Each group was responsible for one finished assignment.

Then I had to come up with assignments that were conducive to group work. When student teaching, I had groups produce essays for or against capital punishment. The brainstorming in the groups that preceded the actual writing wasn't too bad, but getting three people to agree on even the first sentence had been practically impossible. With my language arts assignments, I was more careful. I presented specific elements, such as personal, relative, and demonstrative pronouns, then distributed handouts calling for appropriate pronouns to be inserted in sentences (''Those who hurt others hurt _____.''). I established a time limit, so that groups who didn't finish in class had to do so on their own. When time was up, I collected the papers and then went over them with the class. To be sure, analyzing the types of pronouns was a bit of a drag—I wonder what effect knowing which pronoun is which has on anything?—but I must say that the group work stirred the class in a rather positive way. Even Lonnie got involved with his two friends and actually turned something in.

Grading System

Holding students accountable for daily language arts work posed a problem until I decided to work with points. If a paper met criteria that I established, then I accepted it and gave it one point. Unacceptable papers were returned for another attempt. For instance, one assignment might consist of 20 unfinished sentences to be filled in and 5 original sentences to be written using a certain part of speech. If my criterion was 80 percent accuracy, those papers with at least 20 items correct received one point. I have posted the points, not grades, permanently on a bulletin board so group members know where they stand. The posting also helped solve the problem of coping with students' absences, showing students who missed a day how to keep track of what was due. Posting points took a good deal of time, but luckily I had two seniors assigned to me as teacher assistants. Once I showed them the system, they took full responsibility for keeping it updated.

Tests

The testing procedures that I began in English worked out rather well. The tests that I gave matched what I had been teaching as closely as possible. If in class I'd had the students circle particular types of words in sentences, then my tests also included lots of circling items. If I'd had the students make up their own sentences, then they did likewise on the test. Thus, all who had consistently worked with me in class had a good chance to succeed. However, I also tested students on some material that I had assigned for work at home. This allowed my high-ability students to show what they could do. During the month I made sure to demonstrate test-taking strategies such as returning to difficult multiple choice items and generating key words before writing essay answers. When it came time to report mid-term grades, I included points earned in groups, test scores, and the great intangible, class participation.

As I think about October, I believe my instruction picked up in English but didn't do well in American history. The group work in English is allowing some good interaction among the students as they deal with the rather mundane mechanics of language. But I'm still bound to the text in American history, and I'm having difficulty getting that book to come alive.

November:

Our study of "The New Nation" in American history this month leveled off at a new plateau. My procedure of assigning certain pages and then discussing them just wasn't succeeding. The discussions either ranged far from the topic or I ended up conducting an interrogation that emphasized isolated facts. This month I got tired of discussions and spent most of the time lecturing and showing movies. I began the lectures and movies when we came to the section of the text about the Bill of Rights. We had slogged our way through federalism and checks and balances, and I was getting no response to my questions about the first ten amendments to the Constitution. As a result, I just began talking. There were few interruptions, so I continued. Occasionally someone wanted to know, "Is this going to be on the test?" to which I answered, "Maybe." The next day I showed a surprisingly interesting movie that detailed the contents and implications of the Bill of Rights. Basic liberties such as freedom of speech, protection from unreasonable search and seizure, and due process of law were made somewhat real by the situations enacted in the film. Most of the class actually watched the movie, there were no discipline problems, and my preparation time was practically zero. I'll probably continue with this lecture-and-film procedure a little longer.

Vocabulary instruction took an upswing this month. The word puzzles and searches for definitions had kept everybody well occupied, but little learning seemed to go on. The students rarely remembered the definitions and were at a total loss to explain the terms in their own words. So one day I decided to explain each term by analogizing, that is, by connecting new concepts and terms to something I thought the students had already experienced. For example, *strict construction* and *loose construction* were two high-sounding terms with somewhat vague meanings that came up during our study of the Constitution. "Let's say that you get grounded at home for doing something against the rules," I explained, "and a school club or team that you belong to is going somewhere after school the next day. Would you be able to go?" Judy volunteered the fact that she had never been grounded, but, if she were, her parents probably would make her come home right after classes. On the other hand, Allison contemptuously reported, "They wouldn't dare try to keep

Vocabulary

me in the house every afternoon and evening." Ken reported that it probably would depend on the mood his parents were in each day, and Rod was sure that he could practice with his team but would then need to be home soon afterwards. I pointed out that some families seemed to interpret the "grounding" punishment strictly while others saw it loosely. Thus distinguishing *strict* and *loose constructions* of grounding, I explained how Jefferson's and Hamilton's debate over a federal bank was based on the conflict between strict and loose constructions of the Constitution. This explanation seemed to take hold and I made a mental note to connect more terms with students' lives in that way.

Two words, *party* (as in Federalist Party) and *cabinet*, came up in this unit and deserved special attention. These multiple-meaning words can be really confusing for some students, so I explained their meanings in American history as clearly as possible, pointing out how those meanings differed from general uses of the terms. I reminded the class about the Boston Tea Party and compared that use of the term with its uses in Federalist Party, being a party to a crime, and weekend party. As I explained each term, the students took notes. This way of developing vocabulary definitely makes the students depend on me for information, but there is a lot to learn and sometimes my explanations are the best way to get that information across. In fact, my lectures do seem to be getting the students' attention, but I wonder if this is the best way to teach.

The group work during language skills exercises in English continued nicely this month. Allison brought in some soft rock albums from home, so we play background music during this time. Terry, perhaps the hardest working student in school, really gets involved with these worksheets; whereas Allison more than once questioned the value of knowing the difference between an action verb and an auxiliary verb. "Mr. Mann," she would say, "sometimes I just get tired of answering your paper questions." During our literature study, Allison does a little better. We're into characterization now, having finished theme, plot, and setting, and she does contribute to those discussions.

Comprehension Lesson

One teaching strategy that I tried with characterization worked especially well. I called my strategy an Adjective Checklist. Before having the students read a short story in the anthology, I listed five adjectives on the board: *shrewd*, *brusque*, *honest*, *witty*, and *helpful*. The students and I spent a little time going over those terms by describing behaviors that exemplified each of the five. I then read aloud a brief poem by Shel Silverstein and explained why I thought "helpful" best described the main character in the poem. Lonnie disagreed, saying that "shrewd" was better, but he couldn't support his argument when I pressed him. "What part of the poem supports the fact that he was shrewd?" I asked. Allison stepped in and gave quite a convincing argument for "shrewd" that would never have occurred to me. I accepted her argument and complimented her on her insight into the poem. Only then did I give the assignment, "Read the story on pages 38 to 45 in the anthology and decide which adjective best describes Mr. Steiner, the main character."

The next day we had a lively discussion about whether "witty" or "brusque" best described Mr. Steiner. Students who argued for either adjective came up with some logical reasons for their choices. Finally, Ambrose spoke up. "What's the answer, Mr. Mann?" I knew I was in a dilemma. Giving my answer would limit future discussions because students simply would be trying to anticipate what I would say; on the other hand, not giving an answer seemed unfair because students like to get closure on a problem. Additionally, I must admit that I was becoming used to playing the role of the all-knowing teacher, so not giving the "correct" answer was difficult. My solution was to have students write their choices and justify them on notebook paper. This allowed students to get some closure in their minds, and it allowed me to evaluate their rationales rather than their actual choices.

The adjective checklist continued to work well throughout our study of characterization. It let us cover the traditional aspects of characterization study (physical appearances, motivations, effects on others) while providing a way to analyze characters in real life. The students learned some new vocabulary, and they obtained good insights into the stories. Additionally, our discussions stayed on track without me asking a thousand picky questions. Whenever a student would choose an adjective, I would ask something like, "What makes you think that?" or "What leads you to that conclusion?" Comprehension was directed, and the students' writing consisted of more than completing unfinished sentences or taking notes.

The adjective checklist also worked well with the groups. I brought in several stories written at different levels of difficulty and had each group choose two. Including materials of different levels provided appropriate challenges for my good as well as poor readers. The groups' task was to decide as a group which adjectives from a list of eight gave the best and worst descriptions of the characters I designated. I went from group to group and had them justify their choices to me. Time was short for me to get to all the groups, but I made it. My follow-up test consisted of six adjectives and a two-page story, which I read aloud while the class followed along. The task was to choose the best description and justify it. As I had expected, Allison produced a very insightful paper.

In English our discussions were productive, group members interacted well and completed their tasks, and my grading system was holding up. The students seemed quite alert throughout the class period. Vocabulary study in American history also picked up this month, thanks to analogizing. But I'm still looking for a way to deal with comprehension of the text.

December:

The success we had in English with the adjective checklist made me think twice about the book projects I had assigned. Some good books were being read. Students were picking up old favorites such as *Watership Down, The Pigman,* and *Kon-Tiki* from the school and public library, from each other, and from bookstores. I recommended some newer titles and provided class time for the students to recommend others. However, the reports weren't very compelling. The summaries were mostly adequate, but the brief evaluative statements that I required were on a pretty low level. Students typically stated either that a book was interesting or that it was boring.

Book Projects

So I changed the assignment. Students still needed to read novels out of class, but they had choices of ways to respond to the novels. I divided the assignment among the "big four" literary elements—plot, setting, character, and theme—and provided alternatives for considering those elements. For instance, students could consider setting by diagramming a stage for a scene to be dramatized, or by drawing a map depicting locations in the story. Students analyzed characterization by completing an adjective checklist or by justifying their choices of popular actors and actresses to portray the main characters. Once I got to thinking about it, I saw many options for eliciting responses to stories. Some examples that emerged included the following: select a piece of representative dialogue, choose the book's most important word, describe a change that occurred in a character, explain how a situation you've been in is similar to one in the book, convince a movie producer that your book should be made into a movie, write the book's epilogue. I tried to provide a mix between strongly academic options (What was the theme of the story?) and more artistic ones (Create a mobile that represents the story.).

Thinking Processes

The students seemed to appreciate this new freedom. They produced about the same amount of work as before, but more thinking processes seemed to be in evidence with the new system. Some of the images produced when students dealt with setting and character were outstanding; the connections students drew between their lives and the characters' were sharply drawn; and the hypothetical sales pitches to movie producers were organized well. Moreover, students seemed to like the combination of my clear expectations plus some freedom of choice.

Another major change begun in English this month was to unify what I was teaching. I had felt uncomfortable with the diversity of doing worksheets on superlative degree, collecting projects on whatever book each student chose, and studying the genre of adventure and one or two literary elements in the literature anthology. This fragmented way of doing things was relatively easy to manage, but it lacked the coherence that I thought an English class should have. Science fiction was the next genre in our anthology, so I decided to extend that topic to language arts and the book projects.

Literature

Making the extension to the book projects was not too difficult. I met with the school librarian and the English department head to learn what science fiction was available. We turned up individual copies of numerous books and found a class set of *Flowers for Algernon*. I then announced to my sophomores that December's book projects were to follow the response format that I had begun and were to be based on science fiction novels. Judy reacted to my news in a surprisingly negative way, "Science fiction, yucch! Why do we have to read that stuff?" I explained the value of the topic and informed the class that tying the novels in with the short stories made all kinds of sense—at least in terms of deepening insights into a topic. "Besides," I said, "there are some great science fiction books. *God Stalk, The Beggar Queen,* and *Firestarter* are great, new books, and the *The Martian Chronicles, 20,000 Leagues under the Sea,* and *2001: A Space Odyssey* are practically classics. You'll love them! Trust me."

One way to get students such as Judy into science fiction was for me to read some stories to them. When I told the class my plan, I sensed a "wait and see" attitude. I don't think too many male secondary-school teachers had read to these students. The story I chose was punchy and reasonably short, I reviewed it the night before I presented it, and I read it with as much force as possible. I told myself that I was at a speech contest, the students were the judges, and I intended to impress them. Well, the group attended to every word. It was a great experience! I think they were amazed at how much fun it was to form their own images while listening rather than have a filmmaker form the images for them.

Extending the language skills work to science fiction took more planning on my part, but it seems to have paid off. Writing informal letters and business letters was the unit in our language arts text. I tied letter writing into science fiction by having students compose letters that were related to situations in the stories. For instance, as a group we read a great Ray Bradbury story about a hunter who went back in time to shoot dinosaurs. "OK, group," I said, "we're going to write a letter to a close friend describing the trip." After detailing the purpose, audience, and form of the assignment a bit more, I projected an overhead transparency of a model letter. I pointed out aspects such as where the date went, how to address the letter, how to sign off, and how to develop the composition. My model letter was brief, but it did have an introduction, a chronological description of the trip (which I pointed out as only one way to go), and a summarizing statement at the end. The students then went to their groups for 10 minutes to brainstorm and organize what they intended to say. Finally, 20 minutes of class time was devoted to individuals writing their letters. Rather than grade the letters themselves, I gave one point to each letter written according to the form I'd presented. Students who didn't follow the form were given another chance.

Guided Writing Lesson

The same basic procedure was followed with business letters. I assigned a business letter to a governmental agency requesting a permit to take hunters back in time. Possible governmental objections posed by the story were to be countered in the letter. Again I explained the task, modeled the writing of a business letter, allowed the students to generate and organize information before writing, and then let them write. As with the lesson on informal letters, I took the skill from our language text and applied it to our current topic. I still assigned one or two of the skill book exercises as practice in letter writing, but the skill had already been tied into the content of our study. I don't know why I didn't do this earlier.

And finally, thank goodness for the holiday season! Teaching is hard work, and I was ready for a break. My social life took a dip during the past four months, so I've been trying to revive it during this time. Some college friends came into town, so we had some catching up to do. I invited Kay Bella, a first-year Spanish teacher at school, to one of our parties, and she handled herself well with my rowdy friends. She and I talked shop for a few hours, but that's what we had most in common. I told her how I unified what I taught in English, how the group assignments and book projects worked, and how frustrated I was with American history. She said she had some control problems with her classes, but that basically she was getting along fine. She briefly described how she directed students' reading comprehension. It was fun comparing observations about teaching with her.

January:

Well, I made some major changes in American history this month. At the beginning of the month, students were coming in late to my class and some were even skipping. This upset me because I had thought at least I had kept things moving. I spent a good amount of time preparing my lectures, I always included some humor, and I was familiar with the quirks of every movie projector in the school because I showed so many films. Allison was the one who helped me see the light. She came into class one day muttering about another session of brain death. "Allison, what are you talking about?" I asked. She looked me straight in the eye and replied "When do we get to *do* something in here? All we do is listen to you or some electronic voice." I didn't confront her, but I did think about what she said. Maybe she was right. Perhaps I overreacted to the unsatisfying discussions we had at the beginning of the year. I thought about our discussions in English with the adjective checklist and about what Kay had said about directing comprehension, and I decided to try something similar in American history.

Comprehension Lesson

We were finishing the Civil War and Reconstruction when I first attempted to direct comprehension of part of the text. My planning consisted of several steps. First, I decided what portion of the book my students would read. In September I had had everybody read every page of the text. That was unreasonable because the text simply contained too much information; after all, I too was learning new material. Thus, I decided to show a film about the major Civil War battles, and to have students concentrate their reading on the aftermath of the war. Once I decided to have students read only about Reconstruction, I further pared down the points I wanted them to understand. The text provided more than enough information, so I decided that it would be good for my students to read in order to find out why Reconstruction had ended. Why would a seemingly good thing stop?

Then I had to figure out what my sophomores needed to know in order to get the desired information from the text. I decided to spend some time explaining the reasons for Reconstruction as well as the terms *carpetbagger*, *freedman*, *sharecropper*, *scalawag*, and *Ku Klux Klan*. The first three terms could be presented by pointing out that they were compound words and then explaining the background of the parts of the words. For instance, *free* and *man* gave awfully good clues about the meaning of that word; I just needed to develop them a bit. I found some pictures representing all five of the terms, too. In order to explain the reason for Reconstruction, I decided to draw an analogy between reconstructing the South and making up after a family fight. I intended to point out how the winner actually comes out even further ahead if the loser is welcomed back and the wounds are healed. All of this planning took about an hour. One hour seemed like a lot of time at first, but it occurred to me that if it worked, my life in the classroom would be much more pleasant.

I began the lesson at center stage once again. I informed the class that they needed to know important concepts in order to understand Reconstruction. I then went through my analogy of a family fight, presented the pictures, and pointed out the parts of the compound words. Next, I had them open their books to the pages on Reconstruction in order to survey the information for one minute. Then I set a specific purpose: "I would like you to read these five pages in order to find out why Reconstruction ended. If healing the wounds of a family fight is so important, then why did the healing process stop?" This purpose for reading seemed especially useful because the students couldn't just scan the pages to find a specific fact, nor could they answer my question based on what they knew already. They needed to read the whole passage, and they needed to read between the lines.

As the students were reading, I sat at my desk and read also. This was to model the behavior I wanted them to follow, and it allowed me one more opportunity to brush up on the information. After almost everybody had finished reading, I repeated my original question, "Why did Reconstruction end?" The discussion that followed stayed right on target. Rod didn't interject any comments related to sports, and Ken didn't go off on any tangents, either. Even Terry, who rarely spoke up in class, contributed some thoughts. After a while, I imposed some organization by saying, "OK, let's see if we can list the major reasons on the board." We then listed four major reasons, corruption, incompetence, economics, and changes in leadership. Next I said, "Take another few minutes, reread the text, see if we've listed all the major reasons, and see if these four are correct." Nobody came up with any substantial changes, so the list was left for the class to copy into their notes.

This strategy had many similarities to my lessons with the adjective checklist. Perhaps the biggest similarity was that students knew in general what they were looking for when they were reading. Before, even Judy had seemed to have difficulty separating important from trivial information. That's not surprising when you look carefully at textbooks; they seem to consist of just one darn fact after another. It's also not surprising when you consider the questions I had asked after reading; students needed to memorize the whole passage because they never knew what I might ask about. Setting purposes before reading seemed to help considerably.

I was concerned that my students might come to depend on me totally for direction. What would happen when I wasn't around to tell them what to learn? I liked providing clear, specific direction, but I wanted my students to provide some direction on their own. Because of this concern, I implemented my second big change of the month. I began fading my instruction.

Independence

Fading myself out of center stage and my students in will take place over a long period of time, but this was the month I began to bring my students in on the act of setting purposes for comprehension. After a few weeks of me setting the purposes, I began by having the students set their own. "OK, group, what is the first thing you should do when getting ready to read in order to learn?" I asked. Judy responded that looking over the material in order to gain an impression of what was coming should be done first. Allison spoke up, "Once you know generally what to expect, you should establish some goals about what you intend to learn." When I was reasonably sure that the group knew the strategies for approaching a text, I had them apply those strategies to what we were reading in American history. Rod spoke up, saying he thought they should read in order to determine five key terms from the passage. The group agreed that was a good enough reason for reading, so they got into their books. After reading, I said, "You know that you should follow up to see if you got the information that you set out to get, so let's do it." Students reviewed the information they gathered by listing key terms on the board, and eventually selected five key terms.

My directing comprehension of assigned readings, as well as my fading of that direction, made a big difference in the general tone of the class. Students seemed more involved in the content, and I felt as though I were providing some skills that students could take with them to 11th grade and beyond.

February:

Literature

February in sophomore English class was spent on the skill of persuasive writing and on the general topic of relationships, both among family members and among members of racial groups. Some fine novels deal with both types of relationships, so I recommended older books such as *Black Boy, Roots, I Know Why the Caged Bird Sings*, and *Cry, the Beloved Country*, as well as newer books such as *Who Is Carrie?* and *Chernowitz*. You never know, some assignments really stimulate some students, while leaving others cold. Requiring book projects seems to have worked well for Theresa, my student who rarely spoke. Theresa read *Roll of Thunder Hear My Cry*, and astounded me with a series of pen and ink sketches of scenes from the book. She showed fine technical skill producing the sketches, and her selection of scenes depicting Cassie's encounters with prejudice was just incredible. I showed the drawings to Kay, over in Foreign Languages, who informed me that Theresa always did superior, creative work in her class when they emphasized the cultural aspects of Spanish-speaking countries. Like I said, you never know exactly how things are going to work.

SSR

Fridays were set aside for free reading because I was getting so many complaints from the students about not having time to read after school. I told them that as long as they actually read they could have Fridays to do so, but that I would go back to regular work if they didn't. The time we spent reading—I always had a book going, too—was quite pleasant, so I hope it works out.

Perhaps the most effective lesson in persuasive writing dealt with magazine and newspaper advertising. The language arts book presented the major appeals advertisers use such as bandwagon, testimonial, name calling, and glittering generality. In order to teach these to my classes, I had my teaching assistants go through some magazines and newspapers I had gathered to find examples of each. I listed the appeals on the board and passed around examples of each so the students could experience them directly. Then I gave the following assignment: "We're going to collect advertisements and display them in brochures for a fifth-grade class at our elementary school. Locate at least two ads that exemplify each appeal. Write a brief definition under each example and mount it for display." We devoted three days to completing the brochures, and I delivered the acceptable ones to Connie Tent, a very nice fifth-grade teacher in our district who I had met at a party.

Guided Writing
Lesson

The next step in my lesson on advertising was to have the students compose their own ads exemplifying the various appeals. "Take one short story or novel you've read that deals with relationships and create three different advertisements for it. Pick any three of the appeals that we've studied and use each appeal to sell the same product. For instance, you might use a testimonial, a bandwagon, and a family approach for *Roots*. The audience for your ad consists of other 10th-grade students." Having studied the ads already, the students seemed to have a fairly good idea about how to start. Ken got very enthused and produced ads illustrating all the appeals. Allison pointed out that her one ad incorporated all three appeals.

After everyone had produced three ads, I had the students prepare to work in groups to revise their first efforts. "As you know, no composition is ever perfect after the first attempt, but with a little help from your friends, you might approach perfection on the next attempt or two." I demonstrated how I wanted the group members to work as peer response teams in order to polish each other's work. I displayed an ad for *Cry, the Beloved Country* that I had created for this demonstration and made the following comments: "The most effective aspect of this ad, I think, is its layout. The pictures and lettering are well balanced. The ad is eye-catching. The one thing I would like to know more about is the general topic of the book. The terms 'riveting' and 'sensational' don't provide much insight into the content of the story. I would like to know more about just what in this book is especially riveting and sensational." After commenting this way, I paused and then explained what I had done. My students were aware that I had first commented on positive features, then on the negative. I made it clear that my negative comments were couched as a request for information ("I would like to know more about . . . ") rather than as a direct criticism ("The weakest part of this writing is . . .).

Following this demonstration, I presented a few more ads and had students comment on what they liked and what they wanted to know more about. I then gave the final assignment: "All right, now please get into your groups and do to each other's ads what we just did to mine. However, instead of saying your comments aloud, please write them on a separate sheet of paper. When you get everybody's comments, then redo your ads as you see fit. You are to turn in to me your first drafts, the comments, and your second drafts for each of the three ads."

Most of the groups functioned well with this somewhat dangerous assignment. I was afraid that the comments would either be so snide and hurtful or so gushy and congratulatory that they wouldn't be useful. Lonnie and Allison did start verbally trading insults about each other's work—in a good-natured way, I think—but they stopped when I reminded them that their comments were to be written.

Once the ads were finished, I posted some of the better ones, with their authors' names concealed, on the bulletin board. I hid the authors' names because peer pressure is intense with this age group and displaying work might leave someone open to hurtful comments. On the other hand, I wanted to display some ads in order to model exemplary ones, increase interest in the topic, provide a focus for what we were doing, and just plain dress up the room. Some of the high school classrooms I've been in look more like waiting rooms to contain people for an hour than like places to stimulate learning.

Comprehension Lesson

My comprehension lessons in American history have resulted in some effective discussions. My setting a clear purpose before reading provides a great stabilizer for keeping us on track. One day Kay suggested that I have students predict what they will learn from the passage and then read to see how their predictions come out. She thought the predictions might help students assume control for their own learning, which is my goal in fading instruction. I tried predictions the very next day.

We were studying the Progressives of the early 1900s, and I wanted students to learn about some of the changes legislated by the federal government under Theodore Roosevelt. So after introducing some essential concepts, I asked the class, "What reforms do you think were implemented during Roosevelt's two terms?" I now believe in wait time, but a full 60 seconds was a long time even for me. "Come on, I know you don't know, but what's your best guess?" I prodded. Judy then volunteered that the Pure Food and Drug Act, the Hepburn Act to control freight transportation rates, and the conservation of natural resources might be some of Roosevelt's reforms. Needless to say, her "prediction" was right out of the book, which she confessed to having read the night before as part of her ongoing quest to earn straight As. As Kay and I left school that afternoon, I belittled her suggestion about predictions. "Hugh," she replied, "next time have Judy write on the board what the other students predict. You might also use passages from your classroom magazine because nobody will have a chance to read ahead in them. Why don't you use those magazines for more than a way to keep your students busy?"

Kay really knows how to get my attention! Well, to make a long story short, I did have students predict specific contents of a current events article in response to my question, "What might the administration do in order to calm this latest international disturbance?" If someone accurately predicted one of the plans, I just said "Uh-huh, maybe" and proceeded nonchalantly along. At one point, Ambrose called out, "All right, so what are the administration's plans?" And somebody chimed in with, "Give us the article." It was then that I realized the motivational impact of predictions. I passed out the magazines and the students read the current events article as intently as they had read anything all year.

March:

March is over. In history we finished studying the Depression, the New Deal, and World War II, so we are pretty much on target with regard to covering the content. At the beginning of the year I was concerned about getting through everything, but my decision to direct students' comprehension to the most important information, assign the reading of less important information, and ignore the least important information was a lifesaver. I use the textbook selectively; I am no longer a slave to it. One way I escaped total reliance on the text was by introducing book projects in American history.

A big difference between the American history book projects and the English II book projects concerned the type of book that was appropriate. My **Book Project** English classes had only to read literary materials, that is, novels. But, the history classes could choose either a literary or an expository book. Topical books, biographies, and fiction were fair game for this assignment. I figured that students could learn as much, if not more, from *Johnny Got His Gun* as from some factual treatise on the horrors of war. The only stipulation I set was that I had to approve the book before students began reading it. I granted these approvals before and after class as students brought their books to me for a quick check. My criteria for approval were rather loose; I just didn't want an able student working with an elementary-level picture book, nor a less able student saddled with some graduate-level scholarly tome.

Another difference between the English and the history projects was the format. In English I emphasized literary elements such as plot and setting, but those were not useful for history. In history students had first to summarize their books' contents. I showed them examples of summaries, so I felt reasonably confident that they were familiar with what I expected. Additionally, students were to produce a "creative" response to their book. I passed out a list of possible responses, including visuals, realia, dramatizations, and written or oral compositions. Students might produce a timeline or a collage; they might bring in representative artifacts; they might stage a brief play; or they might write a special dictionary for their book.

The American history book projects are meant to deepen students' understandings of specific aspects of history while allowing me to press on through the different eras. The projects allow both good and poor readers to tackle materials that present appropriate challenges. The projects also allow attention to historical themes rather than just a particular era. For instance, World War II was one of our topics this month, so I promoted *Hiroshima* along with other eras' war-related books such as *The Red Badge of Courage, All Quiet on the Western Front,* and *Warday.* Students who reported on these books invariable commented on the power of their themes.

Vocabulary   Vocabulary still is being emphasized in history. I frequently presented new words and their meanings during the comprehension lessons, and I also spend time focusing on vocabulary whenever a new term is used. Analogies and pictures are used most often when presenting the meanings for the words, and we've put on a few skits to help develop concepts. Rod and Judy presented a well-received skit this past month related to deficit spending. They played a newlywed couple with limited finances wanting to buy a state-of-the-art stereo system. After much debate, they resorted to using a department store credit account and then having to come up with the money later. Rod and Judy then stopped the skit and explained how a married couple using a credit card to buy a stereo is similar to a governmental agency using deficit spending to pay for items such as missiles and freeways.

Whenever possible, I tried to make things real when presenting concepts. To make some of the New Deal legislation come alive, I asked if any student's grandparents had worked in a CCC or WPA project. Terry brought in his grandfather, and I conducted an interview with him. Mr. Donahue related some fascinating stories about why he joined the CCC in the '30s, what the camps were like, and how some of the jobs were completed. I referred to the presentation as "oral history," which seemed to make it more acceptable than "grandpa telling stories."

Class time also was spent with the "alphabet soup" of New Deal innovations so that students would become more aware of abbreviations and acronyms. CCC, WPA, NRA, TVA, and AAA were some of the abbreviations that I presented. Students also came up with contemporary abbreviations such as FBI and CIA as well as acronyms such as NATO and MADD (Mothers Against Drunk Driving). Another vocabulary tactic I used was to highlight common parts of derived words. Many social studies terms contain morphemes that are helpful in figuring out the meanings of new words as well as retrieving the meanings of old ones. During one week with the New Deal, *conservative, unconstitutional, intrastate,* and *progressive* were the key vocabulary terms containing morphemes. I knew I should point out the root word in *conservative* because it is related to several words: conserve, conservation, conservationist, and conservatory. I listed the five words in a column, aligning the shared part, and asked what the words had in common. It was obvious that all five words contained *conserv,* so the discussion then was directed to its meaning. "Keep the same," "preserve," and "traditional" were associated with *conserve.* I closed this 5-minute lesson by drawing attention to the fact that looking for morphemes in words was helpful but occasionally misleading:

"Remember, folks, *undone* means *not done*, but *uncle* does not mean *not cle.*"

In English we continued our study of relationships, and worked on the language skill of reading and writing plays. I must say, most of the students are becoming quite independent with their writing. They are well aware that every composition has a purpose, audience, and form, and they now seem to determine those three aspects automatically before writing. They also generate and organize information on their own before writing. Their revising is becoming automatic, although I do occasionally need to remind them about it. As part of the unit on relationships, we read *West Side Story* in class and I showed a movie of *Romeo and Juliet*. "Hey, Mr. Mann," Ken called out, "why don't you let us write our own play?" "Why not?" I said. "I'll be here to help, but now you all know what you need to do in order to compose a play, so go to it." This was an extremely loose assignment, but I wanted to see just how independent this class was.

To my great satisfaction, the plays turned out quite well! I gave some class time to play production, but some time also was spent outside of school. Some students worked in groups and others worked individually. Some wrote for young children, some for a teenage audience, and some for adults. They all used the same basic form, with stage directions and characters' lines presented as in *West Side Story*. Each group who wanted to present their play to the class practiced it in a conference room in the library, which turned out to be a great stimulus for revision. I didn't pressure all the groups to present their plays because time simply wouldn't allow it. Having some plays presented orally and some only in written form worked out fine. As with other group assignments, points were awarded for acceptable work, although in this case a play was worth five points.

April:

The major emphasis this month in history was on conducting library research. We had done brief projects throughout the year, looking up information about famous people and places and sharing it orally in class, but April was the month for large-scale researching and reporting. I figured students would be reasonably interested in studying the American history unit, "A Decade of Change: 1960-1969," so I launched research projects on that era. One of my first steps was to help students ask researchable questions. First, I told the students about the general nature of the research they would be conducting, then I had them skim the chapter of the text that dealt with the 1960s. I wrote 1960-1970 at the top of the chalkboard and the words *Cuba, equal rights, Berlin, space exploration, John F. Kennedy,* and *Great Society* at the head of columns. "What do you know about these topics?" I asked the class. As information was presented, I placed key words under the headings. *Ted Kennedy, Martin Luther King, Bay of Pigs, Cuban Missile Crisis, Peace Corps,* and *Lee Harvey Oswald* were some of the terms that were listed. I then took

Independence

Research

Identifying Questions

one of the words and asked, "What do you know and what don't you know about this term?" I again listed the information and questions that were presented. Following this class brainstorming, students brainstormed in groups. The lists they made of what they didn't know pointed out the need for research.

The next day I spent more time helping students formulate researchable questions. I reminded the sophomores that questions typically began with a *wh* word (who, what, when, where, and why) and that while *why* could give the most trouble, it could also lead to the most interesting research. Following this brief introduction, I moved into a question-asking exercise. "Meet with one other person about one of the topics you are interested in researching," I directed. "Write down all *wh* questions about the topic that you can think of. For instance, if you took *Peace Corps*, you might ask, 'Where do Peace Corps volunteers work?' 'When did the Peace Corps begin?' 'Why was it begun?' and so on." The two-person teams were given exactly five minutes for brainstorming questions about one topic before I directed them to move to the other person's topic for five minutes. Following this exercise, many of the students had the beginnings of a research project.

Locating Information

Locating information in order to answer questions and generate new questions was the next step. I assumed that everybody had been introduced to aids such as indexes, encyclopedias, and the library card catalog, so I designed a scavenger hunt as a quick and dirty refresher. I came up with questions such as, "What page of our history textbook contains information about the Lusitania?" and "How many books does the library hold on the topic of nuclear energy?" We spent a day scrounging around the library to locate the appropriate information. I reviewed students' answers in class and probed to see whether everyone was comfortable locating information in the traditional sources.

Thinking that the *Readers Guide to Periodical Literature* was new to my sophomores, I asked our librarian to present it to my classes. As for all aids for locating information, the role of key words in using it well became apparent. The students saw that a few key terms were essential for research. For instance, Lonnie wanted to investigate "flower power," which he had heard was a mass movement of the 1960s. He was having trouble getted started, so I suggested looking under *youth movement, counterculture, protest,* and *hippie*.

Along with printed materials, I wanted each student to interview at least one person. I had already demonstrated interviews when Terry's grandfather came to class. The students had seen how I covered the questions I had prepared beforehand, how at certain times I simply said, "Can you tell me more?", and how I explained the presence of my tape recorder. A few students had difficulty locating someone who knew much about their topic (Ambrose was ready to quit after his parents told him they didn't know anything about Cesar Chavez) so I had to be resourceful at times (I suggested that Ambrose interview Kay).

As students began locating information about their topics and refining their questions, the hardest part began—organizing the information. I had been teaching periodically about taking notes from text, so my classes had a bit of a head start on this aspect of organization. One of my more frequent generic purposes for comprehending had been, ''Read in order to choose the three most important words from this section.'' After reading, students would explain why the three words they selected were most important; then I would explain my choices. At first Allison, Judy, and Ken were the only ones to volunteer their most important words, but more students began to open up as they became comfortable with the lesson. In fact, the students and I eventually began producing the same three words for the same reasons, indicating that we were beginning to organize text information in the same way.

Taking good notes from a passage is only the first step in organizing information; putting the notes into a logical framework is the other step. Constructing webs was my answer to organizing the mass of notes that students acquired. When I first introduced webs in class as part of my comprehension lesson plans, I got the ''aha, I understand'' response from several of my slower students. It seemed that for the first time they understood the logic of organizing information on paper. Because we had constructed several webs in class, my suggestion that individuals construct their own webs was readily accepted. Terry created a web that I used as a model. He had taken a large sheet of drafting paper and neatly written his topic, *Beginning the Vietnam War*, in the middle, surrounded by the subtopics, *French withdrawal*, *Ho Chi Minh*, *Ngo Dinh Diem*, and *Gulf of Tonkin Resolution*. He had then written key terms underneath each subtopic. Terry's paper demonstrated how to impose order on the mass of facts and ideas that researchers invariably uncover. He admitted that he probably would need to change his organization as he continued locating information, perhaps adding *Viet Cong*, but he was proud of the initial framework he had produced.

As we moved through the steps of asking questions, locating information, and organizing information, I had the students show me their work so I could help monitor their progress. Staying in touch systematically during these beginning steps seemed valuable as I was able to defuse many potential problems. For instance, Rod had decided to investigate the Soviet Union during the 1960s. ''What do you want to know about the Soviet Union?'' I asked. He replied that he would figure that out after doing some reading. A few days later I had the students turn in statements of their topic and research questions, and Rod still was unsure of what he wanted to do. I met with him briefly the next day, and together we decided that a study of U.S.-Soviet relations on nuclear testing would be interesting and feasible. Helping out during the research process was far more helpful than simply reacting to the finished product.

I also checked on students' webs before giving them the go-ahead to begin writing, a time-consuming but worthwhile procedure. Each student turned in a web that showed the order of presentation of the subtopics, along with the primary information associated with each subtopic. The webs were difficult to interpret because they were only outlines, but I could form impressions about who had a sense of direction and who was floundering. I wrote specific suggestions when I could, and set up brief meetings with those who required more complete overhauls.

Reports Once the webs were approved, students went to work on their written reports. I presented models of reports that my department head had on file so that the class had an idea of what their reports should look like. I required both a first and a second draft. A student of the author's choice and I both reacted to the first draft. The two questions that were to guide the first-draft readers were, "What was the most interesting aspect of this paper?" and "What do I want to know more about?" The students had had experience reacting to others' work, since they had earlier reacted to the advertisements, so things went smoothly.

After responding to the comments about their first drafts, students wrote a second draft and again submitted their papers to another student for a check on the mechanics of spelling, punctuation, and capitalization. The final, polished version was then turned in to me. One thing I learned for next year was to stagger the times that the reports were due. I had two classes working on reports, and the paperwork I faced when all the papers came in at once was staggering.

May:

Good old May, my favorite month! Spring was here in full force and so was baseball season. The baseball practices and games after school added to my responsibilities and decreased my time for lesson planning. It's a good thing that I had been leading my classes to independence, especially during the past few months, because I simply didn't have the time this month to do all the directing that I should have done. On a more valid, defensible line, leading students to independence was one of my goals, so it's good to see that I had made some headway.

Independence Portions of the history text still were required reading, but I didn't preteach as many concepts or set purposes as much as I used to. The students did that for themselves. When I established the fact that the portion of the text on President Reagan's terms of office was to be read, I asked the class, "What do you need to do?" Terry answered, "Look it over, think about what we already know about the topic, and decide what we should read carefully for," which indeed captured the essence of reading for a purpose. "Then go to it," was my directive. After a while, we decided that a timeline was called for, so after reading, one was created on the board, separating the trivial from the noteworthy information.

Vocabulary was handled much the same way as comprehension. Students identified the key terms and proposed ways to handle them. They pointed out the acronym in *Laser* (light amplification by stimulated emission of radiation); identified the root word in *miniaturization*; and connected the changes in lifestyles begun by the computer age with the changes that had occurred at the beginning of the industrial age. My role was simply to keep the class on track as I continually asked, "What terms do you need to know? What can you do to understand and remember each term?" I was comfortable posing such a question because throughout the year I had demonstrated ways to learn vocabulary. Of course, my help still was needed. *Reaganomics* was a term that the students easily separated into *Reagan* and *economics*, but that didn't do much to explain the underlying concept. I had to step in and explain the plan of cutting personal taxes as well as federal spending in order to reduce inflation. Analyzing the morphemes and reading the book simply didn't go far enough for gaining insight into that term.

A practice that I began hesitantly in April but pursued much more confidently in May was journal writing. Most of the writing I had students do consisted of brief entries, taking notes, or producing one- or two-paragraph essays. The research projects involved a good deal of writing, but they occurred too infrequently. The idea of having students informally record their impressions of historical topics really appealed to me. The classes were accustomed to free reading time, so time set aside for free writing was easily accepted. Once journals were started, I occasionally made a specific assignment, such as, "The average life expectancy has increased from about 47 in 1900 to 74 at present. Write a letter to our mayor informing him what the city needs to do in order to handle the increasing numbers of elderly people."

Content Journals

Grading the journals was bound to be a problem, especially with students like Lonnie who won't do anything if it's not for a grade, so I modified the point system I had used for group work. A certain number of pages needed to be filled with some evidence of independent thought in order to deserve one point. At the end of a month, 20 points were possible, so students with 18, 19, or 20 points (that is, those with 90% or more of the possible points) earned an A; those with 80 to 90 percent of the possible points earned a B, and so on. Most students produced the required amounts of writing and got a good grade for their journals. But more importantly, journal writing allowed students the opportunity to think through topics presented in class. It also seems to have promoted independent writing abilities; the most notable difference between the first entries and the later ones was the amount of writing that was produced.

A good deal of writing was being produced independently in my English classes. In fact, this month's book projects consisted of some exceptional pieces of writing. This month's topic in literature was sports, so books such as *Brian's Song* and *Paper Lion* were candidates for book projects. Rod read about George Plimpton, the writer who assumed the role of a football player; he then wrote a poem about Plimpton that paralleled "Casey at the Bat." Allison read a biography of Mary Decker, the distance runner, talked informally with some of her friends, and produced several insights into why individuals might devote themselves to competitive distance running.

Book Project

June:

School is out, baseball season is over (we had a winning season, taking second place in our conference!), and the students have gone to their various summer adventures. As I think back over the year, I realize that class sessions definitely picked up once I got the hang of directing students' comprehension. No more free-floating or interrogating "discussions" for me. The students seemed to appreciate knowing what to look for when they read, and their reactions to the materials certainly improved when they had a preset purpose. Of course, I didn't direct comprehension of everything the class read—book projects and research projects—so I didn't feel as if I were limiting students' opportunities to think for themselves.

Once I integrated skill work with literature topics in English, I felt much better about my writing instruction. Working on sentence structure in the context of meaningful passages, rather than with worksheets, made a lot more sense to me as well as to the students. I seem to have faded my writing instruction more completely than my comprehension instruction. The students could all independently plan, draft, and revise a composition rather well, or at least they all knew the steps to follow! I'm still not sure that they preview a passage, read it, and review it the way I would like. Next year I need to fade my comprehension instruction better.

Developing the students' vocabularies seemed to progress well. Rather than simply have the class copy dictionary definitions, I made every effort to present new terms in meaningful, memorable ways. Analogies, pictures, skits, webs, and morphemes seemed to help the class attach meanings to words as well as words to meanings. As with comprehension, I plan to spend more time next year helping students develop their vocabularies independently. For instance, once I show the class how to form analogies, I will gradually shift that thinking process over to the students.

The book projects, group work, and research projects all went smoothly and students seemed to benefit from them. These projects involved both good and poor readers and writers in activities at appropriate levels of difficulty. I'm convinced that one of secondary-school teachers' biggest challenges is accommodating the wide range of individual differences that each class presents. The projects and my grading system seemed to go far toward meeting those differences.

This last journal entry summarizes the parts of my teaching that I intend to keep and the parts I intend to change. In August I'm going to reread this whole journal, paying special attention to these closing comments. I fully intend to keep refining my instruction. At the end of ten years, I want to be able to say that I had ten years of experience—not one year of experience ten times.

REFERENCES

Adams, R. (1975). *Watership down*. Riverside, NJ; Macmillan.
Alexander, L. (1984). *The beggar queen*. New York: Dutton.

Angelou, M. (1970). *I know why the caged bird sings*. New York: Random House.

Arrick, F. (1981). *Chernowitz*. Scarsdale, NY: Bradbury Press.

Blinn, W. (1972). *Brian's song*. New York: Bantam.

Bradbury, R. (1950). *The Martian chronicles*. Garden City, NY: Doubleday.

Clarke, A. C. (1968). *2001: A space odyssey*. New York: New American Library.

Collier, J. L., & Collier, C. (1984). *Who is Carrie?* New York: Delacorte Press.

Crane, S. (1944). *The red badge of courage*. New York: Heritage.

Haley, A. (1976). *Roots*. Garden City, NY: Doubleday.

Heyerdahl, T. (1950). *Kon-Tiki: Across the Pacific by raft*. Chicago: Rand McNally.

Hodgell, P. C. (1982). *Godstalk*. New York: Antheneum.

Keyes, D. (1966). *Flowers for Algernon*. New York: Harcourt, Brace, & World.

King, S. (1980). *Firestarter*. New York: Viking.

Laurents, A. (1958). *West Side story*. New York: Random House.

Paton, A. (1948). *Cry the beloved country*. New York: Scribner.

Plimpton, G. (1966). *Paper lion*. New York: Harper & Row.

Remarque, E. M. (1983). *All quiet on the Western Front*. New York: Buccaneer. (Original work published in 1929.)

Strieber, W., & Kunetka, J. (1984). *Warday*. New York: Warner Books.

Taylor, M. (1978). *Roll of thunder, hear my cry*. New York: Bantam.

Trumbo, D. (1939). *Johnny got his gun*. New York: Lippincott.

Verne, J. (1925). *Twenty thousand leagues under the sea*. New York: Scribner.

Wright, R. (1945). *Black boy*. New York: Harper & Row.

Zindel, P. (1968). *The pigman*. New York: Harper & Row.

CHAPTER 11

Science and Mathematics

August:

I feel a little strange keeping a journal. I used to keep a diary when I was ten. I wonder if I am regressing. Dr. Knowles, who taught the content area reading and writing course I took in my senior year, suggested that keeping journals allows teachers to do something they seldom have time for—to pause and reflect. He also said that a journal allows you to look back across the year and be reminded of the little triumphs that are frequently overshadowed by the daily problems teachers face. I have decided to keep this journal on just two of my classes this year, one of my regular biology classes and my consumer math class. When Dr. Knowles talked about keeping journals, he suggested we focus on our most challenging classes. From the look of the names on my preliminary rolls, the two classes I've picked should certainly be that!

In the six years I've been teaching, I have vacillated between a textbook approach and a process approach to teaching biology. When I first started, I was strongly influenced by the methods used by my supervising teacher during student teaching. I made a great deal of use of the textbook, supplemented with lectures. Of course we had our lab periods, but these tended to be isolated from the content we were learning. This approach kept the students busy and was obviously what they expected. Soon, however, I found that most students were not learning very much. My below-average students seemed bewildered much of the time. My average and above-average students did satisfactory or even excellent work, but when I referred to something we had studied only a few weeks before, almost all looked blank. Nor were the students very interested in biology. One student said to me that very first year, "Miss Mull, this stuff is as dry as a bone!" Can you imagine how I responded to him? I am ashamed to admit that, out of my frustration, I said sharply, "Well then, why don't you moisten it with a little sweat from your brow!"

It became obvious that to almost all my students, "Mull's bio. class" was either a boring frustration or a dull obstacle course. My hopes of making biology, the study of life, an inspiring and edifying experience seemed no more than a naive dream. I sought advice from the principal, assistant principal, science supervisor, and other teachers, all of whom generally agreed that I was "too idealistic" and should realize that there is a limited amount that can be accomplished with "today's kids." So I continued teaching biology the same way for the next three years until I had become quite adept at assigning the textbook, lecturing, and giving tests. I never became any more satisfied with this way of teaching, however. The summer after my third year of teaching, I had a crisis. I finally made up my mind that I could no longer stand what I was doing. A radical change was in order, and I made it. I swung to the pure process approach that my undergraduate science methods courses had so strongly advocated. Everything we did was hands-on. I brought living things into the classroom and we dissected several plants and animals. We used the microscopes regularly. The students did become more interested, but I soon discovered that while they remembered the hands-on experience, they could not organize their thinking along more global and abstract general principles. In other words, they could not relate the hands-on experiences to a "big picture."

As you can imagine, I gradually began to get frustrated and even cynical. During this time, there was increased pressure in my school system to raise test scores, making me feel that I had to cover everything in the biology curriculum whether my students had time to learn it or not. Trying to cover a lot of curricular ground using demonstrations, experiments, and field trips can really strain a person's system!

This year, when I first walked into my classroom, I found that I had burned out. I couldn't face teaching again. Biology was my major in college and I had always liked it. However, biology is the most often failed high school subject in my state, and it is also the most failed subject in the school where I teach. Students often dread it before they take it, hate it while they take it, and criticize it as they look back on it.

The beginning of school this year was a time of real introspection for me. The more I thought, the more I realized that I had been lying to myself, kidding myself along for at least the previous year. Now I could fool myself no longer. I wanted to do anything but teach. I wanted to be anywhere but walking down those halls into that classroom. I carefully considered my options. I was not tied down with a husband or children. I was only 27 years old. I had a little money saved and my car was relatively new. I was free to resign my job to go wherever I wanted to, change careers completely if I wanted to. I thought of going to work for a biological supply company near where my parents live. On the other hand, I thought that I might like to begin a career in retail sales, selling women's clothes or shoes.

But another force within me pulled strongly in the other direction. I really believed in education as a positive factor in influencing young people. I looked back fondly on the teachers across my school years who had taken an interest in me and taught me things that I needed to know or enjoyed learning. How had they avoided burnout? Or had they? Perhaps they had just hidden it from us. Finally, one night that first week of school, I called one of my teachers whom I remembered particularly fondly and who lives only 25 miles away. She had been my life science teacher in seventh grade. She graciously invited me to her home although I had not seen her in over ten years.

The next evening I arrived at Mrs. Plante's house a little after five o'clock and she welcomed me in. It was so good to see her. Though noticeably older than I had remembered her, her face brought back so many sweet memories to me. We hugged each other and began to catch up on news about my old classmates and other junior-high teachers. Time passed quickly. Before I knew it, it was time for me to go and I had not even broached the subject I had really come to talk about.

"Oh, Mrs. Plante," I exclaimed, "I'm miserable in my job. That's why I really needed to talk with you. How have you stood it all these years?"

"So that's it, Annie," she sighed into her coffee. "Has it been this bad for— how many years have you taught?"

"Five, not counting this one. No, I was pretty happy my first year because I thought I would get better. And I did, but so many students aren't learning very much and they don't particularly like biology or think it's worth much. I just don't think I can stand to do this any more."

"Annie," she asked, "why do you think you became a biology teacher?"

"I always loved the sciences, and biology in particular. I also love kids, especially teenagers. I thought teaching high school biology would be the perfect marriage of those two loves."

"You don't think you're good at teaching, do you?"

"Mrs. Plante, it's strange that you should say that. I get good evaluations and everyone seems reasonably pleased with what I'm doing. But I still feel like a failure almost all the time."

"People who see themselves as professionals are always interested in finding out what needs doing so they can do it. Other people's evaluations aren't good enough for a professional."

"Up to a point, you're right, Mrs. Plante. I'm not satisfied with what I'm accomplishing in my classes even if everyone else is. If this is the best it gets, I want out. Let somebody else mind the mental morgue!"

"Do you think this is the best it gets, Annie?"

"I suppose I'm beginning to think so. Actually, I'm pretty arrogant down inside. I used the traditional method and got pretty good at it. Then I used the vanguard method and got pretty good at that, too. But neither method produced a high-level understanding or appreciation of biology except in one or two students who already knew a lot and were interested when they started."

Suddenly, Mrs. Plante looked very old. "I don't know what to tell you, Annie. Maybe you are too idealistic. Maybe it is too much to expect most students to grasp the big picture of biology and to like it as well."

"That means I have to resign and do something else. Thanks, Mrs. Plante for helping me see what I must do."

We talked longer, but nothing else substantive was said. I had made up my mind and Mrs. Plante seemed to agree with me. I drove home, sat down at the computer to type my letter of resignation, and went to bed.

That night, I had a dream that was to change my life. In the dream, I was led kicking and screaming to a post and tied there. Then a firing squad of two soldiers came and took aim at me. Just as they were about to fire, I realized that one was Dr. Bass, the professor who had taught my science methods class in college, and the other was Mr. DeBoer, my supervising teacher during student teaching. I called out that I had done my best, but they continued to point their rifles at me, frowning. Suddenly, Dr. Knowles, the professor of my content-area reading and writing course, appeared from nowhere and untied me. I grabbed a gun from somewhere to shoot my two executioners, but Dr. Knowles took the gun from me and said, "No, you'll need them both." He walked over to disarm them as well, forcing them to shake hands with each other in spite of their resistance. As their hands finally clasped, he turned to me and asked, "Do you see?" All I could say was, "See what? Tell me what I'm supposed to see!" I said that over and over to no avail until I woke up in a sweat.

My first reaction was to try to forget my dream, but I couldn't get it out of my mind. During breakfast and in the shower, it vividly came back to me, and each time it did, my mind seemed almost ready to understand what Dr. Knowles meant.

As I drove to school, I suddenly remembered something I had once read or heard, "If two intelligent people totally disagree about something, you can be reasonably sure that they are both partly right and partly wrong." In an instant, I saw everything clearly. Textbooks and lectures aren't wrong if properly used, but they can't provide concrete experiences; demonstrations, experiments, and field trips aren't wrong if properly used, but they can't insure high-level thinking. What I needed was a way to integrate the two, to use the strengths of each to compensate for the weaknesses of the other. And Dr. Knowles had taught us how to use direct experiences to build the basis for understanding abstract concepts. He had also taught us that you can't just assign a textbook, you have to be sure that students know their purposes for reading. Writing can also be used to help students organize and integrate information. I remembered with regret how I had yawned through his class, resenting instruction in reading and writing when I wanted to teach biology. I drove right home and dug out my notebook and text from his course.

Then I tore up my letter of resignation. I'll give it a year, I said to myself with determination. If it works, fine. If not, well, I gave it every chance.

September:

Dr. Knowles taught us that main ideas and generalizations are important aids to learning: first, these key concepts are themselves the most important content to be learned; second, knowing the main ideas helps us to learn the

Web less important ideas. As a result, I decided to start out this year by giving my students a firm grasp of the overall structure of biology. Naturally, neither my textbook nor the lab manual provided such a structure. So I had to construct the structure for myself out of both of these sources, my own knowledge, and various other references.

After spending a couple of classes introducing the students to the laboratory, the textbook, and the lab manual, I placed the following diagram on the bulletin board:

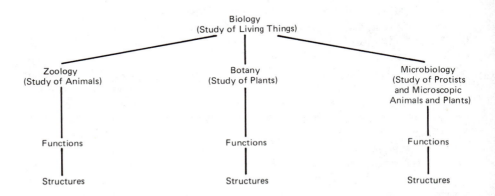

To introduce my students to the structure of biology, I only had to teach them to understand the diagram. First, we discussed the term *biology* itself. What would we study in biology class and what was not included in that discipline? I allowed the students to name all the things they could think of that we would and would not study, and I told them whether they were right or not. Some things they named were not even in the domain of science, though most were. Many of their items fell under other branches of science, such as astronomy, geology, chemistry, or physics. In only one class did they have a good sense of the meaning of biology. Then we spent some time on the terms *zoology* and *botany*. Again, I allowed the students to name a large number of examples and nonexamples, on which I commented.

Direct Experience I then brought out microscopes and asked the students to tell me what they were. They took turns at their tables viewing some prepared slides of common organic and inorganic substances such as hair and dust. When I was sure they understood the term *microscopic*, I introduced them to what I thought would **Vocabulary** be a new domain of life for them, protists. At this point, I only defined protists as "all living things that are neither plants nor animals." Most of them had trouble believing that there could be life that was neither plant nor animal, but I was able to get them to suspend judgment. Based on these understandings, I then led them through a discussion of microbiology and what we would cover under that heading. Finally, they understood that virtually all life that can be seen with the naked eye is either plant or animal, but that microscopic life includes plants, animals, and protists.

I knew that they might have some difficulty understanding what was meant by *functions* and *structures* and I moved to the chalkboard for those lessons. I wrote "functions" at the top of the board, underlined it, and wrote "structures" at the top of the board on the other side, underlining it as well. Under the word "functions" I wrote, "walking," "talking," and "smelling"; under the word "structures" I wrote, "legs," "mouth," and "nose." I then asked for volunteers to explain the difference between functions and structures. In each case, I told them where they were correct and where they still lacked some insight. After a while, they appeared to have a good grasp of the difference, so I wrote "tasting" in the middle of the board. I required each student to take a piece of notebook paper and tear it in half. On one half they were to write a large dark "f" and on the other, an "s." They were given a few seconds to examine the examples still listed on the board; then I had them classify "tasting" by raising the appropriate piece of paper. I did not allow students to show their papers before or after I gave them a signal, but only at that one moment. Then we discussed the correct classification and the reasons for it. I continued to put words in the middle of the board for them to classify until they became automatic at getting them right. Eventually, they were able to classify correctly terms like "heart," "stem," "imagine," and "transpire."

We then returned to the diagram on the bulletin board. I asked them to   **Web** predict what we would study this year in biology. After some discussion, they came to understand that we were going to study the three kinds of living things, animals and plants (both microscopic and not), and protists, and that we would study them by learning the functions that they perform and the structures that enable them to do so. I fielded questions about specific issues, using the diagram whenever possible to show where their question fit into the overall structure of biology. I left the bulletin board up so that students could see at a glance "the big picture" of our year of studying biology.

This process took a lot of time. At first, it was difficult for me not to be impatient, for I remembered that in the past I had spent no more than a few minutes on each of the six terms in the diagram. I had merely defined them, the students had written down these definitions, and we had gone on to other things.

Now that I had decided to teach each of these terms and their interrelationships until the students understood them clearly and could apply them, I was shocked at how long it took. Why, no wonder no one has learned very much biology in my other classes—I've thrown out major concepts as if they were minor facts that only needed to be memorized!

Once the class had a grasp of the diagram, it was assigned to read the portions of the text that pertained to the overall structure of biology, and to how that structure has gradually developed as biology has grown as a science. It's not enough to expose students to a concept; I must continue to work with them on that concept until I am sure that they truly understand it.

Oops! I have been so intent on carrying out my new approach to teaching biology that I have just let my consumer math class ride. Well, they're about to ride me out of town on a rail! I must do something different from what I am doing there, too. The course is supposed to be a practical study of consumer arithmetic for students who are not outstanding in mathematics. So why is the first chapter of the textbook filled with discussions of "interpolating and extrapolating data," and exercises with nothing but confusing word problems to solve? Help!

October:

Word Problems

I began the month in my consumer math class by trying to help my students with word problems. I never realized how much of consumer math consisted of word problems! Word problems present a major difficulty to almost all groups of math students. Fortunately, I came across some research by Ballew and Cunningham (1982) that showed me how to diagnose my students, determining what areas of word problem-solving were holding them back. Because we had not yet begun Chapter 2, I picked out the word problems from that chapter and randomly assigned them to one of three testing conditions as Ballew and Cunningham had done. For test A, I set the word problems up in pure computational form, "the computation test." For test B, I simply wrote down all the numbers from each problem in the order they appeared in the problem. I called this "the problem interpretation test." For test C, I presented the problems exactly as they were in the book (oh, the miracle of copying machines!). Each test had 14 items.

On successive days, I gave the three tests to the class. Test A was merely handed out and taken up after a reasonable time, and I simply graded each problem for the correct answer. When I gave test B, I handed out the mimeographed pages with the numbers on them and read aloud each problem to the students as they followed along, looking at the numbers. By this method I eliminated the need for them to be able to read the problem in order to interpret it. I graded each problem not for correct answers *per se*, but for whether the problem was correctly set up or not; i.e., whether they would have gotten the right answer if they had done the computation properly. When I graded test C, I gave the students two scores, one based on how many problems they had set up correctly (the reading and problem interpretation score) and one based on the number of correct answers (word problem solving score). I came up with the following averages for my class on the four scores generated from the three tests of fourteen problems each:

Computation average score	Problem interpretation average score	Reading and problem interpretation average score	Word problem solving average score
11.7	11.5	9.2	7.4

I was shocked that my students averaged only 7.4 out of 14 word problems correct when they had to do everything independently. Yet, their average score on the computation test shows that they can do the arithmetic that the word problems require; their average score on the problem interpretation test shows that they can generally figure out what computation to do and in what order. Their major difficulty seems to be reading! They did far worse on problem interpretation when they had to read the problems than when I read the problems to them. They also seemed to have difficulty with what Ballew and Cunningham call "integration," the ability to perform arithmetic, problem interpretation, and reading simultaneously, as indicated by the fact that their word problem solving score was lower than any of the other three. For this class, then, I must design activities to improve ability to read word problems and to integrate skills in solving word problems.

Meanwhile, I have been doing a unit on reading and understanding advertisements. My students are so gullible! I have had the hardest time getting them to see past the hype to consider the facts. Finally I decided to require them to rewrite a number of newspaper, magazine, and radio ads, eliminating everything that is not factual information. Then, we talked about making purchasing decisions solely on the factual version of the ad. Most of the time, they realized that they were no longer interested in making the purchase. But some seem to resent their new understanding. Ken and Allison both said that it was more fun to be convinced to buy something than to be so analytical! Maybe when they're earning their own money, they'll feel differently.

Evaluating

Our first major biology unit has been "The Cell." When the students came into the room on the first day of that unit, they found the seven lab tables for seven groups of students. At each table was a scalpel, some forceps, an onion, several glass slides, two eyedroppers, some toothpicks, staining solution, and a microscope. The students followed the directions I had passed out to them, a dittoed sheet that told them to look at a layer of onion tissue and some scrapings from the inside of their cheeks under the microscope. In each case, they looked at the materials both before and after staining them. I explained to them that they were seeing cells—the basic unit of all living things except viruses. Their lab manual contained a drawing of a cheek cell and an onion cell and they were required to find the various parts of these drawn and labeled cells in the real cells they were viewing. I then distributed a set of questions that required them to compare the cells in the onion layer with those from inside their cheeks. Thus I focused their attention on some differences between plant and animal cells.

Direct Experience

Students were also assigned the part of the textbook that described the development of cell theory by various scientists. Their purpose for reading was to write a one-paragraph summary of the major contribution of each scientist. The next day, I selected names at random and had those students read paragraphs they had written about various scientists.

I then reminded them of the difference between functions and structures and explained that the chapter they were going to read next described the functions and structures of the cell. I showed them the following diagram:

function {
    ingestion = cell membrane
    _____ = _____
    _____ = _____
    _____ = _____
    _____ = _____
    _____ = _____
} structure

Their purpose for reading then was to fill in the diagram on paper while they read. The text described functions and structures in a clear and literal fashion, but to understand the particular links between functions and structures required careful reading. I was convinced that this assignment would require students to process more deeply the concepts I considered most important than just telling them to read the chapter would do.

The next day, the students came in and I took up their completed diagrams. With their books closed, they then suggested how to fill in the diagram I had on the board. I did not correct any of their suggestions, just kept them on task and facilitated consensus when they got bogged down. When they had achieved consensus on a completed diagram, we opened our books and made corrections together. Finally, we ended up with a correct diagram.

For the remainder of this unit, I will use a combination of lectures, experiments and demonstrations, and content comprehension lessons like the one above to teach the students about various types of cells. We are making extensive use of the microscopes with both preprepared slides and slides that **Direct** we prepare ourselves. We are also making a detailed study of the structures **Experience** and subfunctions that permit each function of the cell. And we are examining the similarities and differences among plant cells, animal cells, and protists.

November:

In biology, we finished our unit on the cell during the first part of the month. By the end of the unit, most students could label the various structures in a **Tests** drawing of a cell and could write a brief explanation of the function of that structure in various types of cells. The difference between the most and the least successful students was in their understanding of the cell's more complex structures and functions. The range between my top and bottom students is as great as it has been in the past, but the amount learned by the bottom students is far ahead of any year I've ever taught. These methods seem to be working well. My emphasis on main ideas seems to facilitate the learning of **Web** facts and details. The quality of student questions is higher than ever before and they appear much more interested in biology, perhaps because they can always relate what they're learning to the basic structure of the discipline.

Following the unit on the cell, I created a new bulletin board with a new diagram:

Living Things

Animals	Plants	Protists
Invertebrates		
Sponges	Algae	Diatoms
Coelenterates	Fungi	Protozoans
Worms	Mosses and Liverworts	Bacteria
Echinoderms	Ferns	Viruses
Mollusks	Cone-Bearing Plants	
Crustaceans	Flowering Plants	
Arachnids		
Myriapods		
Insects		
Vertebrates		
Fish		
Amphibians		
Reptiles		
Birds		
Mammals		
Non-Humans		
Humans		

I explained to the students that they were now ready to study the structures and functions of the various kinds of plants, animals, and protists. I showed them the diagram and told them the order in which we would investigate these various forms of life during the rest of the year.

I have decided that I want my students to be able to do library research in **Research** biology—a basic skill that all biologists certainly need. Moreover, anyone with questions needs to know how to find accurate answers to them efficiently. Consequently, I developed an approach that requires library research and does not allow mere copying from sources. I gave students a mimeographed copy of the following list:

Fields Related to Biology

Anatomy	Bacteriology	Biochemistry
Biophysics	Botany	Cryobiology
Cytology	Ecology	Embryology
Eugenics	Exobiology	Genetics
Gnotobiotics	Heredity	Histology
Limnology	Marine Biology	Medicine
Microbiology	Molecular Biology	Morphology
Paleontology	Pathology	Phenology
Physiology	Taxidermy	Zoology

Translation Writing

I then wrote the words *compare* and *contrast* on the board and asked them about those words. They generally manifested a good understanding of the terms. I told them that we as a class were going to write a short composition on the board, "comparing and contrasting botany and zoology." They were given three minutes to try to write the first sentence and to list any details they thought should be included. When this brief planning time ended, I took the chalk and stood at the board. "Who has a particularly good first sentence for our composition?"

Allison volunteered that first sentence and I wrote it down as it was dictated to me: "*Botany and zoology are both fields of biology.*"

I then led them to give me sentences comparing what they knew about botany and zoology with what we had already learned. Thus we gradually completed our group composition. My role was only to require consensus and to remind them of the task as often as necessary. Through creating a group composition, every student came to understand what a compare/contrast paper is. I reminded them of the list I had given them and told them to select two fields on which to write a compare/contrast composition based on library research. After some preliminary library research, they submitted their pairs of fields to me for my approval.

Word Problems

In consumer math this month, I have really worked hard on helping my students with word problems. I have consistently used two approaches to improve students' ability to read the problems. First, I have tried to get them to transfer their ability to interpret word problems that they hear to their own reading, as I alternate between having them hear a problem and having them read one. I read the first problem to them and give them time to solve it. All pencils are put down and then a student who I see has it right goes to the board and works that problem. We briefly discuss why it was worked that way. Then students read the next problem to themselves and work it. Again I choose a student to work it correctly on the board. We discuss why that problem was worked that way. The method seems simple, but students do better on the third or fourth independent problem than they did on the first. I believe that they will continue to improve.

I also use an overhead projector so that I can uncover a word problem one clause at a time as we try to solve it as a group. The goal is to solve the problem by seeing as little of the problem as possible. Everyone has to explain any suggestion he or she makes. The students are getting good at using all the information in each word in the problem.

The major factor in integrating skills to solve word problems seems to be lots of successful practice. Unfortunately, that means that only those students for whom word problem solving is already easy can learn to do it well (the rich get richer!). So I have employed two means for providing students with successful practice. First, I have procured math textbooks and workbooks from grades four through eight and have selected consumer-oriented word problems from them. I duplicated these problems on mimeographed copies to give out to my students. They make perfect homework assignments because

Homework

the students can work them successfully and are therefore less likely to "practice their ignorance." I made the mistake of telling Mr. Burr that I was doing this. (He teaches all the other sections of consumer math.) He told me that the students wouldn't do their homework unless it was challenging for them. Rather than arguing with him, I just tried my idea. The proportion of students doing their homework has actually increased since I initiated this practice. I do not understand why we think our top students will perform tasks that they can do well while our bottom students must be given tasks that are nearly impossible for them.

The second thing I did was periodically to assign students to work five problems in class that they have previously solved. This time, however, I place **Word Problems** them under a tight time limit. They must both get the answer right and show all their work to get credit for a problem. I determine their daily grade based on the time they take.

Daily Grade		Time
A	=	2 minutes
B	=	3 minutes
C	=	4 minutes

Missing even one problem because of a careless mistake results in a daily grade of D, regardless of time spent. At the end of each amount of time, students who are finished put down their pencils and turn their papers over. I spend the next minute walking around and writing the number of minutes on the back of each turned-over paper.

This system has really cut down on carelessness, a major problem these students have with word problems. And I am seeing an overall improvement in both their success and their attitude toward word problems. At least now when they miss a word problem, it is usually because of their computation or problem interpretation rather than their reading or integration.

December:

Biology is supposed to be the study of life. This month, I thought it was the study of words! My efforts this year to combine the process and the textbook approach have been largely successful but I have still been concerned about how little some students were learning. Students like Lonnie, Theresa, and Ambrose failed the first nine weeks in spite of all my efforts.

Right after Thanksgiving, I went to an all-day content area reading workshop sponsored by the regional education center. These things are usually a waste of time but I had heard that Dr. Wurdz, the presenter, was quite practical, so I decided to give it a whirl. Am I glad I did! He spent all day convincing us that it is the onslaught of new vocabulary that hurts most students in content **Vocabulary** areas and he targeted the sciences as being particularly at fault. He gave us several passages to read from high-level statistics and management textbooks and none of us could understand a thing we read. It became perfectly clear to me that if you don't have immediate access to the meanings of important words, comprehension of a passage is downright impossible!

Dr. Wurdz also showed us that there are two kinds of vocabulary words, the easy ones to teach and the toughies. The easy words are those for which kids already know the meaning but not the word that represents the meaning. His example was the word *obstreperous*. Many students don't know what the word means but every one of them can practice the concept! The toughies are words for which students lack both the word and the meaning. Of course, of all the disciplines, science is the most plagued by terms with which students have absolutely no experience.

During the workshop, we had to look at a chapter in our textbook to divide the new words into those for which students lacked only the word, and those for which they lacked both word and meaning. The list for one chapter in my text had thirty-two words—of which twenty-four were the tough kind! Then he told us that research showed you can only effectively teach ten words per week! Ten! Most of my chapters have twenty-five to thirty-five words and I certainly can't spend three or four weeks on every chapter. Fortunately, he gave us some rules for getting our list down to the sacred number ten. First, he said, eliminate words for which students already have enough meaning. I didn't think the book would list vocabulary to be taught if most students would know it, but I found that my book had many such words. What tenth-grader doesn't know what a blade or a leaflet is? (I wonder who decides on these vocabulary lists? Have they ever seen a tenth-grader??) Next, he said, eliminate very technical terms that most educated adults don't know and that even teachers have to review before the lesson. (How did he know I had to do that?) These technical terms are defined enough in context for students who can read well to understand them for the moment, and in any case they are not words that anyone remembers. That made sense, although it is hard not to feel guilty about not teaching all these terms. Finally, he said that we needed to read the chapter to see if any important words had been left off the text's vocabulary list. Once again, he was right. My textbook's list had left out the words *broad-leafed*, *narrow-leafed*, and *needle-leafed*. Understanding these words was what the chapter was all about!

By following these new rules, I am now able to get my list of vocabulary words down to about ten per week. I still don't feel quite right about this, but if my students learn 360 new biology words in one year, words that they really know and can use, I guess that is not a bad accomplishment. And I realize that my students must have a good command of these words if they are to understand what they read and what I tell them.

Following is the vocabulary list from our textbook's most recent chapter with the additions and deletions I have made based on these new rules. Words marked ''x'' I have totally eliminated from consideration: we won't discuss it, there won't be activities that use it, and it won't be mentioned on any test

I give. Bracketed words at the end are those I added to the list. For example, I eliminated *fibrovascular bundle* while adding its more common name, *vein*. Then I marked with an asterisk each word that I planned to emphasize in both teaching and testing, leaving the other words to be learned by students on their own. A common word, *leaf*, remained in the list because of the precision of its definition in the chapter.

*abscission	*[broad-leafed plant]	*[compound leaf]
sheath	*[narrow-leafed plant]	*[simple leaf]
cuticle	*[needle-leafed plant]	x bundle
x fibrovascular bundle	blade	*epidermis
x insectivorous plant	epidermal hair	x guttation
*mesophyll	guard cell	leaflet
petiole	leaf	palmate leaf
fiber	palisade mesophyll	x sclerenchyma
sessile leaf	pinnate leaf	spongy
mesophyll	x spine	x succulent leaf
stipule	stoma	*venation
x tendril	x transpiration	*[vein]

Direct Experience

Once I have selected the words I am going to teach, I must be sure to focus on those words. Students have no concept for many of these words. Fortunately, the laboratory part of our course provides them with the real thing on a regular basis. I see now that one reason that my dual-emphasis program is effective is that the laboratory part provides the direct experiences for many new terms. If I don't have the resources or time to develop a concept adequately through direct laboratory experience, I make sure to provide some visual experience for it. This is not too difficult since we have some good films, film loops, and slides in our media center, with more available from our regional education center.

Visual Experience

I have also been using the visuals in our textbook more systematically. Dr. Wurdz suggested that many students simply ignore all photographs, charts, and diagrams in their textbooks. He challenged us to assign some in-class reading and watch what the students did with their eyes as they came to the visuals. Sure enough, many of my poorest students read the text, glanced at a wonderful half-page diagram and continued reading. I could not stand the thought that the students who most needed to build the concepts provided by the visuals in the text were ignoring these visuals. I now do a quick, 5-minute, visuals-only introduction to each chapter. I give the students exactly 5 minutes to look at the visuals and any captions under them and to write down everything they can learn from the visuals only. At the end of the 5 minutes, we go around the room and each person gives me one thing to write on the board until all the information is exhausted (as am I!). I then direct their attention to the information on the board that I consider crucial and ask, "Where in the text did you get this piece of information?" We all look at that visual and discuss it. It is amazing to me how naive my students are in understanding diagrams and charts. After all these years in school, I just assumed they had picked up this skill but many just don't know how to learn from a visual. They will by the time they leave my class!

Vocabulary Word Book

I have had the students begin a vocabulary notebook. This is a bit old-fashioned but I wanted to be sure to focus my attention as well as the students' on the vocabulary, and with so much to do, I was afraid I might lose track of this component. Whenever I begin a new chapter, I put the ten or so selected words on the small bulletin board in the corner and have the students write them in a notebook reserved for vocabulary. The notebook is divided with five pages for each letter of the alphabet and the words are usually entered four words to each page. We enter only the words on the first day of each unit, then fill in the meanings as we do the activities that build meaning for the words. Eventually, for every word, we have written a personal example and a sentence that defines the word. I do not allow them to copy dictionary definitions but sometimes we look up the word to help us formulate our own examples and sentences. We may add whatever we need to make the word clear and easy to remember. If the word is hard to pronounce, we put a phonetic pronunciation next to it. If the word can be illustrated or diagrammed, we do so. If the word has a common morpheme, we highlight it and note its meaning. So far, we have been doing these vocabulary entries together but once the students learn what I expect, I plan to assign the actual writing as homework after I have provided the in-class experience to build meaning. Here are some entries for a few of our words from this month:

abscission (ab si shun)—Example: When a leaf falls off a tree in the fall.
   Sentence: Abscission occurs when any leaf falls off of any plant at any time of the year for any reason.
venation—Example: The hard little tubes you can feel with your fingers when you hold a leaf.
   Sentence: Venation is the arrangement of veins in leaves and is used to identify from which plant a leaf has come.
   Root word: Vein

Tests

I give a weekly vocabulary test on these words, making the test cumulative across all words entered in the notebook so far. This is tough on the kids, but we do some quickie review activities during the last few minutes of each period. Some students are finding that if they study, they can do very well on these tests, which helps their grade since the average vocabulary grade equals one big test grade each quarter. Even Ambrose did well on my last vocabulary test.

Vocabulary

Having become so attuned to vocabulary problems in biology, I couldn't help but notice that my consumer math class's comprehension was also hampered by a lack of technical vocabulary. We are studying taxes (YUK!) and I discovered that students were not clear about the meaning of words like "exemptions" and "withholding." Some students didn't get back money due to them because they couldn't figure out all that gobbledegook on the tax form. I have made a list of crucial tax words and we are working through some realistic student-job tax situations so that they understand what these terms mean. Imagine letting the government keep your money because you couldn't understand the silly form!

January:

Well, we are halfway through the year, and while far from satisfied with everything, I am more content than I have ever been with my teaching. Semester grades were better, too. I have a new grading system that gives students points for effort on their in-class and homework assignments, which I don't grade but simply initial if they appear to demonstrate a good effort. Students must also fix anything that was not right after we go over the work in class, and I require them to turn in their notebook with these initialed and self-corrected assignments. I take a quick glance to see that everything was fixed and again give points toward the final grade. Students also get points for good effort on their laboratory work.

Grading System

Of course, I have grades from our weekly vocabulary tests—which have gotten better each week—as well as chapter and unit test grades. About 80 percent of these test questions concerns the most important information, which we have gone over in class and which everyone should have learned. The other 20 percent comes from reading assignments, which are not completely covered in class.

Tests

I had only three Ds in my biology section and only one in consumer math! I believe that all my students are making more of an effort because they see that their effort pays off. This coming semester, I am going to assign some projects whereby students can extend their knowledge beyond what we are learning in class. It worries me that while students seem less frustrated and a little more motivated, they are not exactly turned on to my subject. I realize that I used to read a lot of books and magazines about biology and famous biologists and I think that is how I became so engrossed in this topic. So I plan to have my students research famous biologists next month and then we will find some way (entertaining, I hope) of sharing what they learn.

Research

I am continuing to stress vocabulary and to teach comprehension lessons on textbook material. This month I did several feature matrix comprehension lessons. This seems to work particularly well in biology, where so much material is a description of different members of a classification and the features that make each distinct. The students enjoy predicting, before they read, where the pluses and minuses will go and their comprehension seems to be much better when they have something specific to look for. Usually, I have them copy the feature matrix from my transparency and fill in their guesses in class;

Comprehension Lesson

then they read the chapter to fill in and correct their matrix for homework. When they come to class, they take out their matrix and I quickly initial those that show a good effort. Then together we fill in my matrix on the transparency, as they show thumbs up for a plus and thumbs down for a minus. As long as there is consensus, we move right through it. When some thumbs are up and some are down, I know that comprehension has broken down and leave that space blank. We then reread the part of the textbook that discusses the point and resolve our disagreement. The students keep the corrected feature matrices in their notebooks and even claim to study them before my tests! This is a very efficient way of organizing a lot of information and helps students who are not good notetakers to keep their information in an organized fashion. Here is one of the feature matrices I used this month:

Arthropods

Features/ Examples	Crustaceans	Myriapods	Arachnids	Insects
Jointed Legs	+	+	+	+
Segmented Bodies	+	+	+	+
Hard Exoskeleton	+	+	+	+
Gills	+	−	−	−
Three pairs of legs	−	−	−	+
Four pairs of legs	−	−	+	−
Antennae	+	+	−	+
Trachae	−	+	+	+
Crabs	+	−	−	−
Centipedes	−	+	−	−
Spiders	−	−	+	+
Termites	−	−	−	+
Shrimp	+	−	−	−
Grasshoppers	−	−	−	+
Millipedes	−	+	−	−
Ticks	−	−	+	−

Three to a Customer

I have used a new review strategy this month that works quite well. It is called three to a customer. You ask the students to write down three things they remember about your topic, limiting them to two minutes. Then you call on different students to tell just one thing each. The goal is to see how many different things the class as a whole can remember. We keep score on a little chart and the competition seems to appeal to them. The first time we did it, they remembered a total of eighteen items, which I recorded. The next time, they remembered twenty-five. This Monday I said, "Let's make sure your brains have not totally atrophied over the weekend. Take out a sheet of paper. You have two minutes to write three things you remember about arthropods." And I heard Rod say, "Twenty-five is the number to beat!" Sure enough, they had a total of twenty-seven different things written down. Now they try hard to remember something unusual or trivial in order to accumulate a large total. A little friendly competition with themselves seems to add to their motivation!

We even had fun in consumer math this month. I am a *Consumer Reports* devotee and as I was looking through their ratings of microwave ovens I realized this was a perfect periodical for my math kids. I found the annual car issue and after leading my kids in a general discussion of which cars they loved and wanted to own (a very hot topic for tenth-graders), I pulled out *Consumer Reports*. I asked them to write down their dream car, how much they thought it would cost, how much they would have to pay for it each month if they borrowed 90 percent at 12 percent interest for 4 years, and what its mile-per-gallon rating, repair record, and crash test ratings were. Then I paired them up with copies of the article and had them work out the real figures! Such a bunch of shocked, disheartened kids you have never seen. Even Ken was momentarily taken aback, until finally he said, "Well, I'll just have to make my first million faster!"

Only Allison was unconcerned. "My father is buying me a Jaguar on my next birthday," she smirked.

February:

February was famous biologist month! When I was a teenager, I loved biology and it has always bothered me that "loved" is hardly the correct verb to describe my teens' reactions to the subject. As I was considering how I came to love biology, I remembered that I got a junior science set for my tenth birthday and that I was always collecting plant and insect specimens and performing various experiments on them. We got *National Geographic* and the *Smithsonian* magazines and they often had fascinating articles on various plant and animal life forms. Mr. Lively, who lived three doors down from us, was a biomedical engineer, and while I wasn't quite sure what a biomedical engineer did, it sure sounded fascinating. In addition, I became interested in biographies, particularly biographies of famous scientists. I read every one I could get my hands on and discovered that these scientists had led very interesting lives. In addition to their important discoveries, many of them were adventurous, courageous people. After reflecting on the development of my love affair with biology, I realized that it had much to do with real things and real people and little to do with biology textbooks and lab reports! I decided to try three ways to develop in my students the fascination I felt when I was their age. The first was the study of famous biologists that we did this month. For the coming weeks, I have planned to have them design and carry out a real experiment of their own, and to deal with some of the career options available to people with training in biology.

Research

I decided that each student would research a famous biologist. I came up with a list of thirty and wrote their names on index cards. Each student would draw a card for his or her assignment. I knew the kids would rather pick their own, but with the exception of Charles Darwin, Louis Pasteur, and Rachel Carson, most students would not have heard of any scientists. I did tell the kids they could try to get someone to swap with them.

Deciding how to have the students share what they learned was a difficult task. I remembered the term papers I had to write, and the oral reports I had to stand up and give with my knees knocking and my voice breaking. Somehow I knew that these traditional methods of reporting did nothing to promote attitudes of excitement! I worried for several days and then I found the answer in the letter announcing my tenth-year high school reunion. "At least I won't get any prizes," I chuckled, as I remembered the awards for "parent of the most kids" and "traveled farthest" that are usual at these affairs. Then I realized that I might just have found the gimmick to get my kids excited about their biologists.

After I explained to their skeptical looks that each person was to become an expert on one biologist, I told them that we would give prizes for these biologists' various accomplishments. I asked them to help me think of some awards we could give and suggested that we include demographic data, such as who had lived the longest, as well as more subjective data, such as who had made the biological discovery of greatest importance. I wrote these two things on the board and asked them to brainstorm other possible awards. They were slow to start but once they got started, you couldn't stop them. Here is the list we finally made from the students' brainstorming:

Most Ancient (one born longest ago)
Most Recent
Oldest
Youngest
Most married (Most husbands or wives!) [Lonnie suggested this one]
Most Blessed (Most children) [Ken was serious; I tried not to laugh]
Tallest
Shortest
Heaviest
Richest
Most Degrees Earned
Most Important Biological Discovery
Most Adventurous Life
Most Interesting Life
Most Tragic Life
Best Biologist (Life-long contribution)

Once the list was made, I turned the awards into questions. I put these on dittos and left room for the students to write their answers. For the subjective awards, the questions were worded as follows: "What did your scientist do that qualifies him or her for the Most Adventurous Life award?" Students were asked to write answers to all demographic questions, plus a sentence or two for any nominations they wanted to make. Ambrose asked if that meant they didn't have to write anything if they didn't want to nominate their scientist for any of the subjective awards. "You must nominate for at least one," was my exasperated response. I asked them to use three or more sources of research to list and number these sources, and to attach this list to the dittoed sheets. Then they only needed to write down the number of the source next to each question they answered. If the information was found in more than one source, they only needed to list one source but could include more.

Students had two weeks to complete their library research. I asked them to keep secret what they found out so that the awards would be a surprise for everyone. They were not very enthusiastic to begin with, but as awards day got closer, I heard people saying things like, "I've got the Most Adventurous Life sewed up!"

For the demographic awards, we went down the list and each student who thought his or her scientist was in contention gave the data required. These awards were granted automatically. For the more subjective awards, students had one minute to nominate their candidate and to argue that he or she deserved the award. All the students then voted. In some cases, I believe they were voting for the popularity of the student researcher rather than for the merit of the biologist but, all in all, they enjoyed it. Most important, they learned that biologists are real people, many of whom lead fascinating lives. Mission accomplished.

March:

Independence

My two greatest accomplishments this month were both in the cause of independence. I am pleased with how much better my students are learning and with their improved motivation, but I do feel that I am spoon-feeding them a bit too much. I decided to try to equip them with some strategies they could use to become more independent learners. I told them that they would not always have good old Miss Mull to identify vocabulary and help them to summarize and review their work. (I didn't tell them that if they took Chemistry next year, they would have good old Mrs. "Some got it and some don't" Hardy!)

Vocabulary

For vocabulary, I first showed them how I selected the ten words. (Don't tell Dr. Wurdz, but sometimes I just have to have eleven or twelve. This is compensated for by the one time I had only nine!) We took the list for the last chapter and I showed them how I first eliminate those words they already know. (Judy made a disparaging remark about the people who made that vocabulary list not knowing anything about how much tenth-graders knew. I ignored it but thought, "Smart kid!") Then I showed them how I eliminated very technical terms. This was hard for my students because all the words looked technical to them, but we decided that if a term only occurred once or twice, was defined by the context, and was a very picky detail, it could be eliminated. Getting them to see that there were some words they needed to add was harder. "Aren't there enough already?" Ambrose asked. I had them read the introduction and summary for each chapter, however, to find the chapter's key words. Most saw that these words had to be added to the list. Once we did this, we still often had more than ten or twelve, so we eliminated a few more picky terms—those only used in one small part of the chapter—and got the final list.

I had shown them all this for last week's chapter. This week I paired them up with their lab partners and had them go through it all again for this week's chapter. I gave them 10 minutes to work and then put the words suggested by the pairs on the board. There was general agreement on most words (Thank goodness!) and of course some overlap on the close calls. All in all, I thought they did a good job of deciding what the important vocabulary was. I then had them write these words on the appropriate vocabulary notebook pages as we have since December, and I led them to complete these entries with personal examples, sentence definitions, and whatever else was helpful.

After three weeks of having the students pick the words, I decided it was time for them to decide on their own vocabulary entries. After the words were picked, I assigned each pair of students one word (two pairs overlapped) and had them decide what to write for that vocabulary entry. I encouraged them to use their textbook and classroom reference books. I instructed them to provide their own personal examples to serve as models for everyone else, and a definitional sentence that gave the crucial information. I reminded them that we included phonetic spelling when the word had a tricky pronunciation, illustrations or diagrams when possible, and morphemic information when helpful. I then gave each pair a transparency on which to write the notebook entry they thought everyone should use. They did a very good job and I intend to continue this paired working during April. In May, I will have the students come up with notebook entries on their own.

The other strategy for promoting independence is 5-minute summary writing. At the end of class a couple of times a week, I reserve 5 minutes for them to summarize in their notebooks the major things they learned that day. We did a few of these as group summaries so that they would get the idea, then I turned them loose. At the beginning of the next class, I picked two students to read their summaries as a review of what we have learned. The students are not exactly wild about this writing but they are getting better at it. I intend to suggest that they take 5 minutes to write summaries at the end of other classes even when it is not assigned so that they will have something to review. There is usually some dead time at the end of most classes—but not mine! I wonder how many will write summaries if not forced to. Oh well, if only two or three learn to use this strategy, that is two or three more than would have if I hadn't taught them!

April:

While my students continued to learn new content in biology this month (we were just beginning our study of human biology), I also emphasized application of the content they had already learned. In April I tried to move them into seeing themselves as potential biological scientists. Most of our experiments and demonstrations have been more or less prescribed. While the hands-on biology we did certainly improved learning and attitudes, the students have rarely participated in actually designing experiments to investigate hypotheses that interest them. They had been studying biology without learning how to be biologists!

Thinking Processes

Knowing how difficult this assignment would be, I began April by telling the students to conduct and report on an original experiment investigating a particular hypothesis. Then I began the process of teaching them how to do the assignment.

Research

First, they needed to understand what a hypothesis is and where one comes from. After a brief discussion, I saw why scientists like Edison have always emphasized "perspiration" over "inspiration" when explaining their achievements. My students certainly attributed much to scientific inspiration. Most seemed to think that ideas just "popped into biologists' heads." I told them that scientists are no different than other curious and observant people. Imagine, I explained, that a person was watering some house plants some years ago and a child asked why plants have to be watered. The adult could simply have said, "Because they will die if they are not watered."

Children being persistent, however, the child might have asked, "Why will they die without water?"

Then the adult might have explained to the child why he or she needs water and that plants need water for similar reasons. So far the adult is answering the child's questions based on the adult's general knowledge. But what if the child than asked, "After I drink water, it goes out when I use the bathroom. What do plants do with the water after they drink it?"

The adult, after thinking a moment, might have said, "I don't know. That is a very good question. Let's find out."

Imagine, then, that the adult looked in various books to find the answer and discovered that the answer was not available. Let's say that the adult thought and thought about what might happen to the water and finally guessed that the water might be given off into the air from the leaves, like sweating. Then let's say that the adult designed an experiment to see if leaves give off water into the air and finds out that they do.

After this explanation, I asked them to help me to use it as an illustration. Any curious and observant person, even a child, has questions about living things and how they function, I explained. Then I tried to convince them that all scientific investigation begins with a question about something.

Furthermore, I explained that adults are different from children only because, by going to school, they have learned the answers to certain common questions that curious and observant people have. They do not have to be constantly confused by the world in which they live, but instead can look around them and realize that they have a certain degree of understanding of their environment. This, I said, is the major reason that everyone is required to study science in school.

At this point, I explained why it is important that people learn how to use libraries and other sources of information so that they can learn answers to questions that they do not remember or never learned. So far, so good.

But, I asked them, what happens when you ask a question whose answer you cannot find? You must try to develop your own answer by thinking about what you know. The answer you come up with is called a *hypothesis*.

At this point, I wrote on the board:

hypothesis—A possible answer to a previously unanswered question.

I gave the students the opportunity to come up with hypotheses that some scientist had once developed about the same material we had studied in biology up to that point. We discussed each one, focusing the question and finding the precise wording for a possible answer. Each of these possible answers we labeled as having once been a hypothesis.

Ambrose raised an important question during these discussions, "How do you know which questions have already been answered?"

I referred him back to our previous discussion of the adult and child and showed him that there are only two ways: either know an area of biology so well that you know what is known and what is not, or go to the library and do research until you are convinced that you are now aware of what is and isn't known.

"So that's why biologists have to go to graduate school!" remarked Terry.

I strongly supported that comment.

"But we haven't been to graduate school yet!" said Ambrose in his "I'm just about to give up" voice.

"No," I agreed, "but actually that will make it easier for you. You see, we really won't be able to answer questions that haven't yet been answered about biology. You don't and even I don't have the knowledge or equipment necessary to do new research in biology. You do have a lot of questions, however, that you don't have answers to. You've been asking me such questions all year! It is those questions for which you will develop first hypotheses, and then experiments. Besides, even famous scientists replicate experiments in order to check results."

I had gone through the units we had studied and chosen those that could be investigated by the students. I reminded them of a unit and asked them to think of important questions they still had. We listed these on the board. Through a process of brainstorming and selection, we developed quite a list of questions across the several units I had chosen. Each student then picked a question for which he or she had to think of a possible answer (hypothesis) that could be investigated by a simple experiment.

We then went back to the story of the adult and child. As a group, we planned an experiment to determine whether plant leaves give off the water that the plant has taken in. I insisted that they design the experiment themselves. I only kept them on task by making them vote on decisions instead of endlessly arguing about them. They had to see any weaknesses themselves and try to repair them. Once they had the basic design of the experiment, I then gave my suggestions for improvements. I was very proud of them. They were able to figure out that they had to have some way to water the plant without getting water into the air at the same time. They had also determined that the air around the plant would have to be contained so that water could not get in from any other source. Finally, they figured out that they had to have a control, a space just like that occupied by the plant, but without a plant in it.

So we obtained large plastic containers, put water in two of them, and covered them with wax paper. Then we cut a hole in one of the pieces of wax paper and inserted a small plant so that the roots went in the water in the container and the top stuck out above the wax paper. We used petroleum jelly to seal around the base of the plant so that no water could get out of the bottom container. We covered the two bottom containers with two top containers, turned them upside down, and sealed around where they joined with more petroleum jelly. Naturally, it wasn't long before the inside of the top container with the plant in it began to fog up with moisture, but the container without the plant remained dry just as the hypothesis would lead one to predict.

Direct Experience

Once we had completed our class investigation, I modeled how to write up the report on a sheet I had made up for this purpose. I also had several students find books that described similar investigations, including results against which we could check our own results.

They then started on their individual investigations. I required them to get an approval from me at each of three points. I had to approve of the question each chose to prevent unnecessary duplication and to make sure that it was not too broad. Then I had to approve of the hypothesis that each one developed. I wanted to make sure it was their own hypothesis and not one they had copied from somewhere. And I wanted the hypothesis to be one they could design an experiment to investigate. Whether it was the correct answer to their question or not made no difference to me. Finally, I had to approve the design of their experiments. Here was where I did most of my teaching this month. Reasoning with them and holding conferences about their experiments took a lot of time but I believe they learned a lot from designing them. They met in small groups to get feedback from one another while I met with individuals. After I approved the design of an experiment, I set a day for that student to set up the experiment in the lab. After everything was completed, I required them to report the results of their investigations on a sheet with the following entries:

Question:
Hypothesis:
Experiment:
Data:
Interpretation:

These reports were shared with their lab partners first and revised based on those comments. I read them to make comments and they revised them again. Finally, we published these research reports in a class book called *Our Biology Experiments* which we shared with everyone who was interested and some who were not. Our librarian even put a copy in the science section of our library! We ended the month with quite a sense of accomplishment and admiration for biological scientists.

May:

May is probably the best month for teaching biology, not just because it is almost the end of the year, but because the new life is everywhere and it is impossible not to be excited about life—and its science this month. We have had many things to do this month so I didn't begin anything new except for their research on careers in biology. This was part of my plan to get them excited about biology. Since the famous biologists' awards had worked so well, I decided to use the same format. I wrote various careers biologists could pursue (nutritionist, teacher, animal husbandry specialist, microbiologist, etc.) on index cards and let each student pick one. We then brainstormed a list of questions in the form of awards. The list again included objective features (highest paid, most job mobility) as well as subjective features (most prestigious, most dangerous). When we had the brainstormed list completed on the board, someone suggested that we have "booby prizes," too. We ended up deciding to try to find out about both the high and the low end for each of the career features.

The students researched the career they had picked (or "gotten stuck with," as Lonnie put it), filling in the information on a dittoed sheet. They noted sources as they had done for the famous biologists project. They had more trouble finding information this time and Paige Turner, the librarian, and I had to help them. We also made some calls to our state employment office and interviewed some people in biological careers.

When the data was compiled, we gave awards and booby prizes in each category. What category of career do you think came up with the lowest pay and was voted to have the lowest prestige? *Teacher* won these two booby prizes hands down, naturally! I was not surprised that teaching was at the bottom, but I was reminded of the enormous salaries many biologists make. It's a good thing that I didn't do this last year when I was at such a low point in my job satisfaction! Rod was very worried about my low salary and prestige,

Research

but Allison told him not to worry because I had "chosen" to do this and had my summers completely free!

After the awards were given, I had each student write a one-paragraph essay indicating which career they would choose if they were to pursue work in biology. They had to state the career choice and at least three reasons why. We made a tally of the various careers chosen and there was a great deal of diversity. Several students told me that they had no idea there were so many interesting and well-paying jobs for biologists and were seriously considering pursuing the career they had selected!

This month, I had students select independently the vocabulary words they thought we needed to learn and write those entries in their notebooks. Most did quite well but I wonder if they will make the effort to do this next year when they are not required to. They have gotten very good at writing a 5-minute summary of the important information learned; I think many of them will continue to do this because they see how useful it is when it comes time to study for a test. They even tell me that writing the summary helps them to sort out what is important and to organize the information. I have certainly found that writing this journal this year has helped me to organize my own thoughts and to reflect upon what is most important.

Vocabulary

I have continued to work on vocabulary with my consumer math class. I am constantly amazed at how little they understand such common terms as *interest*, *dividends*, and *balance*. I think next year if I teach a section of consumer math, I will start a vocabulary notebook with them at the beginning of the year. I will also use *Consumer Reports* earlier and more frequently. Their interest always piques when I use real-life newspapers and magazines to let them see how crucial is their ability to compute what things cost and where money comes from and goes.

I did do one new thing in consumer math over the past two months. I had each student study stocks and then select some stock to buy with an imaginary $500. We checked stock prices regularly and charted the growth or decline of our stocks. The students got very excited, almost as if they were actually making or losing that money. Although their money investment wasn't real, the investment of time and energy in choosing and following the stock was, and their motivation to learn about the world of money grew. I just wish I had had five hundred real dollars and had invested them in Rod's stock. The boy is uncannily lucky. His stock split and he almost doubled his money. My imaginary stock, on the other hand, is now behind 46.40!

Direct Experience

June:

Well, as Allison said, "She gets the whole summer off!" And thank goodness for that! Even with a good year like this one, I am ready for the change of pace in June. This summer will be a real change of pace. I am once again playing the role of student—complaining about "meaningless assignments" and "boring textbooks."

I had been toying all spring with the idea of going back to school to pursue graduate work in science education. Once I knew that I found teaching fulfilling and that you could teach even below-average students to understand and appreciate biology, I began to wonder why everyone who taught biology didn't feel this way. I concluded that we ourselves hadn't been taught well, and hadn't been taught how to teach well. Suddenly I wanted to run out and gather up teachers and teachers-to-be and teach them everything that was such a struggle for me to learn. I might never have gotten past the mulling-it-over stage had I not run into Dr. Knowles at a political rally. I was so shocked to see him there—he looked just like he did when I had him for content area reading and writing in my senior year! He even remembered my name and seemed pleased to see someone he knew since he had just moved into town. "I got tired of living in such a small university community," he explained. "I have always liked this little town and have decided that a 30-minute commute is worth it to live where real people live."

We talked for almost an hour after the meeting. I told him my life history, or at least my teaching history. He was fascinated with how I had realized that I had to provide the students with real experiences with science while simultaneously providing activities in reading, listening, and helping them think the material through. I almost told him about the dream in which he forced me to deal with the two components, but I wasn't quite sure enough of him to share that. I did tell him that I had started keeping a journal as he had suggested and how much it had helped me to reflect upon what I was doing.

After standing and talking on the steps for almost an hour, he began to look impatient. I realized I had been babbling on and that he had probably just been polite. I apologized but he only laughed and said, "I'm not bored—just famished. I came straight from the university to this meeting." We went to my favorite Italian restaurant and I told him even more. (Well, he is such an enthusiastic listener and asked question after question!) Finally, I told him about my frustrations with how teachers were taught. He said, "I know just how you feel and there is only one thing to do about that!" So now I am enrolled in a graduate program—though if I only take courses in summers or in the evenings, I will be old and decrepit before I finish! Some days I commute in with Jer (that's Dr. Knowles' first name and he insists he can't spend an hour in the car with someone who calls him "Dr."!) and that is usually the hour in which I learn the most. He has so many good ideas—I don't remember him being so fascinating when I was in his class. Next year, he is going to come and watch me teach. Horrors!! He is even talking about designing an experiment to see if students are learning more content and—as important to both of us—if their attitudes toward biology are improving. It is going to be such a super summer and next year should be even better than last. I must call Mrs. Plante and catch her up on my life. She would love Jer. I think I will invite her and Jer for dinner.

REFERENCES

Ballew, H., & Cunningham, J. W. (1982). Diagnosing strengths and weaknesses of sixth-grade students in solving word problems. *Journal for Research in Mathematics Education, 13*, 202–210.

SUGGESTED READINGS

The following readings are reports of actual experiences in schools. These accounts cover teachers' and students' experiences with all aspects of the school day; the accounts are not restricted to reading and writing in the content areas. We include these because we believe that you need to know about the realities of working with administrators, other teachers, and groups of students. The following books describe those realities clearly. Although the accounts frequently are critical of public schooling, they are quite informative about the pleasures and the pressures of teaching.

The following description of teaching during the mid-1800s points out how far some aspects of the teaching profession have progressed. It graphically portrays the primitive conditions early American teachers endured.

Woody, T. (1954). Country schoolmaster of long ago. *History of Education Journal, 5*, 41–53.

The following books deal specifically with modern secondary schools. The author of the first book was a university-level researcher who became the confidante of several high school students while attending classes with them. The second book is an edited collection of real teachers' journal entries. Its title comes from the hard-bitten advice sometimes offered to beginning teachers.

Cusick, P. (1973). *Inside high school.* New York: Holt, Rinehart & Winston.
Ryan, K. (Ed.). (1980). *Don't smile until Christmas.* Chicago: University of Chicago Press.

These last books are based on elementary-school experiences. The first is an inspiring account by one teacher of her experiences instructing disadvantaged children through an integrated reading and writing approach. The other two are more jaundiced reports of teachers' concerns about issues such as classroom control and the status of teachers in the community and the school.

Ashton-Warner, S. (1963). *Teacher.* New York: Simon and Schuster.
Eddy, E. M. (1969). *Becoming a teacher.* New York: Teachers College Press.
McPherson, G. (1972). *Small town teacher.* Cambridge, MA: Harvard University Press.

Index

り